Becoming Neighbors in a Mexican American Community

Becoming Neighbors
in a Mexican American Community

Power
Conflict
and
Solidarity

Gilda L. Ochoa

University of Texas Press, Austin

A section from a poem by Pat Mora, "Legal Alien," first published in the volume *Chants,* appears in Chapter 4. It is reprinted with permission from the publisher (Houston: Arte Público Press—University of Houston, 1985).

First edition, 2004

Requests for permission to reproduce material from this work should be sent to Permissions, University of Texas Press, Box 7819, Austin, TX 78713-7819.

♾ The paper used in this book meets the minimum requirements of ANSI/NISO Z39.48-1992 (R1997) (Permanence of Paper).

Library of Congress Cataloging-in-Publication Data

Ochoa, Gilda L., 1965–
Becoming neighbors in a Mexican American community : power, conflict, and solidarity / Gilda L. Ochoa.— 1st ed.
    p.   cm.
Includes bibliographical references (p.   ) and index.
ISBN 978-0-292-70168-7
ISBN 0-292-70168-3 (pbk. : alk. paper)
1. Mexican Americans—California—La Puente—Social conditions. 2. Mexican Americans—California—La Puente—Politics and government. 3. Immigrants—California—La Puente—Social conditions. 4. Ethnic neighborhoods—California—La Puente. 5. Community life—California—La Puente. 6. Social conflict—California—La Puente. 7. La Puente (Calif.)—Social conditions. 8. La Puente (Calif.)—Politics and government. I. Title.
F869.L124 O28   2004
305.868′72079493—dc22   2003017903

*For past, present, and future generations of La Puente residents,
including Henry José Ochoa (1935–1989), Francesca Palazzolo Ochoa,
Enrique C. Ochoa, and Eduardo Ruiz*

Contents

List of Illustrations

Tables

Photographs

Acknowledgments

From conception to completion, this book has benefited from the help and support of many people. Without their assistance and encouragement, I could not have written it. First of all, I am deeply indebted to all of the residents of La Puente and the surrounding communities who opened their doors and shared their stories and knowledge with me. Also, individuals from the La Puente Valley Historical Society, the Hacienda–La Puente Unified School District, the Workman and Temple Family Homestead Museum, and the Claremont Colleges' Honnold Library each introduced me to their archives and made available crucial documents.

From the early stages of this project, I was fortunate to have been guided by several supportive individuals. While I was at UCLA, Vilma Ortiz, my graduate advisor, was instrumental in guiding me toward the skills, knowledge, and determination to carry out this work. Edward Telles, John Horton, and Karen Brodkin, my dissertation committee members, shared with me their insights and suggestions as well.

Pomona College has been an environment conducive to teaching, researching, and writing. Travel and research grants in addition to Pomona College's Steele Leave were crucial for allotting me the necessary time and resources to complete this project. I appreciate the support from students and colleagues, particularly in the Intercollegiate Department of Chicana/o Studies and the Department of Sociology. I have also been fortunate to have worked with many wonderful research assistants, most of whom were funded through Pomona College. Four who assisted me in the final stages of this project were Emily de Ayora, Juanita del Toro, Dianna Moreno, and Daniela Pineda. In particular, Daniela Pineda's critical and thoughtful readings of earlier drafts of this work were extremely helpful.

During the 2000–2001 academic year, colleagues at UC Irvine's Chicano/Latino Studies Program provided a welcoming atmosphere in which I was able to complete a final draft of this book. Director Leo Chavez, Program Manager Stella Ginez, and Professors Gilbert Gonzalez and Raúl Fernández were instrumental in arranging for my stay as a visiting scholar and in helping to foster a stimulating working environment.

Over the years, the following friends and colleagues have offered advice and encouragement: Estela Ballon, Ray Buriel, Edith Chen, José Calderon, José De Paz, Yvonne Garcia, Jill Grigsby, Sondra Hale, Ester Hernandez, Manuel Maldonado, Daniel Malpica, Lynn Rapaport, María Soldatenko, Garrett Terrones, Alicia Velázquez, and Kris Zentgraf. I am especially grateful to Kimberly Nettles, who painstakingly read multiple versions of this work, each time providing invaluable comments.

My work has benefited from the financial support of institutions including the American Sociological Association's Minority Fellowship Program, the Inter-University Program for Latino Research, the Social Science Research Council, UCLA's Center for the Study of Women and Women's Studies Program, Pomona College, and the John Randolph Haynes and Dora Haynes Faculty Fellowship.

Special thanks to the University of Texas Press, especially to Theresa May, Lynne Chapman, Allison Faust, and Tana Silva. This book was improved by the thoughtful suggestions of Martha Menchaca and an anonymous reviewer.

My family has inspired and sustained this work. My parents, Henry José Ochoa and Francesca Palazzolo Ochoa, nurtured the sense of home and community that impelled me to research the very communities, La Puente and Hacienda Heights, in which they settled and worked. My brother, Enrique C. Ochoa, a Latin American historian, has read and commented on multiple versions of this work and has always offered encouraging and helpful advice. Finally, thanks to Eduardo Ruiz, who accompanied me on my return to La Puente in 1995 and assisted in some of the data collection process. I especially appreciated his words of encouragement at those critical moments of research and writing.

Becoming Neighbors in a Mexican American Community

Chapter 1

Introducing *Becoming Neighbors*

> One gets sad because one is humiliated here, and unfortunately
> one's own race is doing the humiliating. I have been humiliated
> many times because I can't speak English.
>
> SARA VALDEZ, Mexican immigrant

Migrating from Cuernavaca, Mexico, to escape an abusive husband and
with hopes of "earning enough money to eat," thirty-six-year-old Sara Valdez arrived in 1989 in La Puente, a city in Los Angeles County, California.[1]
After acquiring a job in a neighborhood restaurant, she encouraged other
family members to join her. She now lives with her two teenage children
and her cousin in a converted two-car garage. She works from 5 P.M. until
midnight, more than forty hours a week, as a waitress.

Sitting at her kitchen table, Sara speaks candidly about the difficulties
she has encountered in the United States. As her voice cracks and tears well
up in her eyes, she describes the humiliation she experiences because of her
current economic situation and her limited English-speaking skills. Living
and working in La Puente, a largely Mexican-origin community, Sara explains how it is "established" Mexican Americans who have humiliated her.[2]
Sorrowfully, she shares:

> One's own people discriminate. It's sad. These are people that clearly
> are established. They have businesses and their own homes. They look
> down on one because of one's bad economic situation.

The *coraje* (courage out of anger) that led Sara Valdez to travel thousands of
miles to leave her abusive husband is what she is drawing on now to com-
bat the ridicule she currently faces. After long nights at work, she studies
English at a local school:

> It's a little hard to go to school because I usually get home from work at
> midnight, but sometimes as late as 2 A.M. It's hard to get up, but I am
> going to school because of *coraje*. I want to improve myself and have a
> better job for my children, so I tell myself, "What do you have to do to
> improve?" Because since I came here, I've been in the same little hole.

1

I've gotten angry because they humiliate us and I ask, "Why?" And then I push my tiredness, and I go on.

Having lived in the United States ten years longer than Sara, María Ramos also migrated as a single woman, but she has a different story to tell. In 1979 she left her home in Jalisco, Mexico, at the age of twenty-two. The second-oldest of ten children, she crossed the U.S.-Mexican border, "running like contraband," to assist her parents economically. She met her husband, also a Mexican immigrant, in Los Angeles, and after living in East Los Angeles and various San Gabriel Valley cities, they purchased a home in La Puente in 1990. Mexican Americans facilitated her family's settlement in their new city. Gratefully, María retold how her Mexican American real estate agent was instrumental in placing her children into schools that were within walking distance. She also spoke fondly of a past Mexican American school board member who ensured that her oldest son was enrolled in a special program that provided assistance for his speech impediment.

It was in 1992 that I met both Sara Valdez and María Ramos. I was interviewing Mexican immigrant women as part of a project I was completing on immigrant settlement and incorporation in the United States. Looking at these women's experiences in a larger context, we see that they are a reflection and a manifestation of some of the macro-level dynamics occurring in California around immigration, language, and race/ethnic relations.[3] At the time that these two women shared their stories with me, California was in the midst of an economic recession, and anti-immigrant sentiment was on the rise. Mexican immigrants were the targets of such xenophobia and nativist sentiment. They were being accused of taking jobs away from U.S. citizens and of draining public services. Such anti-immigrant sentiment and the resulting legislation stemmed from societal concerns over the supposed detrimental impacts of immigrants on the U.S. economy, the dominant culture, and the national image.

For many California voters, such misperceptions diverted attention away from the ongoing impacts of global economic transformations. Such transformations have included the shifting of manufacturing jobs and transnational corporations from the United States into countries throughout Latin America. The North American Free Trade Agreement (NAFTA) implemented in 1994 has hastened the movement of factories into Latin America as companies cross borders in their quest for maximum profits. Such U.S. capitalist expansion has increased the wage gap and further destabilized economies in Latin America, perhaps fostering additional immigration to the United States (J. Gonzalez 2000).

Current racial/ethnic demographics indicating that more than one-third of California residents are Latina/o have led some conservative groups to fret over what has been referred to as the "browning" of California and what these demographic changes mean for the hegemony of the English language, Anglo culture, and Whites.[4] Among some, at issue is the belief that the growth of the Latina/o population and the Spanish language will result in the disuniting, the fragmenting, or the Balkanization of the United States (see Schlesinger 1991). In the 1990s such sentiment resulted in the passage of three California propositions—one that sought to deny undocumented immigrants access to public services, such as excluding children from the public school system (Proposition 187), another that eliminated affirmative action in schools and workplaces (Proposition 209), and a third that stemmed from the larger English-only movement and aimed to eliminate bilingual education (Proposition 227).[5] All three propositions demonstrate that schools—as institutions that focus on socializing groups into society— have been primary locales where the debates on immigration and language have taken place. Since women are typically responsible for the health and education of the family and are often considered the transmitters of language, by attempting to limit social service and bilingual education, these propositions specifically targeted Latinas and the reproduction and welfare of Latina/o families (L. R. Chavez 1998; M. D. Gonzales 1999).

While the experiences of Sara Valdez speak to the impact that such a hostile climate has had on her life, when we compare her experiences with the ones shared by María Ramos, these disparate accounts might be attributed to the individual differences between these two women, including variations in class position, length of time in the United States, and English language skills. However, upon closer consideration, their narratives suggest something more—the oftentimes unspoken and understudied influences that Mexican Americans may have on the experiences of Mexican immigrants and on their integration into the United States. When looked at together, the narratives of these two women raise questions such as: What might lead some Mexican Americans to ridicule immigrants who speak Spanish? Why might others identify with immigrants such that they feel a sense of connectedness and a desire to provide assistance or to counter anti-immigrant sentiment?

Although questions such as these emerged from my interviews with Mexican immigrant women, when I turned to the academic scholarship to shed light on them, I found that despite the enduring presence of the Mexican-origin community and the burgeoning body of work on Mexican Americans and Mexican immigrants, research on the relationships between these two groups has been limited (Browning and de la Garza 1986; Gutiérrez 1995).[6] Much of this scholarship has either focused on the impact of immigration on the wages and employment opportunities of Mexican Americans (Browning and de la Garza 1986; Sullivan 1986; G. Cardenas, de la Garza, and Hansen 1986; Poston, Rogers, and Cullen 1986; G. Cardenas 1986; N. Rodriguez 1986) or has quantitatively examined Mexican Americans' attitudes toward immigrants (Miller, Polinard, and Wrinkle 1984; Polinard, Wrinkle, and de la Garza 1984; Citrin, Reingold, and Green 1990; de la Garza et al. 1991; Espenshade and Calhoun 1993; Binder, Polinard, and Wrinkle 1997). While this work has illustrated the heterogeneity and complexity among the Mexican-origin population, the tendency has been to focus on the labor market. Notably absent is an understanding of how individual Mexican Americans and established communities have reacted to Mexican immigrants (Gutiérrez 1995) and a qualitative analysis of the everyday attitudes and interactions that occur in arenas which are often significant for women's lives—such as neighborhoods, schools, and churches (for exceptions see Menchaca 1995; Pardo 1998). As such, scant literature exists on Mexican Americans' perceptions of immigrants and on the factors and processes that might explain the experiences shared by women such as Sara Valdez and María Ramos.

There are several explanations for the limited work on Mexican American–Mexican immigrant relations. One explanation is that the dominant society has only recently made the distinction between U.S. residents of Mexican descent and Mexican immigrants (Gutiérrez 1995). Thus, within academic scholarship and public discourse, the diversity within the Mexican-origin community has sometimes been overlooked.

Second, much of the race/ethnic relations scholarship has been framed in opposition to or in comparison to Whites. In fact, up until the 1970s, scholars were largely concerned with White-Black and White–Mexican American relationships. While more recently there is an increasing body of literature on relationships among groups of color (for examples see Johnson and Oliver 1989; Lamphere 1992; Horton 1995; Saito 1998), some scholars are still working within the traditional Black-White paradigm of race relations. For example, rather than understanding the experiences of Mexican Americans and Mexican immigrants on their own terms, a few have framed the debate around whether the experiences of Mexican Americans are more like those encountered by Whites or by African Americans. Such binary thinking has tended to prevent an analysis of the heterogeneity among the Mexican-origin community and has centered the experiences of Whites, making their experiences the norm by which other racial/ethnic groups are compared.

Another explanation for the limited amount of work is that the study of Mexican Americans and Mexican immigrants has tended to be compartmentalized into two separate bodies of research, one that focuses on Mexican Americans as ethnic minorities and another which centers the experiences of undocumented and documented immigrants (Browning and de la Garza 1986). More recently, the sociological scholarship has turned to the important analysis of the children of immigrants (see Portes and Rumbaut 2001). However, with its emphasis on the "new second generation," this work typically neglects the experiences of Mexican American families and communities that have a long history in the United States.

In response to these trends in the literature, scholars have called for empirical research that explores the attitudes and perceptions of established Mexican Americans toward Mexicanas/os (Mindiola and Martinez 1986, 4; Niemann et al. 1999, 57) and for more ethnographies on Mexican-origin communities to better understand the group's heterogeneity (Zavella 1994). Moving beyond these dichotomies (Mexican American–White and Black–White) and centering the experiences of Mexican Americans, *Becoming Neighbors* adds to the growing scholarship on the perceptions of established residents of color to the movement of newcomers into their communities (for examples see Lamphere 1992; Horton 1995; Saito 1998).

Focusing on the city of La Puente, this book examines the experiences of Mexican Americans and their everyday attitudes toward and interactions with Mexican immigrants. In telling this story, this book addresses some of the gaps in the literature and heeds the calls for additional research. It does so by focusing on how Mexican Americans are negotiating their relationships with Mexican immigrants in the midst of dominant structures and ideologies. To this end, several questions guide this work: (1) How do Mexican Americans characterize their attitudes and interactions with Mexican immigrants? (2) What factors and situations are influencing Mexican American–Mexican immigrant relationships? In particular, how have dominant ideologies and practices impacted intra-ethnic relations?[7] How are Mexican Americans' perceptions of self related to their attitudes toward immigrants? (3) How are Mexican Americans influencing the adaptation processes of immigrants? and (4) How are established Mexican-origin communities negotiating the changing demographics?

By centering the dynamics occurring within a community rather than solely in the labor market, this book offers insight on the processes and relationships in arenas such as schools, neighborhoods, and churches. Studies documenting relationships within the labor market have tended to provide important macro-structural analyses without significant consideration of workers' attitudes and interactions outside of the workplace. Likewise, given women's gender role responsibilities, which typically include community engagement, by exploring how Mexican Americans are negotiating their relationships with immigrants at an interpersonal level in the places where they shop, worship, learn, raise their families, and live, a nuanced understanding of women's centrality in Mexican American–Mexican immigrant relationships emerges.

The Setting

La Puente provides an ideal site to consider intra-ethnic relations among Mexican Americans and Mexican immigrants.[8] The city is twenty miles southeast of downtown Los Angeles in the Eastern San Gabriel Valley, and it is bordered by the cities of West Covina and City of Industry. Valley Boulevard, a main industrial thoroughfare, and railroad tracks run along the southern section of La Puente, largely through the nonresidential city of Industry, physically demarcating La Puente from its middle-class, unincorporated neighbor, Hacienda Heights. Surrounded by three major freeways, the San Bernardino (Interstate 10), the San Gabriel River (Interstate 605), and the Pomona (Interstate 60), La Puente is three and a half square miles and has more than forty thousand residents.

During a time when the United States is growing increasingly multiracial/multiethnic, it is important to examine the factors, processes, and situations influencing conflict and solidarity among diverse populations. Moreover, the demographic shifts and political climate within the Los Angeles area make it a critical place to explore the complexities of contemporary race/ethnic relations, and the dynamics and processes under which Mexican Americans and Mexican immigrants are becoming neighbors.

Demographic shifts have altered the racial/ethnic composition of the Los Angeles area such that the Latina/o population is expected to surpass the White population by 2 million by the year 2010 (Sabagh and Bozorgmehr 1996, 104). Currently, 45 percent of Los Angeles residents are Latina/o, and nearly three-quarters (72 percent) of the Latina/o population in the county of Los Angeles are of Mexican descent. As a result of immigration and the natural birth rate, the Mexican-origin population is the fastest-growing ethnic group in the twentieth century, numbering more than 3 million in the county (U.S. Bureau of the Census, 2001). As the largest group in the area, some refer to Los Angeles as the "Chicano capital" of the United States (Moore and Vigil 1993).

In Los Angeles, immigration and demographic changes have been occurring in conjunction with a restructuring of the U.S. economy and a backlash against immigrants and people of color. Because of the shift from an economic base of durable goods manufacturing to a service-based economy, cities throughout Los Angeles County have been experiencing a decline in high-wage, stable, and unionized manufacturing and industrial jobs and decreases in middle management and white-collar jobs. As in the past, immigrants and people of color have been blamed for this changing economy. This scapegoating has manifested in waves of nativism and state propositions such as the "Save Our State Initiative," Proposition 187, described earlier. For the Mexican-origin community, nowhere has this scapegoating been more evident than in Southern California (Acuña 1996).

La Puente is a microcosm of the shifts occurring in cities throughout Los Angeles County. From the time of its founding as a Mexican rancho in 1845, La Puente has had a Mexican-origin community—though after the U.S. conquest, this community became increasingly segregated—geographically, socially, economically, and politically (Sandoval 1994). By 1970, nearly half of La Puente's residents were Latina/o (U.S. Bureau of the Census 1971). Since that time period, more established Mexican Americans have been joined by Mexican immigrant neighbors, while large numbers of Whites have left the city. These changing demographics are apparent in La Puente schools, where the 2001-2002 Latina/o student population was nearly 90 percent and the percentage of students designated as English-language learners was about 35 percent (California Department of Education 2001b). The city's logo, "Where the past meets the future," captures these changing demographics, and it raises questions about how community residents and institutions are responding to these shifts.

Qualitative Research Methods

Most of the data for this manuscript comes from interviews, ethnographic fieldwork, and printed materials collected between 1994 and 1996 and again in 2000 and 2001. I conducted sixty-four in-depth, semistructured, open-ended interviews with Mexican Americans and Mexican immigrants in La Puente.[9] I also completed twenty-five informal and formal interviews with residents of various racial/ethnic backgrounds. Interviews were conducted in either English or Spanish, according to residents' preferences.[10] The interviews ranged from thirty minutes to four hours, averaging ninety minutes in length. While participants had the option of being interviewed in their homes, in my home, at local restaurants, at city offices, or at local schools, most opted to meet me in their homes. All of the formal interviews were audio-taped, fully transcribed, and subsequently analyzed for recurring themes and patterns. The quotations appearing throughout this book are verbatim from the transcripts.[11]

Residents were asked open-ended questions on racial/ethnic identity, race/ethnic relations, their experiences in La Puente, and their attitudes on issues such as bilingual education, affirmative action, Proposition 187, and immigration. I used the grounded theory approach commonly used in qualitative research that stresses "discovery and theory development" rather than hypothesis testing (Charmaz 1983, 111). The format of the interviews was designed to allow people the flexibility to construct their own categories and meanings of the topics discussed and to speak about their experiences and perceptions in ways that are significant to them (Lofland and Lofland 1984). One of the advantages of utilizing semistructured and open-ended interviews over other methods is that they provide a space for individuals to voice their perceptions and experiences, opening up the possibilities for a deeper understanding of intra-ethnic relations. The decision to use the voices of the participants through extensive quotes throughout this book is consistent with my goal of placing Mexican Americans at the center of this study.

While interviews form the basis of this book, as a La Puente resident I attended city council meetings, community meetings, parent meetings, community-wide events, and school-based meetings in order to better understand the circumstances that influence group relations.[12] As well as being extremely interested in the issues discussed at these meetings, my attendance was critical in strengthening my understanding of the dynamics occurring in the city.

Most of my participant observations focused on the schools because this was one arena that many residents discussed. While there are three school districts in the area, the majority of La Puente residents attend schools in the Hacienda–La Puente Unified School District (HLPUSD).[13] Therefore, I focused my observations on this school district, attending district board meetings and parent advisory meetings at one of the two main high schools. Following these meetings, several individuals invited me to their homes and to local schools where two parent groups were forming—Parents for Quality Education and Puente Parents.

Several additional data sources were utilized to provide a structural context for understanding intra-ethnic relations. Historical information contextualizes the city and the experiences of its residents. Census data demonstrate the city's changing demographics. Finally, local newspapers and school records provide information on past and present events. This use of macro-level data to understand micro-level qualitative observations and in-depth interviews is characteristic of recent approaches to urban ethnographies (for examples, see Burawoy et al. 1991; Lamphere 1992; Goode and

Becoming Neighbors in a Mexican American Community

Schneider 1994; Horton 1995; Bourgois 1996; Saito 1998) and is useful for providing a broader understanding of how prevailing ideologies and structural factors may influence individual attitudes and interactions between immigrants and established residents (Lamphere 1992).

I do not claim that this study is exhaustive or generally applicable to all Mexican Americans. Rather, I seek to provide in it, as a qualitative study, a detailed understanding of how a group of Mexican Americans and one Los Angeles community are contending with race/ethnic relations in the midst of demographics shifts and in relationship to social, cultural, and economic transformations. Thus, this study's findings provide insight into the complexities of intra-ethnic relations and should be seen as part of the growing body of scholarship on Mexican-origin communities. It is my hope that the stories that unfold here may lead others to unravel the dynamics occurring in different communities and among future generations of Mexican Americans.

The Participants

For this study, I interviewed both Mexican Americans and Mexican immigrants in the La Puente area. However, throughout the data analysis and writing process, it became apparent that it would be difficult to adequately include the detailed narratives of both U.S.-born individuals and immigrants on their own terms. Therefore, it is Mexican Americans—individuals of Mexican descent who were born and raised in the United States—whose stories take center stage in this book. While a systematic analysis of Mexican immigrants' attitudes toward and interactions with Mexican Americans are saved for another time, interviews with immigrants new to the United States and with those who have spent most of their lives here, long-term immigrants, are included to provide a larger context for understanding Mexican Americans' experiences. Also, in Chapter 7, as La Puente residents work collectively to impact change, we hear from Mexican Americans and Mexican immigrants and are offered insight into what the future suggests for intra-group relations and collective action.

The majority of Mexican Americans whose personal narratives inform this book live in single-story, three-bedroom tract homes. Their homes were built when most La Puente houses were constructed, during the 1950s post–World War II housing boom. At the time that we met, many respondents were in the process of buying their homes or were living with their parents. Many are longtime residents, living in the city for an average of thirty-one years. Nine of the individuals were born and raised in La Puente.

As illustrated in Table 1.1, the thirty-nine Mexican American respondents are diverse in terms of age, generation, level of education, and occupation. Their ages range from fourteen to seventy-six years. At the time of their interview, their mean age was forty-six, placing their average year of birth in the 1950s. Sixty-two percent are second generation, having at least one parent who emigrated from Mexico. Thirty-three percent are third-generation and 5 percent are fourth- and fifth-generation Mexican American. While places of birth vary, 97 percent were born in the Southwest, in the states of California (74 percent), Texas (10 percent), New Mexico (8 percent), and Arizona (5 percent). Of those born in California, 72 percent were born in the Greater Los Angeles area. With respect to educational level, nearly 60 percent completed at least one year of college, mostly at local community colleges or public universities; 5 percent were still in high school at the time of the interview. The average year of schooling was nearly fourteen, with 15 percent of the respondents having earned postgraduate degrees. Regarding occupations, more than 40 percent were engaged in sales or such administrative support positions as clerical workers and instructional aides. The second most common occupational category was managerial and professional, which included elementary school principals, teachers, and the chief financial officer of a local family business.

These individuals expressed a range of language skills—from speaking only English, to understanding Spanish, to being able to converse in both English and Spanish. When asked if they spoke Spanish, 74 percent reported that they did, though they described their levels of fluency in various ways. and some expressed their desires to improve their Spanish-language skills. Some explained that they spoke enough Spanish "to get by" but that they were unsure of themselves when they did speak it. Others spoke Spanish on a daily basis with their in-laws or neighbors or at their work sites.

As well as interviewing Mexican Americans, I completed twenty-five in-depth interviews with Mexican immigrants. These included interviews with nine fairly recent immigrants who at the time of their interviews had been in the United States from one to ten years and fourteen interviews with immigrants who had spent most of their lives in the United States. However, since the focus of this book is on Mexican Americans, Table 1.2 includes only the demographic backgrounds of those immigrants whose experiences, attitudes, and activities are explicitly included in the book.

Though this research has come to an end, I remain a La Puente resident. I am deeply indebted to all who have opened their doors to me. While I began this project with an interest in better understanding intra-ethnic attitudes and interactions, through listening, observing, and learning it became apparent that I could not dissociate intra-ethnic relations from a discussion of the role of schools in structuring relationships.

Table I.I *Demographic Characteristics of Mexican American Respondents*

Name	Age	No. of Children	Generation in U.S.	Years of Education	Occupation
Alberto Perez	42	2	2nd	18	Court production manager
Ann O'Brien	68	2	2nd	12	Beautician
Art Marquez	40	3	2nd	13	Sales representative
Carlos Mendoza	75	6	2nd	12	Retired school custodian
Cristina Saldana	70	4	3rd	10	Retired quality control inspector
David Galvez	27	2	2nd	16	Middle school teacher
Deana Martinez	36	3	4th	13	Clerk
Delia Centeno	52	4	2nd	14	Licensed vocational nurse
Denise Villarreal	46	0	3rd	18	Elementary school principal
Diane Gallardo	55	3	2nd	13	Security clerk
Diego Tellez	44	0	2nd	16	Executive director of nonprofit organization
Erica Handel	62	2	3rd	14	Elementary instructional aide
Frank Gallegos	52	0	2nd	15	Chief financial officer
Gary Mesa	32	0	3rd	14	Information systems specialist
Geraldo Romero	23	0	2nd	16	High school teacher
Gloria Dominguez	65	3	2nd	12	Retired elementary instructional aide
Ilene Gómez	55	1	2nd	20	Education consultant
Irene Renteria-Salazar	35	2	2nd	16	Risk analyst
Jane Hanson	55	1	3rd	13	Elementary instructional aide
Joe Zavala	69	4	3rd	12	Retired supervisor of operations

Table 1.1 Continued

Name	Age	No. of Children	Generation in U.S.	Years of Education	Occupation
John Palomares	36	1	2nd	12	Hairstylist
Leticia Mendoza	76	6	3rd	12	Retired school food worker
Lois Sandoval	43	2	2nd	12	Biller
Lourdes Fernandez	41	3	3rd	18	Elementary school principal
Margarita Villa	29	0	2nd	16	Middle school teacher
Marie Rogers	58	3	2nd	12	Retired factory worker
Mary Marquez	40	3	3rd	13	Purchasing clerk
Mel Sandoval	15	0	3rd	11+	High school student
Mireya Pardo	23	0	2nd	11	Clothes salesperson
Nicole Sandoval	14	0	3rd	10+	High school student
Pete Saldana	69	4	5th	8	Retired foreman
Ray Sanchez	60	3	2nd	14	Retired car salesperson
Rita Lopez Tellez	36	0	2nd	18	Self-employed consultant
Roberta Zavala	47	0	3rd	18	Elementary school principal
Rosario Jones	30	1	2nd	12	Service representative
Shirley Garcia	29	2	3rd	14	Homemaker
Silvia Bravo	62	5	2nd	12	Retired secretary
Susan Martin-Riley	50	4	2nd	DNR	Piano teacher
Sylvia Espinosa	31	2	2nd	13	Customer service representative

Schools Structuring Intra-Ethnic Relations

Since this study focuses on the perceptions and experiences of adults—rather than of youth—some may wonder why the schooling process and experiences within schools are a main topic of examination throughout this book. While I did not set out to focus on schools, conversations with resi-

Table I.2 *Demographic Characteristics of Selected Mexican Immigrant Respondents*

Name	Age	No. of Children	Years in the U.S.	Years of Education	Occupation
Francisco Delgado	43	7	31	16	U.S. Postal worker
George Lopez	44	4	42	16	Department of Corrections
Joaquin Macias	44	3	30	18	Executive director of community organization
María Ramos	35	3	13	3	Garment worker
Miriam Flores	36	1	4	15	Homemaker
Raquel Heinrich	40	2	21	16	Union representative
Roberto Delgado	46	5	31	12	U.S. Postal worker
Sara Valdez	36	2	3	6	Waitress

dents and struggles around bilingual education made it evident that it would be difficult to complete a community study on intra-ethnic relations without considering the dynamics within schools. Throughout their interviews, a significant number of people vividly reflected on their own schooling. They remembered experiences of language repression where they were punished by school officials, held back in school, or ridiculed by their peers for speaking Spanish. Some recounted teachers' stereotyped perceptions of Mexican-origin students, and a few discussed the Eurocentric course curriculum that prevailed throughout their K-12 education. These early experiences have stayed with them as adults, and they easily recalled them when asked to talk about their Spanish language abilities and their educational experiences.

When they were not reflecting on their own educational experiences, residents discussed the education that their children and grandchildren were receiving or their contemporary observations as school officials. For example, those who had children enrolled in local schools had much to say about the relatively low quality of education that they believed their children were receiving in comparison to students in wealthier schools and in other districts. In addition, individuals who were working in the La Puente-area schools (as instructional aides, teachers, or school principals) drew on their daily activities to describe their views on bilingual education, their perceptions of teachers' interactions with Mexican-origin parents and students, and their attempts to foster positive Mexican American–Mexican immigrant relationships.

Aside from being an issue of importance for La Puente residents, schooling proves to be a critical topic to explore in a study on intra-ethnic relations for two additional reasons. First of all, as an institution, the educational system is a reflection of the larger society. The structure of schools, their policies, and their practices mirror and reproduce the dominant values, ideologies, and inequalities apparent in the social, political, and economic structures of the United States (Bowles and Gintis 1976; Giroux 1983). For example, a key function of schools has been socialization where an emphasis has been placed on integrating immigrants and groups of color into society by teaching them the dominant values, attitudes, norms, and expectations (Parsons 1951). This has been carried out through "Americanization" and "newcomer" programs designed to teach the English language and U.S. laws and customs. As a result, school policies and practices such as Americanization, the emphasis on assimilation, and the differential placement of students into different career and college tracks have worked in ways to reinforce racial/ethnic hierarchies and dominant structures of society (Oakes 1985; G. Gonzalez 1990; Valenzuela 1999). Such practices have hindered the educational and economic advancement of the Mexican-origin population and have influenced Mexican Americans' perceptions of self, their experiences with the Spanish language, and their intra-ethnic relations with immigrants.[14]

Likewise, when we consider who has been in decision-making positions, Whites, Mexican Americans, and Mexican immigrants tend to possess unequal status and authority in schools. Therefore, consideration of the dynamics occurring within schools highlights the ways that interactions may be influenced by the structure of organizations and differences in race/ethnicity, generation, class position, and access to power (Lamphere 1992). By focusing on individuals' experiences in schools, then, we acquire a greater understanding of the macroscopic issues and dynamics occurring in society and their implications for Mexican Americans.

Finally, since schools are designed to serve the community, they are among the few public arenas where established residents and immigrants engage in sustained interaction (Goode, Schneider, and Blanc 1992, 176). Nevertheless, little of the research on schools has focused on race/ethnic relationships. Instead, the tendency has been to understand the factors influencing educational outcomes (for examples see Gándara 1995; Romo and Falbo 1996; Darder, Torres, and Gutiérrez 1997). Thus, this study also contributes to the small but growing qualitative scholarship on how schooling influences race/ethnic relations (see Goode, Schneider, and Blanc 1992; Valenzuela 1999). In this case, we see the current and long-term influences of school policies and practices on race/ethnic relations among a group of Mexican American adults.

Focus and Organization of the Book

In the chapters that follow, I argue that Mexican Americans' identities, attitudes, and interactions with immigrants may be situationally specific and are influenced by structural factors (such as exploitation, inequality, racism, and discrimination), dominant ideologies (such as assimilation and Anglo superiority or white supremacy), and cultural commonalities with immigrants (in particular, the Spanish language).[15] Within this context, the in-depth interviews and participant observations reveal the dynamics and processes under which Mexican Americans in this study are actively engaged in negotiating, building, and strengthening their relationships with immigrants. As well as documenting the possibilities for Mexican American–Mexican immigrant solidarity, *Becoming Neighbors* illustrates how identities and relationships may vary historically, geographically, generationally, and situationally.

A continuum of conflict and solidarity is used to capture respondents' varied, multifaceted, and at times overlapping attitudes. Their attitudes toward Mexican immigrants fall along a continuum of conflict and solidarity that includes antagonism, a shared connection, and political mobilization. While many express beliefs that fall more readily along one end of the continuum than the other, individuals' attitudes tend not to be mutually exclusive or static. Their attitudes cannot be used to categorize or typologize people. Rather, their beliefs and behaviors are oftentimes situational and are influenced by external factors and a shared connection to the Spanish language. To capture this fluidity, *Becoming Neighbors* is organized into eight chapters around this conflict-solidarity continuum and the factors, processes, and situations influencing conflict, solidarity, and mobilization.

Chapter 2, "Theorizing about Mexican American–Mexican Immigrant Relations in 'Occupied Mexico,'" provides the theoretical framework for understanding Mexican American–Mexican immigrant relations in California. Emphasizing the significance of U.S. colonization, exploitation, racism, and discrimination on the unique experiences of the Mexican-origin community, this chapter documents the limits of dominant race/ethnicity frameworks that have tended to focus on cultural factors and assimilation. It argues for an integrated approach that considers how structural factors and dominant ideologies have influenced the life chances and experiences of Mexican Americans. It is these same external processes, combined with cultural factors, which have historically and are contemporarily influencing identities, attitudes, and interactions. An assimilationist imperative has impacted some respondents' beliefs that immigrants should "become Americans" by learning English and the dominant customs and values; for others, the adoption of a power-conflict perspective has strengthened their sense of connection with immigrants, their critique of the racial/ethnic hierarchy that perpetuates the assimilationist imperative, and their commitment for social justice.

In Chapter 3, " 'Where the Past Meets the Future,' " I trace La Puente's history from its early days as a Mexican rancho to its current status as a U.S. city. The information presented on the persistence of asymmetrical power relations—illustrated in the area's history of exclusion and in the contemporary debates surrounding the Spanish language and Mexican immigrants—gives a backdrop for understanding respondents' narratives.

Part of the process of understanding intra-ethnic relations involves considering Mexican Americans' self-concepts and the factors and processes influencing their racial/ethnic identities. Chapter 4, " 'This Is Who I Am,' " introduces the reader to how respondents are negotiating racial/ethnic identities in the context of structural constraints and narrow and exclusionary constructions of Mexicanness and Americanness. Despite top-down, static, and inaccurate racial/ethnic categorizations, Mexican Americans are challenging stereotypes and naming themselves, and some are claiming an oppositional Chicana/o identity. What begins to become apparent in this chapter are the connections between identity and race/ethnic relations and the factors and processes influencing Mexican American–Mexican immigrant relations, in particular the role of schools.

Chapter 5, " 'Between a Rock and a Hard Place, with No Easy Answers,' " starts to explicitly consider Mexican Americans' perceptions of immigrants. Throughout the analysis, I emphasize the institutional factors and ideological processes fostering the conflictual attitudes and interactions articulated by some. This chapter includes a discussion of how the dominant emphasis on assimilation and the structure of schools and school policies may shape intra-ethnic relations.

Moving along the conflict-solidarity continuum, Chapter 6, " 'We Can't Forget Our Roots,' " examines the processes that may account for Mexican Americans' expressions of solidarity with immigrants in spite of the hierarchical and exclusionary factors described in Chapter 5. Centered in this chapter are the ways that some respondents are building community in their everyday lives by creating inclusive spaces, challenging anti-Mexican and anti-immigrant sentiment, and maintaining or reclaiming the Spanish language.

Chapter 7, "Constructing Puentes," focuses on the dynamics occurring in the neighborhood schools and how in some situations, school district policies have resulted in political activism. In the case profiled in this chapter, community residents protested attempts by the local school board to establish an English-only policy. While this chapter demonstrates how the intersection of shared cultural factors and similar structural factors and ideological processes resulted in a sense of solidarity among a group of working-class individuals of Mexican descent, it also illustrates the significance of gender differences by analyzing the diverse organizing philosophies and strategies of the two parent groups that emerged, one organized primarily by men and the other by women. By exploring how gender is related to intra-ethnic mobilization, this chapter sheds light on the ways that men and women are building community.

In the final chapter I discuss the practical and policy implications of this study, paying particular attention to issues of language and schooling as they are connected to power and control. Based on the research findings, I argue for bilingual education, for creating inclusive public spaces, for institutions that reflect the interests of the communities that they service, and for a critical and engaged education that is grounded in the histories, lives, and experiences of groups of color, the working class, and women. As communities become increasingly multiracial/ethnic, so must the policies and practices of institutions. Community leaders must enact a model of "power sharing" (Shor 1996, 200). This would involve bringing together residents as partners as opposed to audience members or consumers in school activities and policies. To the extent that La Puente and other communities move in this direction, the potential exists for engaged and politicized residents that may be in positions to foster alliances not only within the Mexican-origin community but cross-racially/ethnically and across classes.

Chapter 2

Theorizing about Mexican American–Mexican Immigrant Relations in "Occupied Mexico"

> If they're going to be here, they should learn the language and not have everything geared to them in Spanish. I hate that . . . They want to bring their customs here instead of getting used to our customs.
>
> SILVIA BRAVO, sixty-two-year-old Mexican American

> The United States is the land of milk and honey. I'll never memorize what it says on the Statue of Liberty, "bring me your huddled masses," and we have always accepted people as long as [they] are European. My father will tell you that this is occupied Mexico. "You're lucky we [Mexicans] have let you stay here this long," he'll tell people.
>
> DENISE VILLARREAL, forty-six-year-old Mexican American

The views of La Puente residents Silvia Bravo and Denise Villarreal represent two of the most popular perspectives on race/ethnic relations, the assimilationist and the power-conflict perspective. While each perspective has numerous variations, they nonetheless represent two distinct approaches that are used by members of the academic community and by the general public to understand race/ethnic relations and immigration (Mario Barrera 1979; Frankenberg 1993; Omi and Winant 1994).[1]

As Silvia Bravo's comments illustrate, the assimilationist perspective tends to be characterized by an emphasis on integrating into U.S. society by acquiring the English language and middle-class, Anglo American values and traditions. Assimilationists often equate the experiences of Mexicans with those of Southern and Eastern European immigrants at the turn of the twentieth century. The underlying belief is that Mexicans, like Irish, Italian, and Jewish Americans, will gradually assimilate into the dominant society. The process of assimilation is perceived as inevitable and desirable, reinforcing the perception of meritocracy and that all racial/ethnic groups have equal opportunities to "become American."[2] Oftentimes underlying this perspective is the ideology of Anglo superiority where the Spanish language and other Mexican cultural practices are seen as distinct and inferior to the English language and dominant U.S. values.

While they also vary, power-conflict views such as Denise Villarreal expresses contest the assimilationist perspective by delineating the vastly different forms of incorporation and receptions encountered by Southern and Eastern Europeans and Mexicans in what her father refers to as "occupied Mexico." Power-conflict theorists focus on the persisting inequalities of power and resources as they are structured in society.

The two perspectives articulated by Silvia and Denise have influenced and reflect respondents' worldviews. Since assimilation has been the prevailing expectation in the United States, the La Puente residents included in this work are negotiating their acceptance, perpetuation, and rejection of assimilation and its corollary ideology — Anglo superiority. For Mexican Americans such as Denise Villarreal who are chafing against the racial/ethnic hierarchy underlying the emphasis on assimilation, their sense of intra-ethnic solidarity and political mobilization are connected to their adoption of various power-conflict views of race/ethnic relations.

To analyze Mexican Americans' relations with Mexican immigrants, I draw on both the assimilationist and power-conflict paradigms. Individuals such as Silvia Bravo who support the underlying tenets of the assimilationist paradigm contend that they have "played by the rules," have learned the English language, and so should others. They are typically more likely to express intra-ethnic antagonism for what they perceive as greater individual and institutional acceptance of the Spanish language. Likewise, individuals such as Denise Villarreal who challenge the assimilationist paradigm and see the historical and contemporary commonalities that Mexican Americans and Mexican immigrants share are more likely to be creating public spaces where the Spanish language can flourish and to be uniting with immigrants in the struggle for social justice.[3]

Though these two paradigms are useful for providing a framework for conceptualizing respondents' narratives, given the position of Mexican Americans in the United States' racial/ethnic hierarchy, this study moves away from the assimilationist approach. To better understand the complexities of race/ethnic relations, I adopt what Almaguer (1994) describes as an "integrated approach." This integrated power-conflict perspective emphasizes the significance of structural factors and ideological processes on race/ethnic relations. While I also consider the salience of cultural factors (language, traditions, and values), I do so within the context of these structural factors and ideological processes.

Organized into four main sections, this chapter presents the theoretical framework used in this study. The first part of the chapter includes a discussion of the two dominant frameworks of race/ethnic relations, the assimilationist and power-conflict paradigms. Since these paradigms have been significant in influencing people's beliefs and because they effectively capture respondents' perspectives and behaviors, this section frames the narratives presented in the upcoming chapters.

Building from this discussion, the second section of the chapter concentrates on my use of an integrated power-conflict paradigm to understand Mexican American–Mexican immigrant relations. Within this section, I draw on the existing theoretical, historical, and empirical scholarship to illustrate how Mexican American's experiences and intra-ethnic relations have been influenced by a history of conquest and colonization, a pattern of labor exploitation, the persistence of individual and institutional racism and discrimination, and a history of resistance. Cultural factors, in particular the Spanish language, are also considered.

Following a discussion of how these interrelated factors and processes have created and maintained a system of inequality, including a racial/ethnic hierarchy that has granted superior status to the English language and Anglo Americans, I consider in the third section how historically Mexican Americans' negotiations with these macroscopic factors have resulted in patterns of intra-group conflict, identification, mobilization, and resistance. At times, U.S. policies and practices and the prevailing belief systems have explicitly divided the Mexican-origin population. In other ways, it has been organizations and individuals that have tried to distance themselves from immigrants in an attempt to integrate into the dominant society. Historical and contemporary patterns reveal that while Mexican American–Mexican immigrant solidarity has always existed, it becomes increasingly evident in situations where practices and beliefs are perceived to indiscriminately target or restrict the life chances of all individuals of Mexican descent.

This chapter concludes by highlighting the importance of the contemporary scholarship on micro attitudes and routine exchanges in community arenas. This conclusion leads to the subsequent chapters that explore how within the macroscopic context outlined in this chapter Mexican American men and women are negotiating race/ethnic relations in their everyday lives. For a better understanding of the dominant frameworks influencing academic scholarship and Mexican American–Mexican immigrant relations, we now turn to a discussion of the underlying tenets of the assimilation and power-conflict perspectives.

The Assimilationist Paradigm: The Emphasis on Culture

> Some say that Chicanos are no different from other immigrants who arrived in the United States impoverished, and who managed by hard work to gain advantages for their children, taking the first step toward assimilation. (Estrada et al. 1981, 128)

Since the early post–World War II era, the assimilationist paradigm has been the dominant theoretical framework conceptualizing race/ethnic relations (Yetman 1991), and Americanization and the emphasis on cultural assimilation has been its prevailing practice (G. Gonzalez 1990).[4] The assimilationist paradigm is premised on the idea of "sameness," in which the experiences of groups of color in the United States are equated with the experiences of Southern, Central, and Eastern European immigrants (Frankenberg 1993, 14). The belief is that ethnic succession is the eventual outcome for all groups.

While all new groups certainly undergo a period of hardship when they enter the United States, the assumption of the assimilationist paradigm is that immigrants from Mexico, for example, will eventually integrate into the dominant society as it is believed that Irish, Italian, and Jewish immigrant groups did before them. As groups acculturate by adopting the characteristics of the dominant group—including the values, beliefs, language, and behaviors—cultural differences are thought to become less important. Groups are then expected to assimilate structurally by entering into the organizations, institutional activities, and general life of the dominant society. This straight-line theory of assimilation assumes that over time, immigrants, their children, and their grandchildren become less ethnically identifiable (Park 1950; Gordon 1964). As immigrants and their children learn the dominant culture and lose their traditional ways, it is believed that the established majority will become less hostile toward them. It is further argued by some that racial or ethnic groups who have not acquired socioeconomic parity or structural integration maintain distinct cultural characteristics which are at odds with the values and norms necessary to gain entrance into the dominant society (Glazer and Moynihan 1975; Sowell 1981; Harrison 1999).

In explaining the position of the Mexican-origin population in the United States, social scientists working within this assimilationist model have tended to focus on presumed cultural "deficiencies" (Mario Barrera 1979). Some have attributed a lack of structural assimilation into the dominant society to a belief that Mexicans are too "clannish" or "present time oriented" (Madsen 1964; Heller 1966). Today, some scholars still believe that the "malfunctioning" of the Mexican-origin family or the maintenance of the Spanish language has prevented advancement (Chavez 1991). Overall, greater acculturation, "modernization," and "becoming American" have been trumpeted as prerequisites to acquiring complete structural integration and success.

Generally, the assimilationist model is based on the ideas of meritocracy and of integration into the dominant society as a racially neutral process that is necessary, inevitable, and desirable. By focusing on supposed cultural aspects, this perspective reinforces a hierarchy in which the dominant values, traditions, language, and aspirations are seen as superior. Within this paradigm, "Mexican culture" and "American culture" are often portrayed as static and dichotomous, without consideration for their heterogeneity, intersectionality, or simultaneity—that is, the ways they are diverse and in flux, influence one another, and may overlap.

This paradigm also tends to neglect the distinct social factors and processes that have resulted in migration as well as the different conditions that groups have faced while in the United States (Blauner 1972; Mario Barrera 1979; Steinberg 1989; Portes and Rumbaut 1990). By failing to sufficiently analyze differing historical backgrounds and material conditions, assimilationists have tended to blame individuals and distinct racial/ethnic groups for their position in society. For the Mexican-origin population, in which the asymmetrical power relationships between the United States and Mexico have endured and been linked socially, economically, and culturally, the assimilationist model does not capture the macroscopic factors influencing individuals, families, communities, and migration patterns.

The popularity of the assimilationist model has fluctuated over the past thirty years. As Omi and Winant (1994) have described, in the mid-1960s and early 1970s, it declined in acceptance as academics and activists directly challenged it with power-conflict frameworks that provided class- and nation-based analyses for understanding race/ethnic relations. Nevertheless, since the late 1970s and the 1980s, there has been a resurgence in the assimilationist paradigm's fundamental tenets under the guise of neo-conservatism and the emphasis on being "color-blind" or "power-evasive" —not seeing color or racial hierarchies (Frankenberg 1993; Omi and Winant 1994).[5] Today, such a perspective is evident in the writings of Chavez (1991) and Skerry (1993), who argue that the experiences of Mexican Americans are similar to the experiences of European Americans and that they too are joining the American mainstream but are being seduced by Mexican American leaders and the political system to characterize themselves as a minority group that is victim to discrimination. This perspective is represented in the following passage:

Can Mexican Americans have it both ways? Should they? If their experience is in many ways similar to that of typical immigrant groups, then what entitles them to the same protections that the nation has, with considerable reluctance and controversy, given to blacks in recognition of the debilitating effects of slavery and Jim Crow? (Skerry 1993, 8-9)

Despite its fluctuations in academic discourse, the emphasis on assimilation remains a dominant expectation. It continues to guide and shape organizational practices and policies as well as individual worldviews, expectations, and behaviors (see Valenzuela 1999). Most recently in California, the movement for a "Racial Privacy" initiative epitomizes this power-evasive approach. Supported by Ward Connerly, the same person who led the Proposition 209 campaign to eliminate affirmative action, this initiative would prohibit state agencies from collecting racial and ethnic data. It advocates a "color-blind" society without interrogating historical, organizational, and structural racial/ethnic discrimination.

As will become clear in Chapter 5, the ideology and practice of assimilation and Americanization have influenced respondents' perceptions of and interactions with Mexican immigrants. While the Spanish-speaking abilities of some individuals may have been affected because of the emphasis on assimilation and a pattern of language repression, a few have accepted the dominant discourse such that they too advocate that immigrants should "learn American customs." As illustrated below, a power-conflict framework, though to a lesser extent than the assimilationist paradigm, has also influenced race/ethnic relations scholarship. It is an approach that has affected popular discourse, and it captures the perceptions of a number of La Puente residents.

The Power-Conflict Paradigm: The Emphasis on Structural Factors and Ideological Processes

[Southern, Central, and Eastern European] immigrants were disparaged for their cultural peculiarities, and the implied message was, "You will become like us whether you want to or not." When it came to racial minorities, however, the unspoken dictum was, "No matter how much like us you are, you will remain apart." (Steinberg 1989, 42)

As illustrated in Steinberg's (1989) *Ethnic Myth,* power-conflict theorists have critiqued the assimilationist paradigm for its failure to explain the experiences of Mexican Americans and other groups of color. Critics argue that most assimilationists do not sufficiently analyze the system of inequality or the historical backgrounds and material conditions of different racial/ ethnic groups. As various sociologists have argued, such factors are significant for understanding why groups of color in the United States have generally not achieved the same level of social, political, and economic integration experienced by earlier European immigrants (Blauner 1972; Lieberson 1980; Omi and Winant 1994; Steinberg 1989; Almaguer 1994).

Specifically reacting to the application of the straight-line theory of assimilation to groups of color, power-conflict theorists have argued that differences in initial forms of incorporation into the United States, coupled with the imposition of various racial ideologies—used to justify domination—have been critical in fostering distinct experiences for groups of color and previous groups of European immigrants (Blauner 1972; Camarillo 1984; Almaguer 1994). While most Europeans immigrated individually and relatively voluntarily, the history of Mexican Americans in the United States is marked with conquest and exclusion. In his theory of internal colonialism, Blauner (1972) explains that as a result of these historical variations, the labor forces in the Western Hemisphere became organized by race and color. Free labor became associated with White Europeans, and unfree labor was equated with people of color (57). Also, the destruction and transformation of the cultures of groups of colors by colonizers resulted in the enhancement of the dominant culture, further legitimization of the cultural oppression of the colonized groups, and an increase in racial notions of superiority and inferiority (66–68). Racializing ideologies such as Manifest Destiny, assimilation, Anglo superiority, and the color-evasive rhetoric have justified and perpetuated a racial hierarchy that has subordinated groups of color to Whites (Almaguer 1994; Menchaca 1995).

Since the assimilationist paradigm does not capture the complexity of the experiences of the Mexican-origin population, to understand Mexican American–Mexican immigrant relations I use an integrated power-conflict perspective. This umbrella approach emphasizes the impacts of historical events, structural factors, and dominant ideologies that emerge throughout time and remain significant today. As the following section indicates, these include U.S. colonialism, patterns of labor exploitation—highlighted in the cycle of Mexican immigrant recruitment and deportation—the persistence of individual and institutional racism and discrimination, and a history of resistance as exemplified by the Chicana/o movement. It is my contention that these events and factors have influenced the experiences of Mexican Americans and, as a result, their attitudes toward and interactions with immigrants. While these macro forces are interrelated, for purposes of elaboration I discuss each of them separately. With these historical events and macroscopic factors and processes as a framework, I then discuss the salience of cultural commonalities on intra-ethnic relations.

An Integrated Power-Conflict Approach

A History of Colonialism: The U.S. Conquest of Northern Mexico

As power-conflict theorists have argued, the nineteenth-century United States military conquest of northern Mexico had a transformative impact on the experiences of people of Mexican descent (Blauner 1972; Mario Barrera 1979). The conflict—referred to in the United States as the Mexican American War and in Mexico as the War of the North American Invasion—ended in 1848 with the signing of the Treaty of Guadalupe Hidalgo. This treaty forced Mexico to give up the present-day states of Arizona, California, Nevada, New Mexico, Texas, and Utah and parts of Colorado to the United States in return for fifteen million dollars (Acuña 1988, 19). As such, this treaty politically separated communities of Mexicans who were living and would eventually live in the newly constructed United States from those who resided in Mexico.

The ideology of Manifest Destiny was employed to justify the conquest of northern Mexico. As Almaguer (1994) writes, "European Americans saw it as their manifest destiny, their mission, to settle the entire North American continent with a homogenous population" (32). Thus, the United States' conquest of more than half of Mexico is an explicit expression of Manifest Destiny from this time period. However, "symbolically, the notion of manifest destiny implied the domination of civilization over nature, Christianity over heathenism, progress over backwardness and Whites over Mexicans and Native Americans" (33).

The underlying tenets of Manifest Destiny helped to rationalize and to support a racial/ethnic hierarchy that placed Whites and Anglo practices, values, and beliefs above the Californio elite, who included Mexican and Spanish landowners in California, above the Mexican working class, and above African Americans, Asian immigrants, and Native Americans (D. J. Weber 1973; Ruiz 1998). As a result of these class and color distinctions, the Mexican working class, despite being granted citizenship rights in what was now the United States, encountered prejudice and discrimination comparable to those experienced by other racialized groups in California (Vigil 1980; Almaguer 1994). Initially, the more accepted Californio elite, who were deemed "half civilized" because of their Europeanized culture and ancestry, were briefly able to avoid and contest the discriminatory legislation that subordinated other groups of color (D. J. Weber 1973; Almaguer 1994).

Shortly after the U.S. conquest, the California gold rush brought with it economic competition that resulted in a wave of anti-Mexicanism. With the exception perhaps of the wealthy Californios, White newcomers to California stopped distinguishing between Californios and Mexican immigrants, and in the minds of many, they all became "greasers" or "foreigners," regardless of generation. In the gold mines, such anti-Mexican sentiment manifested itself in lynchings, beatings, and robberies of Mexican American and Mexican immigrant miners. The California Legislature also initiated a Foreign Miners' Tax in 1850 that was used to target Chinese as well as Spanish-speaking miners. This prejudice and discrimination against the Spanish-speaking population was prevalent throughout California. However, their weight was borne differently according to class and color differences: it was largely working-class Mexicans whose individual rights were violated in everyday spheres, while for the most part, light-skinned, wealthy Californios were forced to struggle to maintain control of their land (D. J. Weber 1973).

California statehood quickly altered much of the Californio elite's political influence as the Mexican land titles that were to be protected under the Treaty of Guadalupe Hidalgo were transferred on a massive scale from the Spanish-speaking population to Anglos between 1848 and 1880 (Griswold del Castillo 1990; Almaguer 1994). Expensive litigation used to defend land grants, removal of unlawful "squatters," the imposition of property taxes, and sales of land for debts reduced many Mexicans in the Southwest to a landless people who became politically and economically powerless and had a foreign language and culture imposed on them (Pitt 1966; D. J. Weber 1973; Mario Barrera 1979, Estrada et. al. 1981; Almaguer 1994). As historians have described, southern California was transformed from "Mexican pueblos to American barrios" (Camarillo 1979) as Mexicans became "foreigners in their native land" (D. J. Weber 1973).

Scholars have documented that for the Mexican-origin population in the newly conquered territory, ethnic identity and intra-ethnic relations were influenced by their distinct class positions and placements on the racial/ethnic hierarchy as well as the prejudice and discrimination they experienced by European Americans. In some cases, a collective sense of ethnic awareness developed in response to such unequal treatment (Gutiérrez 1995; Ruiz 1998).

Before U.S. annexation, Mexicans referred to themselves largely in regional or local terms such as Californios, Tejanos, or Nuevomexicanos rather than with the Republic of Mexico (D. J. Weber 1982; Gutiérrez 1995). However, by the 1850s, Mexicans in the United States started to refer to themselves as a community distinct from Anglos, using terms such as "Mexicano" and "La Raza" to refer to Mexicans in Mexico and in the United States (Gutiérrez 1995). Aware of Anglo perceptions, working-class Mexicans attempted to limit contact with them by residing in ethnic neighborhoods where they continued to engage in traditional cultural practices. Some began to organize based on this collective identity, forming voluntary associations and newspapers (D. J. Weber 1973; Gutiérrez 1995). This shared sense of ethnic consciousness has been attributed to the challenge of adapting to a new social order and the prejudice and discrimination Mexicans encountered, including the persisting perception that Mexicans, despite their historical connection to the area, were "foreigners" or "non-Americans" (Gamio 1971; Gutiérrez 1995). At times, this collective consciousness stemmed from the desire to assert a positive group image to contradict Anglos' disparaging perceptions. Thus, a shared sense of identity emerged among the Mexican-origin population in response to the U.S. conquest and encounters with exclusionary ideologies and practices (Gutiérrez 1995).

However, among some in the Mexican-origin community, internal divisions linked largely to class position and region persisted such that many of the Californio elite and light-skinned Mexicans tended to refer to themselves as "Spanish" in an attempt to distance themselves from "Mexicanos," a term adopted by more working-class Mexican individuals and communities (Gamio 1971; Gutiérrez 1995). As the Californio elite began to lose their economic and political status in the United States, it is believed that descendants of these wealthy families attempted to maintain their previous status distinctions even more (McWilliams 1990; Gutiérrez 1995). Frequently earning the gratitude of Anglos, the more highly regarded Californios were known to have participated in vigilante groups against Mexican Americans who were believed to be involved in what has been called "social banditry" (D. J. Weber 1973, 206–207). In a display of resistance to Anglo control over the Southwest and Anglos' acts of discrimination, some Mexicans engaged in social banditry that involved "committing antisocial acts against the society that victimized them" (Acuña 1988, 42).

Current racial/ethnic relations have their origins in this history of conquest and exploitation (Blauner 1972, 29). For Mexicans, a history of forced, exclusionary, and exploitative integration into the United States is exemplified by their current social, economic, and political status in the United States and by dominant perceptions such that some U.S. residents may continue to define and treat Mexicans as foreigners. The enduring asymmetrical power and economic relations between the United States and

Mexico are further elucidated in the historical patterns of U.S. recruitment and deportation of Mexican immigrants.

Patterns of Labor Exploitation: Cycles of Recruitment and Deportation

Since the conquest, the U.S. government and capitalists have engaged in a pattern of recruitment and deportation of Mexicans depending on the demands of the domestic economy and labor market conditions. When there has been a need for laborers, the United States has turned to Mexico. However, during economic downturns, Mexican immigrants and Mexican Americans have oftentimes been scapegoated and "repatriated" or deported. This "revolving door strategy" (Cockcroft 1986) of migration, which has coincided with the ideology of White supremacy and with racial discrimination against the Mexican-origin community, has reproduced race/ethnic and class inequality and the image of Mexicans as "forever foreigners" and as "disposable labor."

The first major wave of Mexican immigration occurred between World War I and the Great Depression. During this period, Mexican immigration to the United States, mostly to the Southwest, was a result of economic and political problems in Mexico and inflated labor demands in the United States (Estrada et al. 1981; Monto 1994). In particular, the economic, political, and social disruption of the Mexican Revolution (1910–1920), the desire of Southwestern employers for cheap labor, and the labor shortage associated with World War I were key factors that encouraged northward migration (Mario Barrera 1979). Pressure from industrialists and agriculturists led U.S. officials to waive sections of the literacy provisions of the 1917 Immigration Act for Mexican immigrants, and labor contractors actively recruited Mexicans for work in agriculture, railroads, mining, meat-packing houses, brickyards, and canneries (Ruiz 1987; Zavella 1987; Calavita 1992). Between 1917 and 1921, the years these exceptions were in force, more than 72,000 Mexicans were registered as temporary contract workers in the U.S. Southwest and Midwest (Cardoso 1980, 48). Thousands more crossed the border to work without documents.

During times of economic hardship, Mexicans were blamed by state officials, the media, and Anglos in general for economic and social problems. In Los Angeles in the 1910s, Anglos attributed the social problems caused by industrial expansion to the arrival of 50,000 Mexicans, although, as Acuña (1988) describes, 500,000 Anglos also were arriving (160). In 1929 Congress passed a law making it a felony for Mexicans to enter the United States without documents, thereby transforming Mexican immigrants from migratory workers into "criminals" or "illegal aliens" in a land that was once their own (Mirandé 1985, 51–52). Such laws explicitly divided the Mexican-origin population in the United States and those in Mexico and drew distinctions between documented and undocumented immigrants.

During the economic depression of the 1930s, scapegoating and anti-Mexican sentiment in the United States increased. As the Great Depression led to high unemployment rates, nativists argued that Mexicans were taking jobs away from "citizens," that they were in the United States "illegally," and that they should not benefit from public services. Such sentiment was directed at both Mexican immigrants and Mexican Americans and resulted in the repatriation and deportation during the 1930s of nearly one million people of Mexican descent, including Mexican American children (Balderrama and Rodríquez 1995, 158). In March 1931 the first repatriation train that was organized by the Los Angeles County Welfare Department left, and by September 1931, 50,000 Mexicans and their Mexican American children had been repatriated from Los Angeles. This represented about a third of the Mexican-origin population in Los Angeles (ibid., 104). As a result of repatriations and restricted immigration, by 1940 the Mexican-origin population in the United States declined to about half of what it had been in the previous decade (González 1983, 71). The propaganda used to advocate and justify such expulsions reinforced the image of Mexican immigrants and Mexican Americans as "non-Americans," "aliens," and "the other" (Guerin-Gonzales 1994).

Despite the anti-immigrant and anti-Mexican sentiment of the 1930s, the onset of World War II brought new labor demands. In 1942 the United States government initiated the Bracero Program, a contract worker program with Mexico, and thousands of Mexican workers were recruited. This program, which lasted from 1942 to 1964, provided Mexicans with temporary work visas and the United States with a cheap reserve army of labor to replace Mexican Americans who fought in World War II and Japanese Americans who were interned in concentration camps (Acuña 1988; Amott and Matthaei 1991). The governments of the United States and Mexico in 1942 formed a preliminary agreement, the Emergency Labor Program. Since this program was seen as offsetting the labor shortage created by the war, nativist groups tended not to reject to the importation of temporary workers. Under this program, about 200,000 braceros were brought to work in the United States from 1942 to 1947 (Acuña 1988, 262).

The Bracero Program was formalized in 1951 and officially continued until 1964 (Mario Barrera 1979, 116–117). Between 1942 and 1964, five million braceros with temporary labor contracts entered the United States (Calavita 1992, 1), along with about five million more Mexicans who entered without documents, to meet the demands of U.S. agribusiness (Hondagneu-Sotelo 1994, 22–23). The program was eventually terminated because of a decreased demand for farm labor due to mechanization and an increased opposition by U.S. workers and because growers feared militancy among Mexican workers (Acuña 1988; Amott and Matthaei 1991). Despite this, many Mexicans continued to migrate to the United States as undocumented workers, relying on contacts made during the program. Thus, the Bracero Program has been described as setting the foundation for future migration by providing both a psychological and a social bridge between the United States and the generation of children whose parents migrated during the program (Mario Barrera 1979; Chavez 1998). Furthermore, the family, job, and community networks that developed during this twenty-two-year period facilitated the migration of other undocumented and documented immigrants (Massey et al. 1987; Chavez 1998).

During part of the same period as the Bracero Program, anti-communist sentiment and the post–Korean War recession from 1953 to 1955 resulted in another wave of mass deportations by the Immigration and Naturalization Service (INS). Newspapers agitated anti-immigrant sentiment by calling for the expulsion of Mexican immigrants and depicting undocumented workers as dangerous. During this so-called "Operation Wetback," the INS deported 875,000 Mexicans in 1953. In 1954 the INS deported 1,035,282; in 1955 more than 250,000 Mexicans were deported, and in 1956 the number was over 90,000 (Acuña 1988, 267). In 1952 the McCarran-Walter Act enabled the Justice Department to deport politically "undesirable aliens and naturalized citizens," resulting in the deportation of many Mexican immigrants active in labor organizing (Acuña 1996, 113).

During the 1960s, documented and undocumented Mexican immigrants continued to enter the United States. Los Angeles was the preferred destination, and the Mexican-origin population in the county increased from 576,717 in 1960 to 1,228,593 in 1970 (Acuña 1996, 114). Compared to previous waves of Mexican migration, this phase was characterized by a greater representation of women, families, and children (Portes and Bach 1985; Durand and Massey 1992; Hondagneu-Sotelo 1994). A significant number were related to individuals who had worked in the United States as part of the Bracero Program. They legalized their status through their employers and were now able to bring their families to the United States under the family reunification preference system established in 1965. As Hondagneu-Sotelo (1994) documents in her study of a northern California city, this larger percentage of women and family migration resulted in the establishment of a number of permanent communities.

The 1970s economic recession in the United States and structural changes in the economy led to the scapegoating once again of Mexicans (Gutiérrez 1995; Acuña 1996). These economic changes included a shift from a manufacturing- to a service-based economy. Such a shift has led to a decline in production of durable goods in high-wage, unionized jobs and a relocation of industry from central cities to U.S. suburbs and international locations (Wilson 1978; Kasarda 1989; Morales and Ong 1993). Besides these changes, there also has been a gradual movement of undocumented workers from agricultural work to service-sector jobs in urban locales (Hondagneu-Sotelo 1994). Another important aspect of economic restructuring has been the growth of highly competitive small-scale assembly industries in large cities such as Los Angeles. These industries are part of an increasingly globalized economy and labor market that attract what Sassen (1998) has described as large numbers of low-wage laborers to these "global cities."

Such economic shifts, along with the growth in the Mexican-origin population, resulted in sensationalized newspaper stories of Mexican immigrants who were described as threatening the United States, taking jobs away from Americans, and not paying taxes. In response to and as a reflection of such media and public hysteria, the Immigration and Naturalization Service conducted neighborhood sweeps in predominantly Mexican American communities and deported undocumented immigrants. From 1971 through 1973, the INS apprehended 1,377,964 undocumented immigrants (Acuña 1996, 114). Simultaneously, some state governments proposed the creation of a national identification card (Gutiérrez 1995; Acuña 1996).

Throughout the mid-1980s, the media and politicians continued to perpetuate stereotyped perceptions of immigrants as threats to public safety and as a cause of social problems. Such sentiment led Congress to pass key legislation directly affecting the lives of undocumented immigrants. In an attempt to regulate illegal immigration, Congress passed the Immigration Reform and Control Act (IRCA) in 1986 (Donato 1993, 751). A restrictionist policy, IRCA was intended to reduce undocumented immigration by imposing employer sanctions against those who knowingly hired undocumented workers and providing amnesty to immigrants who qualified under Congress' stipulations. Applicants could apply for amnesty by proving continuous residence since January 1982 or by validating that they had engaged in farm work for ninety days between May 1, 1985 and May 1, 1986. By January 1989, of the 2.96 million people who had applied for amnesty, 70 percent were Mexican immigrants (McWilliams 1990, 328–330). Despite its makers' intentions, IRCA did not curb immigration, and some employers worked around the strict immigration policies to hire undocumented immigrants to fill labor-intensive jobs in the service sector (Hondagneu-Sotelo 1994; Acuña 1996).

The 1990s brought a resurgence of anti-immigrant sentiment. An economic recession in California in the early 1990s worsened the scapegoating of immigrants, particularly those from Latin America, in the form of a "Save Our State" initiative that was approved by 59 percent of the voters on November 8, 1994. This initiative, known as Proposition 187, barred undocumented residents from receiving public education, health care, and other publicly funded services (Alvarez and Butterfield 2000, 168). While most aspects of the proposition were ruled unconstitutional, it contributed to a climate in which Latinas/os are suspect, discriminated against, and not considered "Americans."

At the crux of this history of a revolving-door policy toward immigration is the maintenance of unequal power and economic relations between the United States and Mexico. In the final decades of the twentieth century, U.S. transnational corporations, with the support of governmental policies, deindustrialized the United States and moved many of their manufacturing plants to destinations including "free trade zones." These free trade zones, numbering two hundred in Mexico in 1992, are industrial regions where minimal or no tariffs are paid to export materials and where environmental and child labor laws are routinely violated. The U.S. Congress approved the North American Free Trade Agreement (NAFTA), which went into effect in 1994. NAFTA's aim is to remove tariff barriers among Mexico, Canada, and the United States. While supporters of such neo-liberal policies argue that they will benefit U.S. residents and will limit emigration from Mexico, these policies have spurred internal migration as subsistence farmers have been pushed off their land and have not been able to compete with U.S. agriculturalists. Likewise, increases in international migration have been positively correlated with the increases in U.S. factories and businesses in Mexico. Part of this international movement of people may be attributed to the fact that internal migration from the countryside to free trade zones often exposes individuals to the English language and to television images of the United States as the land of opportunity where they might earn higher wages for similar work. Despite the reduction of barriers for corporations and capital to move across borders, the movement of Mexicans into the United States continues to be restricted, and more expensive surveillance technology has forced some migrants to seek other, more dangerous routes to enter the United States (J. Gonzalez 2000, 228–245).

U.S. political and economic interests have influenced migration patterns and have determined what Portes and Rumbaut (1990) describe as "the context of reception" under which immigrants enter the United States. The oftentimes hostile reception encountered by Mexican immigrants reproduced the racial/ethnic and class hierarchies that emerged during the nineteenth-century conquest of northern Mexico. For the Mexican-origin population in the United States, these hierarchies have shaped and continue to influence individuals' everyday lives as they contend not only with economic inequality but also with individual and institutional forms of racism and discrimination.

The U.S. System of Racism and Discrimination

The racial/ethnic hierarchy and class distinctions evident in the years following the U.S. conquest set the stage for the policies, practices, and ideologies evident throughout the twentieth century. Since the conquest, the Mexican-origin population has faced a system of racism and discrimination in the United States that includes national, cultural, and racial oppression (E. Martínez 1995).

Through the 1950s, the life chances of Mexicans were constrained by overt exclusionary practices. As a result of discriminatory policies and practices, Mexicans were segregated into jobs that were dangerous, labor-intensive, seasonal, and poorly paid (Guerin-Gonzales 1994). They were placed into "Mexican classrooms" or "Mexican schools" where an emphasis was placed on vocational education (G. Gonzalez 1990). They were prevented from purchasing homes in certain communities, and in public facilities, individuals of darker complexion and who did not speak English were required to sit in segregated sections in movie theaters and were excluded from public swimming pools or were only allowed to use the pool just before it was cleaned (Camarillo 1979).

While today such exclusionary practices may not be as overt, some nonetheless persist. For example, as scholars have documented, de jure segregation has become de facto segregation in the school system (G. Gonzalez 1990). In fact, since the 1970s, Latina/o segregation has increased such that "Latina/o students are significantly more segregated than African Americans" (Orfield and Yun 1999, 27).[6] California schools in particular are approaching what Orfield and Yun (1999) describe as "hypersegregation." Just as de facto segregation persists in the overrepresentation of Mexican-origin students in underfunded urban schools, they also may experience segregation within schools in the form of curriculum tracking that can lead to their overrepresentation in vocational and non–college preparatory courses and course placements that may be racially skewed to their disadvantage (Oakes 1985; Orfield 1996).

The history of racism and discrimination against the Mexican-origin community has involved such violence and hate crimes as lynchings and police brutality. At times, the violence has been sanctioned by institutions and exacerbated by the media. The June 1943 Servicemen's Rampage in Los Angeles, more commonly known as the Zoot Suit Riots, is one such example. In his account of this period, Escobar (1999) explains how servicemen, cheered on by the police, local authorities, and the press, went into Mexican-origin communities, attacked and tore off the clothing of Mexican men, women, and children. African Americans and Filipinos also were targets of these attacks. Police abetted such atrocities by inciting riots with encouraging and provocative statements, standing by during the assaults, or arriving at the scene of these beatings after servicemen left and then arresting the victims—Mexican American youth. Local newspapers' anti-Mexican articles and stories about an alleged Mexican American crime wave fueled these rampages by fostering public hysteria against Mexicans.

Dominant ideologies, in particular the assimilationist ideology, have helped to rationalize these exclusionary practices and to reproduce inequality. For example, throughout the history of the United States, "Anglo conformity" has been the most prevailing ideology of assimilation (Gordon 1961). This ideology is the worldview that the English language and English-oriented cultural patterns should be maintained as dominant and standard in the United States. Underlying this ideology is the narrow construction of the United States' cultural, national, and racial identity as Anglo and White. Oftentimes connected with these ideas is the belief of Anglo racial and cultural superiority. Examples of the institutionalization of Anglo conformity include Americanization programs that emphasized cultural and linguistic acculturation and English-only movements that strive to maintain English as the primary language and to prohibit the speaking of other languages in public places such as schools and work sites.[7]

More recently, these underlying beliefs have persisted in the prevailing ideology of power evasiveness. As part of the assimilationist ideology, the dominant assumptions of a power-evasive perspective are that "we are all the same," that there is "a level playing field," and that racism is a thing of the past. Within this framework, people may say that they do not see race (Sleeter 1993), or they may equate being color-conscious with being racist (Blauner 1999). Socially constructed power differentials and racism are camouflaged and not acknowledged (Frankenberg 1993; Omi and Winant 1994). Thus, by failing to consider the larger societal factors that impact people's lives differently depending on their social locations—their position in society based on race/ethnicity, class, gender, etc., this discourse blames people of color for their positions in society and reinforces the prevailing notions of rugged individualism and meritocracy (Frankenberg 1993; P. McIntosh 1995). Individual and cultural factors, as opposed to historical, political, economic, and social ones, are used to explain group position.

Protest and Resistance: The Chicano Movement

In response to these multiple forms of racism and discrimination, there is a long history of resistance and collective action on the part of Mexican Americans. While protest movements have existed since the conquest, during the first half of the twentieth century there was an emergence of regional and national organizations—many of which reflected the assimilationist ethos of the larger society.[8] For example, as historians have recounted, the League of Latin American Citizens (LULAC), a primarily middle-class group founded in 1929, exemplified integrationist attitudes by advocating that parents teach their children the English language and by allowing only English-speaking U.S. citizens to become members (M. García 1989; Gutiérrez 1995).[9] Operating in a society that supported English only, English was declared the official language at LULAC meetings, and members believed that only by learning English could Mexican Americans become full U.S. citizens (Orozco 1992).[10]

However, political activity in the 1960s and 1970s challenged this emphasis on assimilation, integration, and immigrant restrictions that were advanced by the larger society, in schools, and by many middle-class and integrationist Mexican American organizations. As the 1950s came to an end and as the Black civil rights movement gained national attention, many began to feel that Mexican American organizations were not pressing hard enough to acquire civil rights (McLemore and Romo 1985). As a result, activists advocated for more aggressive organizing tactics, a stronger assertion of Mexican identity, and mobilizing as an interest group (Gutiérrez 1995, 181). It was within this context that the Chicano movement, with its anti-assimilationist, power-conflict perspective, emerged, dramatically altering perspectives on race/ethnic relations.

In the 1960s Chicana/o youth, motivated and inspired by the Black civil rights movement, by the farmworkers movement, and by land rights struggles in New Mexico, began their own radical movements (M. García 1994; Ruiz 1998). By the middle to late 1960s, Mexican American high school and college students were increasingly voicing their dissatisfaction with discrimination and inferior education through the formation of student organizations, the promotion of Chicana/o self-determination, student protests, school strikes, and the adoption of a Chicana/o identity (Gómez-Quiñones 1990; Gutiérrez 1995; Ruiz 1998). Historically used as a pejorative term applied to working-class Mexicans north of the Rio Grande or playfully by working-class Mexican Americans to refer to one another, in the 1960s the term "Chicano" was given political connotations by young activists who advocated self-determination, cultural pride, and ethnic solidarity (Gómez-Quiñones 1990; Gutiérrez 1995). Growing increasingly frustrated from experiencing discrimination and impatient with assimilationist policies, this Chicano generation rejected the acculturating tendencies of the previous generation and disparaged those who distanced themselves from their Mexican ancestry by identifying as "Latin American" or "Spanish-speaking" (Alvarez 1971).

Students involved in the Chicano movement argued for increasing the educational opportunities of Mexicans and establishing educational programs on Chicana/o history and experiences. In Los Angeles more than ten thousand students "blew out" of high schools to call attention to the racist attitudes and behaviors of the primarily White teaching staff, the course curriculum that ignored Chicana/o history and experiences, and the poor quality of education that Mexican students were receiving. In accordance with their commitment to confronting inequality, acquiring social justice, and rejecting assimilation, beginning in 1969 student organizations were changing their names to El Movimiento Estudiantil Chicano de Aztlán, or MEChA (Gómez-Quiñones 1990).

Following the school walkouts, Chicana/o activists continued to organize around a number of issues, one being the U.S. military involvement in Vietnam. In response to the disproportionate number of Mexican American casualties in the Vietnam War and in support for the Vietnamese struggle for national liberation, anti-war activists organized the August 29, 1970, National Chicano Moratorium. The moratorium brought together nearly thirty thousand people, including student activists, members of the United Farm Workers, and Mexican Americans from throughout the Southwest. It became not only an anti-war protest but also a public affirmation of the Chicano movement (Gómez-Quiñones 1990, 124). As a result, public officials denounced it, and the police used forceful means to disperse the crowd.

Not all people of Mexican-origin supported the tactics and ideologies of the Chicano movement. Some of the members and supporters of more established Mexican American organizations such as the GI Forum, LULAC, and other civil rights organizations were among the critics who felt that the Chicano movement was unrealistic and anti-American because of its nationalist focus (Gutiérrez 1995). Chicana feminists also criticized the lack of an analysis of sexism and the sexist and heterosexist ideologies and practices that were oftentimes replicated within the movement (A. García 1989; Zavella

1993; E. Martínez 1998; Ruiz 1998). Despite some of these problems, the movement has been described as effective for raising public awareness of the structural factors affecting the Mexican-origin community, eventually leading to the establishment of Chicano studies courses and departments, bilingual education classes, and affirmative action policies (E. Martínez 1998).

The Chicano movement also applied pressure to more assimilationist Mexican American organizations to reconsider their strategies for change, and it highlighted the historical, economic, and cultural connections that Mexican Americans and Mexican immigrants share (Gutiérrez 1995). Marxists within the movement emphasized the generally working-class connections Mexican Americans and Mexican immigrants shared and advocated strategies that fostered greater class consciousness (Gómez-Quiñones 1990). One organization established in 1968 that is credited for being the first during this era to systematically explore the relationships between Mexican immigration, ethnic identity, and Mexican Americans was El Centro de Acción Autonoma–Hermandad General de Trabajadores (the Center for Autonomous Social Action, CASA). Building class-based coalitions with Latino immigrants and Mexican Americans, CASA looked to the exploitation inherent in capitalism to understand the social position of Mexicans in the United States (Gutiérrez 1995; Ruiz 1998).

Influenced by the ideologies and practices of Chicana/o activists who drew on Mexican symbols and emphasized ethnic and class solidarity, more traditional Mexican American organizations such as the GI Forum and LULAC began to change their previous restrictionist views on immigration. Remembering the attacks on Mexican nationals in the 1930s and 1950s, Mexican Americans in the 1970s spoke out against anti-immigrant legislation and expressed concern for the civil and human rights of all people of Mexican descent in the United States. While in the past, restrictive legislation against immigrants was favored by integrationists who tended to believe that immigration was detrimental to the economic, political, and social position of U.S.-born Mexicans, these groups increasingly focused their critique on the government and the ways that such policies would negatively impact U.S. citizens of Mexican descent (Gutiérrez 1995).

While they remained ideologically and politically divided on many issues, traditional Mexican American organizations joined forces with Chicana/o groups to pressure César Chávez and the United Farm Workers (UFW) to reconsider their anti-immigrant position. Chávez and the UFW, from its inception in 1962, favored immigrant restrictions for fear that undocumented immigrants would limit unionization attempts. However, by the 1970s the UFW reversed its position by expressing solidarity with undocumented immigrants and by critiquing the state and federal governments' anti-immigrant legislation (Gutiérrez 1995).

Despite this general consensus on Mexican immigration, Mexican Americans, Chicanas/os, and immigrants continued to differ over how to work toward change, some advocating integration, others self-determination (Gutiérrez 1995). However, the practices and ideologies endorsed by the Chicano movement and other progressive movements have had a significant impact on public and academic rethinking of the assimilationist paradigm. These movements raised awareness of the structural factors and ideological processes that have limited the opportunities of groups of color in the United States. Thus, beginning in the 1960s such power-conflict approaches to race/ethnic relations have influenced academic scholarship and have been used by anti-racist and cultural nationalist activists (Omi and Winant 1994).

Today, power-conflict worldviews that include an awareness of structural inequality and a concern for social justice are apparent in the perspectives of La Puente residents such as Denise Villarreal, whose quote began this chapter. Most clearly elucidated in chapters 6 and 7, this perspective has enabled community-building and Mexican American–Mexican immigrant solidarity in opposition to racial/ethnic stereotypes, anti-Mexican sentiment, and educational inequality. For some, such a macro-historical and structural approach also involves challenging the assimilationist imperative and fighting to maintain the use of the Spanish language. While to understand intra-ethnic relations I adopt an integrated power-conflict perspective, given respondents' emphasis on the Spanish language it is also important to consider the significance of culture within this macro context.

In the Context of Structural Factors and Ideological Processes: The Significance of Cultural Commonalities on Group Relations

While assimilationists have tended to focus on cultural factors and power-conflict theorists on structural factors, scholars of panethnicity, or a "politico-cultural collectivity made up of people of several, hitherto distinct, tribal or national origins," have considered the relative significance of both cultural and structural factors (Espiritu 1992, 2; Lopez and Espiritu 1990; Padilla 1985). For example, focusing on the creation of a panethnic Latino identity among Mexican Americans and Puerto Ricans in Chicago, Padilla (1985) describes how the "interplay" between cultural and structural similarities may lead to the manifestation of group identity in specific situations and given certain social conditions (153). However, he argues that the Spanish language alone is not the defining factor that results in Latino political consciousness and mobilization. Similar to Lopez and Espiritu (1990), he attributes Latino politicization to shared structural commonalities—in particular, economic inequality and political exclusion (Padilla 1985, 153).

As in Padilla (1985), the findings for this work illustrate the significance of cultural factors on group identity. Likewise, in contrast to assimilationists who only focus on culture or who adopt the ideology of "cultural deficiency," my approach involves considering the cultural heterogeneity and fluidity among the Mexican-origin population as well as the social construction of culture and the salience of cultural commonalities within the larger framework of structural factors and ideological processes. Thus, though there is much variation in Spanish-language fluency, a common language—the Spanish language or a symbolic commitment to the Spanish language—can be a strong basis for group unity (Lopez and Espiritu 1990). As Padilla (1985) documents and as is the case in La Puente, this basis for group unity exists within a sociopolitical and economic context of inequality and repression of the use of the Spanish language. The subordination of the Spanish language is most recently illustrated in the English-only movement that resulted in the passage of two California propositions—the 1986 proposition declaring English the official language and the 1998 "English for the Children" proposition that severely restricted the teaching of bilingual education. Thus, in considering cultural factors, my approach pays attention to macroscopic factors and processes and also leaves space for a more contextualized analysis of the significance of cultural factors on group relations.

Before moving to a discussion of contemporary Mexican American–Mexican immigrant relations and the significance of structural factors, ideological processes, and their intersection with cultural factors, the following section reviews some of the existing scholarship to present a historical overview on Mexican American–Mexican immigrant relations. As such, it raises questions on how the historical patterns characterizing intra-ethnic relations compare with the contemporary findings presented in this study.

Mexican American–Mexican Immigrant Relations: A Historical Overview

As historical studies have documented, Mexican American–Mexican immigrant relations have been complex (D. J. Weber 1973; Gutiérrez 1995; Ruiz 1998). They have been influenced by society's perceptions of immigration and dominant practices toward the Mexican-origin community. Considering the impacts of social, cultural, and political contexts on Mexican American–Mexican immigrant relations, Gutiérrez (1995) writes that

Mexican Americans have been "torn between the strong cultural affinities they felt toward Mexico and Mexicans on one hand and their desire to be accepted . . . as equal members of American society on the other" (70). According to Gutiérrez, variations in class position, region, and culture among Mexican Americans have been connected to their differing perceptions of immigrants. A review of this historical scholarship and Mexican American–Mexican immigrant relations over time is helpful for understanding this complexity. Such a review also reveals how much of this research has tended to focus on Mexican-origin activists and organizations, leaving out the more micro everyday activities and attitudes that are centered in *Becoming Neighbors*.

Writing about Mexican American–Mexican immigrant relations during the 1910s and 1920s, the first major wave of Mexican immigration, historians recount the multifaceted character of intra-ethnic interactions. They describe how as a result of chain migration, the establishment of communities in the United States, and circular migration, the distinctions between Mexicans born in the United States and in Mexico were oftentimes blurred (Ruiz 1998). Living together in the same segregated areas, speaking Spanish, intermarrying, building fictive kin networks, and not being distinguished by Anglos (Gómez 1992), many Mexican American and immigrant families were intertwined (Ruiz 1998), shared a sense of ethnic identity (Weber 1994), and referred to themselves collectively as "La Raza" (Gamio 1971). Thus, there was a significant percentage of Mexican Americans who maintained strong cultural ties to Mexico and who empathized with immigrants (D. J. Weber 1973), and it was not uncommon for U.S.-born Mexicans and Mexican immigrants to establish and participate in the same organizations (Orozco 1992). Nevertheless, economic competition with immigrants and the possible extension of Anglo's negative views onto them concerned some Mexican Americans (Gamio 1971; Camarillo 1979; Gutiérrez 1995), resulting in immigrant-differentiation by more established residents who identified not as Mexican but as Spanish, Spanish-American, or Latin American (D. J. Weber 1973).

As Gutiérrez (1995) describes, during the 1930s Depression and repatriation drives in the United States, Mexican Americans' responses to immigrants remained polarized. Among working-class Mexican Americans and immigrants, there was a sense of commonality based on a shared cultural background and class position along with similar experiences of discrimination. Working-class individuals and groups generally thought that there were more commonalities that united the Mexican-origin community than differences. However, some Mexican Americans exhibited the belief that as citizens who were denied full acceptance into the United States, Mexican Americans should focus their energy on attempting to assimilate into the dominant society. For some this involved distinguishing themselves from immigrants.

Scholars have recounted how the Bracero Program pitted migrant workers against Mexican Americans. It was believed that the Bracero Program created a social and economic hierarchy within the Mexican-origin community that favored agribusiness (Mirandé 1985, 67). The 1940s, when the Bracero Program began, has been identified as marking a unique shift in terms of ethnic identity for the Mexican-origin community (Gómez 1992). During this period, Mexican Americans outnumbered Mexican immigrants (M. García 1985, 202) and an emerging middle class began to develop a sense of being American (Gómez 1992).

As examined in detail by Gutiérrez (1995), some of the beliefs of this emerging middle class were reflected in two key integrationist Mexican American organizations of the 1940s and 1950s, the GI Forum and LULAC. These organizations considered Mexican immigration to be the most important factor impacting Mexican Americans, and soon after the GI Forum was established in 1949, it applied pressure to convince Congress to end the Bracero Program and to instill strict regulations on immigration from Mexico. Not unlike some of the sentiments expressed during the first great wave of Mexican immigration in the 1910s and 1920s, members of the GI Forum and LULAC believed that the civil rights of Mexican Americans must be upheld and that the Bracero Program and undocumented immigration negatively affected their social, political, and economic position (Gutiérrez 1995, 155–157; M. García 1994). LULAC, the most visible Mexican American organization against the Bracero Program, stressed the differences between Mexican Americans and Mexican immigrants while strongly endorsing assimilation and restrictive immigration policies (Muñoz 1989; Gutiérrez 1995).

Gutiérrez (1995) notes that during this same period a significant proportion of the Mexican-origin community maintained the Spanish language, religious practices, and Mexican traditions as well as a strong sense of ethnic identity and connection with immigrants. Some of these same individuals allied with political activists to assist braceros and to support the rights of immigrants. He provides the example of the Community Service Organization (CSO), which supported the elimination of the Bracero Program but provided assistance to residents regardless of their documentation status. Unlike the GI Forum and LULAC, the CSO attempted to unite Mexican immigrants and Mexican Americans, and it encouraged the participation of all residents by not imposing citizenship requirements for membership (170). A small but growing number of Mexican Americans also linked the exploitation and discrimination experienced by immigrants with the civil rights abuses encountered by Mexican Americans.

The searches, seizures, and deportations of the 1950s under Operation Wetback fostered a climate where all people of Mexican descent were suspected of being undocumented (Acuña 1988). According to Gutiérrez (1995), such practices reinforced the realization that while the Mexican-origin community is heterogeneous in some ways, Mexican Americans and immigrants are inextricably linked and may be subjected to similar practices. Thus, the passage of the McCarran Walter Act and the INS sweeps during Operation Wetback resulted in a shift in the ideological positions of Mexican American organizations regarding immigrants. For Mexican American organizations including LULAC and the GI Forum, the government's treatment of non-U.S. citizens served as a catalyst for the evolution of a broader-based civil rights movement, one that included the rights of Mexican immigrants and that affirmed Mexican descent (Gutiérrez 1995, 172–178).

Scholars have illustrated how during the Chicano movement and throughout the 1980s, some Chicanas/os worked in solidarity with Mexican immigrants and Central American groups or engaged in grassroots and labor struggles comprised of Mexican Americans and Mexican immigrants (Kingsolver 1989; E. Martínez 1998; Pardo 1998; Ruiz 1998). They have also documented how with the emergence of the conservative 1980s, activism and public protests of the Chicana/o generation declined (Acuña 1988; E. Martínez 1998) and was replaced by what Gómez (1992) has referred to as "the Hispanic generation." Mexican American middle-class professionals, leaders, and politicians were believed to be adapting to the dominant ideologies of the period by focusing not on reform through grassroots organizing but on integration through electoral politics (Gómez 1992). At times this translated into divisions where more established Mexican Americans attempted to distinguish themselves from immigrants and supported movements to deny them services (E. Martínez 1998).

In a study of Santa Paula in the middle to late 1980s, Menchaca (1989, 1995) found considerable divisions between Mexican Americans and Mexican immigrants. Due to the ranking of cultures that places Anglo culture over Mexican culture, Mexican immigrants who were unfamiliar with or had not assimilated to the Anglo norms, practices, and values were seen as culturally "backward" by the "Americanized" Chicanas/os (Menchaca 1989, 218). Moreover, Menchaca claims that those who were proficient in English were ascribed higher social prestige. Thus, a clear demarcation existed between Chicanas/os and immigrants.[11] Immigrants were admitted into the social circles of Chicanas/os only after they learned the practices and traditions of the United States–born Mexicans. Despite such intra-group conflict, at times of crisis when Anglos in Santa Paula attempted to impose unequal policies or practices on those of Mexican origin, group cohesion resulted. Such ethnic solidarity was also evident in Santa Paula during movements for farmworker housing, braceros' rights, and the elimination of social segregation (Menchaca 1995).

Focusing on the 1992 Los Angeles uprisings, Oliver, Johnson, and Farrell (1993) recount how Mexican American political leaders from East Los Angeles attempted to distance themselves from Mexican and Central American immigrants residing in South Central Los Angeles. Much of the looting, firebombing, and violence that followed the announcement of the not-guilty verdict in the trial of four police officers accused of using excessive force in the arrest of African American motorist Rodney King was centered in South Central Los Angeles, Koreatown, and Pico-Union (see also Johnson et al. 1992). In comparison to the historically Mexican American community of East Los Angeles, these communities consist of African American and, more recently, immigrants from Mexico and Central America who are less likely to be homeowners and U.S. citizens. Such class and generational distinctions among the Mexican-origin and the broader Latina/o community became evident when East Los Angeles Mexican American leaders remained silent about the involvement of some recent Mexican and Central American immigrants in the uprisings.

Much of this history on Mexican American–Mexican immigrant relationships has been framed around the politics and ideologies of Mexican-origin organizations and activists. Such a discussion is important for providing a general overview. However, it tends to overlook the more micro everyday activities, attitudes, and lives of community members. In addition, it may camouflage the ways that women, who have not always been in traditionally defined political or leadership positions, may negotiate and articulate intra-ethnic relations. By focusing on individual attitudes and practices in the current scene, not only are we brought up to date on contemporary Mexican Americans' perceptions of Mexican immigrants, but we are provided with the narratives and experiences of Mexican American women and men.

Understanding Mexican Americans' Identities and Intra-Group Relations in Contemporary Society

The history of Mexicans in the United States is one rife with labor exploitation, discrimination, racism, and resistance. Exclusion and barriers in housing, employment, schooling, and public facilities have coexisted with the recruitment and deportation of immigrants, depending on the social, economic, and political climate. Such practices have been justified by ideologies that have reinforced and maintained a system of inequality that has been linked to race/ethnicity and class. Awareness of this macro context is critical for revealing the historical and material conditions that have shaped and constrained the experiences of Mexicans and Mexican American–Mexican immigrant relationships.

This macroscopic context has set the parameters that influence respondents' attitudes and interactions, but given their distinct experiences and social positions, individuals and communities are actively engaged in accepting, reacting to, and contesting social structures and dominant frameworks.

In the upcoming chapters that examine La Puente residents' complex and multifaceted processes of becoming neighbors, the structural factors, ideological processes, and cultural commonalities influencing intra-ethnic relations throughout history appear in the contemporary scene. As with the past, members of the Mexican-origin community continue to maneuver around such constraints to construct identities, attitudes, and relationships that are meaningful to them. The competing academic and popular frameworks on race/ethnic relations—the assimilationist and power-conflict paradigms—appear throughout respondents' narratives. The dynamics occurring within La Puente, California, are a reflection of the macro processes described in this chapter. To acquire a greater understanding of how these dynamics have played out at the community and individual levels, we move next to the city of La Puente.

Chapter 3

"Where the Past Meets the Future": Centering La Puente

> They keep coming—two million illegal immigrants in California. The federal government won't stop them at the border, yet requires us to pay billions to take care of them.
>
> LAURA ANGELICA SIMÓN, director of video *Fear and Learning at Hoover Elementary*, 1996

Television commercials endorsing California's Proposition 187, dubbed the "Save Our State" (SOS) initiative, played frequently during the fall of 1994—the period in which I began to systematically interview La Puente residents and to attend community events. During this period California was experiencing the most severe economic crisis since the Great Depression, and Proposition 187 effectively diverted attention away from the nearly one million jobs that had been lost in the early 1990s (Alvarez and Butterfield 2000, 168). Designed to eliminate social services to undocumented immigrants, Proposition 187 was premised on the belief that immigrants were spreading diseases, draining social services, crowding schools, and stealing jobs. Mexican immigrants already in the United States and Mexican immigration became the targets of this proposition and scapegoats for the declining economy. Though Proposition 187 was approved by a majority of voters, 77 percent of voting Latinas/os opposed the proposition (Acuña 1996, 160). It was just one of several California propositions during the 1990s that directly impacted the Mexican-origin community.

On the heels of the SOS initiative, California voters approved the 1996 ballot initiative to eliminate affirmative action, Proposition 209. This proposition, named the California Civil Rights Initiative (CCRI), appropriated the language of the civil rights movements and Martin Luther King Jr. and advocated that people "be judged by the content of their character, not the color of their skin." Proponents combined such color-evasive rhetoric with the dominant myth of meritocracy. They equated affirmative action with racial preferences for people of color and discrimination against White men. Seventy-six percent of Latina/o voters opposed Proposition 209 (Acuña 1998, 9).

In 1998, stemming from the larger "English-only" movement, bilingual education was severely limited in California by the passage of the "English for the Children" initiative, Proposition 227. Sixty-three percent of Latina/o voters opposed the elimination of bilingual education (Davis 2000, 122), with 37 percent voting in favor of the proposition. Although a significant proportion of the Latina/o voting population opposed these high-profile propositions, there has been some division among the diverse population, and it is reflected in such voting patterns. According to E. Martínez (1998), this division among Latina/o voters has continued such that "since 1980 an approximately 40 percent conservative vote by Latinos on national and state issues has been fairly predictable" (200–201).

Despite Latinas/os general opposition to these propositions, all three passed. Even though such propositions specifically targeted and would affect Mexican Americans and Mexican immigrants, public opinion outside of the Mexican-origin community was determining the fate and experiences of Mexican families and children. For example, 80 percent of those who voted in the 1994 California elections were middle-class Whites (Acuña 1996, 160). Striking a cord in many, these state propositions received much attention and sparked heated debates about rights, citizenship, and "Americanism." Just as the debates surrounding these issues swept across California, they also crept into the city of La Puente, into residents' homes, churches, schools, and city offices. While only half of the approximately 10,000 registered voters in La Puente voted on these propositions, they too were divided.[1]

In the context of changing demographics and economic downturns, these debates are not new. As we saw in the previous chapter, these debates have been waged throughout history and have resulted in the dispossession of land and experiences of exploitation, racism, and discrimination. Historically, in communities such as La Puente, such oppression has taken the forms of segregation and of restricting public use of the Spanish language. Contemporarily, it persists in attempts to exclude Mexican immigrants from equal facilities and to force the learning and speaking of English instead of Spanish.

This chapter tells the story of La Puente from its time as a Mexican rancho to its status as a U.S. city with a predominantly Mexican-origin population. Organized chronologically, it provides a historical, demographic, and economic profile of the area. Following a discussion of the racial/ethnic and class hierarchies of the 1800s and early 1900s, the memories of older La Puente residents illustrate the history of Mexicans' exclusion. As the chapter progresses into the contemporary scene, an emphasis is placed on the transformation of La Puente from an agricultural area to a suburban, working-class Mexican-origin community. Just as the Spanish language and "the Mexican situation" were issues of concern included in the 1940s school board minutes, contemporary debates on similar topics are being waged by city and school officials and among community residents. By exploring these historical and contemporary patterns, we see that the social relations in La Puente reflect the class and racial/ethnic inequality of the history of California. We also acquire a greater understanding of the continuity and change of La Puente, including the asymmetrical power relations that have characterized the area.

La Puente: From Rancho to City

The Early Years

As has been the case throughout the Southwest, the history of La Puente is one of conquest, labor exploitation, racism, and discrimination. The establishment of the San Gabriel Mission in 1771 and the Christianizing attempts by the missionaries had a devastating impact on the indigenous population that had inhabited the land. Following Mexico's independence from Spain in 1821, further transformations occurred, influencing class and race/ethnic relations (Camarillo 1979; Almaguer 1994). These transformations included the introduction of the land-tenure system and the secularization of the Spanish missions. In 1824 the Mexican National Congress granted large tracts of land and encouraged settlement in Alta California (Almaguer 1994, 47), and the 1834 Secularization Proclamation led to the breakup of the California missions (Camarillo 1979, 9). The La Puente Valley represented one of the largest areas that had been part of the San Gabriel Mission and was described by some as having "the richest soil in America" (Rowland 1958, 8).

Following the Secularization Proclamation, which stated that half of the mission lands were to be divided among the colonists and Native Americans who had lived on the mission (Camarillo 1979, 9), the original residents of the area had sought to acquire Mexican land grants for Rancho La Puente. Dismissing the residents' claims, the nearly 50,000 acres of land that constituted Rancho La Puente were granted by the Mexican government to two Anglos new to California, John Rowland and William Workman (C. McIntosh 1960, 1; La Puente Valley Historical Society 1976, 9–10).

Aspiring rancheros, Rowland and Workman came to the Los Angeles area in 1841 with a group of twenty-five people (including other speculators, families, and servants) from New Mexico (Rowland 1958, 8).[2] Having converted to Catholicism and becoming Mexican nationals, they married

Mexican women of elite families, María de la Encarnación Martínez and Nicolasa Urioste, respectively.[3] Since they had lived long enough in New Mexico to become Mexican citizens, Rowland and Workman were eligible to receive land grants from the Mexican government (McIntosh 1960, 1). It is described that through their strategically acquired status, political maneuvering, and their offer of money, Rowland and Workman secured the land grant for Rancho La Puente in July 22, 1845 (La Puente Valley Historical Society 1976, 11).[4]

The granting of large areas of land to individuals such as Rowland and Workman resulted in greater concentrations of wealth and power. These two Anglo-Mexican families who were assimilated into Mexican society shared their class position with other rancheros in the area who were often Spanish and mestizo (Spanish and Indian) Californios (Camarillo 1979). In contrast, Native Americans were relegated to laborer status, and those who worked on Rancho La Puente were said to have been paid in merchandise (Rowland 1958, 37). Working-class Mexicans also played a critical role in the formation of La Puente, as they too constituted the labor used by Rowland and Workman in their ranching businesses and later in the agricultural industry (Sandoval 1994).[5] The wealthy families of La Puente lived in fort-like residences enclosed behind adobe walls that separated them from the homes of Native Americans and of other Mexicans. In 1868 Rowland and Workman divided the land grants between themselves. Rowland took the eastern section of the rancho—from which a section was mapped as the Puente town site in 1886 (Rowland 1958).[6]

Through the 1860s the area's economy was based on cattle raising (Camarillo 1979; Almaguer 1994), and this was the case in Puente as well (Radford 1984). However, floods and a severe drought in the early 1860s devastated the pastoral economy as large numbers of cattle, horses, and sheep died (Almaguer 1994, 85). Over the next seventy to eighty years, agriculture became the economic base, and in Puente it centered around citrus fruits, walnuts, and avocados.[7]

By the turn of the century, along with the walnut and citrus industries, the population of Puente was also growing. The Rowland Township, used as a reporting base by the United States Census through 1930 and larger than the Puente Township, indicates that the population in 1890 was 736. By 1910 the population had more than doubled to 1,823—with about 200 people living in Puente. In 1920 the Rowland Township had increased to 2,545 (Riley 1962, 16). Among the groups now residing in Puente were Anglo as well as French, Basque, Italian, and Mexican families. Between 1890 and 1970 European Americans constituted the majority of the population, and they came to be the majority of the landowners in Puente, while Mexicans were largely agricultural laborers (Sandoval 1994, 29).

During the 1910s and 1920s, part of the population growth was attributable to the Mexican-origin population, which increased in large part as a result of migration and labor recruitment. The desire of Southwestern employers for cheap labor and the labor shortage associated with World War I led contractors to actively recruit Mexicans for work, and in Puente's walnut industry, Mexican workers provided much of the labor. In 1925 nearly 2,500 Mexican men, women, and children "picked, hulled, sacked, and delivered" walnut crops to the walnut-packing house (Pinheiro 1960, 85).[8] A third-generation La Puente resident, Roberta Zavala, described the work lives of her grandparents, who were among the migrant farm laborers who eventually settled in Puente:

> They were the orchard pickers, the walnuts, the oranges, whatever was in season. Then they moved from place to place in Southern California, and they just liked the La Puente area.

In an interview in 2001, a descendant of the original Rowland family recalled the Mexican migrant workers whom her grandparents employed to pick walnuts on their 160-acre ranch in Puente:

> There were always people that were hired to help . . . It was usually the same group of people who came. In the eucalyptus grove that my grandfather planted, there were three little they looked like dollhouses. They were little wood and corrugated tin houses, and the migrant workers would stay there in those little houses. The houses were there in expectation that these people would come. It was a routine that they had . . . I've been told it was the same families. My mother said that they saw children born, children next year one year old, next year two, and so on.

The recruitment and confinement of Mexican workers into such manual labor and under a secondary wage scale maintained class and racial/ethnic inequality.

Overall, these early racial/ethnic and class dynamics in Puente capture the long Mexican presence in the area (including established residents, as in the Rowland and Workman families and Mexican immigrants), as well as the race/ethnic, class, and immigrant distinctions within the community. Similar to other communities, as the Mexican population and the agricultural industry in Puente grew in the 1920s, institutionalized segregation increased, especially within the education system (see Menchaca 1995).

Hudson Primary Building, 1930s

Remembering a History of Exclusion: Carlos and Leticia Mendoza

Along with the segregation of Mexicans into low-wage and labor-intensive occupations, Puente was also residentially segregated. Seventy-five- and seventy-six-year-old Carlos and Leticia Mendoza had much to say in an interview in 2000 about living under segregation in Puente through the 1950s. The son of immigrants, Carlos Mendoza was born in Puente, the location his parents moved to at the turn of the twentieth century. A third-generation Mexican American Puente resident, Leticia Mendoza moved with her family to the region in the 1880s.

The Mendozas remember that the Mexican-origin community was confined to certain residential areas, businesses, churches and schools, as Leticia Mendoza describes the circumstances:

> We had a barrio, and it was from Central up to Valley Boulevard. We were not allowed to buy a home outside of Central. We were all segregated. We all lived in this barrio, and we all knew each other. The area isn't that big. Where the library is now, that was our school, called Central School.

The Puente barrio described by the Mendozas was bordered by Main Street —the town's center—to the east and railroad tracks and Valley Boulevard— the key access ways to Los Angeles—to the south. The roads that surrounded this community merged on a third side and looked out to the walnut, citrus, and avocado fields (Sandoval 1994).

As the Mexican-origin population throughout the Southwest grew, school boards established segregated schools or classrooms that focused on teaching Mexican-origin students manual labor, hygiene, and the English language (G. Gonzalez 1990; Menchaca 1995; Ruiz 1998). A 1930s study found that segregation existed in 85 percent of the school districts surveyed in the Southwest (G. Gonzalez 1990, 21). As the Mendozas recount, the Hudson Elementary School District in Puente was no different. The first Puente school was opened in 1889. It was a one-room school, and in 1910, to accommodate the growing community, a new and larger Hudson School replaced the first one (La Puente Valley Historical Society 1976, 16).

In 1920, Central Avenue Americanization School, a segregated school attended by Mexican and Japanese students, was built.[9]

A student at Central in the 1920s and 1930s, Leticia Mendoza recalls the segregation that existed within the Hudson Elementary School District:

> Our school was called Central School, and we were segregated. Only Mexicans and Japanese went there . . . The Japanese could not go with the White either. The White went to Hudson School. That was the name of their school. We went to school together through grammar school.

A review of the Hudson Elementary School District minutes from the 1920s through the 1940s illustrates that discussions surrounding the segregation of Mexican students in Puente were scarcely documented. However, during a 1943 board meeting, school board trustees requested that the district superintendent inform Mexican parents that they were to send their children to what was described as "the Mexican School," Central Avenue:

> The Mexican Situation was discussed at length concerning the segregation of Mexican children. The Board requested the superintendent to write letters to parents of Mexican Extraction suggesting that they have their children attend the Mexican School, and that their cooperation was desired. (Hudson Elementary School District 1943)

Central Avenue Americanization School, 1930s

Americanization was a primary goal of Central Avenue School. The focus of instruction was the English language, American citizenship, and respect for California and the United States. The Hudson Elementary School District superintendent from 1931 to 1945, Douglas P. Lucas, explained that the additional money and time given to the operation of Central Avenue School was premised on the perception that the Mexican-origin community accepted authority and would not resist segregation and Americanization (Lucas, n.d.).

Americanization programs reached beyond students in the classroom. Supporters of Americanization also sought to change Mexican families and homes (G. Gonzalez 1990; Sánchez 1993). According to District Superintendent D. P. Lucas, the aims of Central Avenue School were similar:

> Mexican tots who were among the first pupils at Central have carried to their homes the type of instruction that is imparted in the school. These boys and girls, some of them, have grown to manhood and womanhood and have been able to create an entirely different attitude toward the institutions of the state than their parents hitherto had experienced. Because of this type of Americanization in the schools, there is certain to be a definite increase in cooperation in the homes of the coming generation. (Lucas, n.d., 5)

Thus, as described by G. Gonzalez (1990), the purposes of Americanization were twofold: to eliminate the linguistic and cultural practices of the Mexican-origin community and to maintain the existing economic, social, and political order in which Mexican Americans fulfilled the role of low-wage and subordinated labor.

To satisfy the economic demands of agriculturalists, school hours were shortened during the walnut-picking season in Puente (Hudson Elementary School District September 14, 1939). A Central Avenue teacher from 1928 to 1948 recalls: "School here in Puente operated on short session, 8 A.M. to 12, so children could pick nuts on nearby ranches" (quoted in Fields and Guerrero 1978, 45). In agricultural towns throughout California, these half-day schools were adapted to grower demands for child labor in the fields (G. Gonzalez 1990). In Puente, half-day schools existed until the early forties (Riley 1962, 21).

As well as being separate, the facilities at Central Avenue School and Hudson School were unequal, a pattern not uncommon during this era (G. Gonzalez 1990). A respondent who had attended Hudson School during the time that the Mendozas were at Central said during an interview in 2001 that Central's wood-frame building was inferior to Hudson's cement

Americanization was a primary goal of Central Avenue School. The focus of instruction was the English language, American citizenship, and respect for California and the United States. The Hudson Elementary School District superintendent from 1931 to 1945, Douglas P. Lucas, explained that the additional money and time given to the operation of Central Avenue School was premised on the perception that the Mexican-origin community accepted authority and would not resist segregation and Americanization (Lucas, n.d.).

Americanization programs reached beyond students in the classroom. Supporters of Americanization also sought to change Mexican families and homes (G. Gonzalez 1990; Sánchez 1993). According to District Superintendent D. P. Lucas, the aims of Central Avenue School were similar:

> Mexican tots who were among the first pupils at Central have carried to their homes the type of instruction that is imparted in the school. These boys and girls, some of them, have grown to manhood and womanhood and have been able to create an entirely different attitude toward the institutions of the state than their parents hitherto had experienced. Because of this type of Americanization in the schools, there is certain to be a definite increase in cooperation in the homes of the coming generation. (Lucas, n.d., 5)

Thus, as described by G. Gonzalez (1990), the purposes of Americanization were twofold: to eliminate the linguistic and cultural practices of the Mexican-origin community and to maintain the existing economic, social, and political order in which Mexican Americans fulfilled the role of low-wage and subordinated labor.

To satisfy the economic demands of agriculturalists, school hours were shortened during the walnut-picking season in Puente (Hudson Elementary School District September 14, 1939). A Central Avenue teacher from 1928 to 1948 recalls: "School here in Puente operated on short session, 8 A.M. to 12, so children could pick nuts on nearby ranches" (quoted in Fields and Guerrero 1978, 45). In agricultural towns throughout California, these half-day schools were adapted to grower demands for child labor in the fields (G. Gonzalez 1990). In Puente, half-day schools existed until the early forties (Riley 1962, 21).

As well as being separate, the facilities at Central Avenue School and Hudson School were unequal, a pattern not uncommon during this era (G. Gonzalez 1990). A respondent who had attended Hudson School during the time that the Mendozas were at Central said during an interview in 2001 that Central's wood-frame building was inferior to Hudson's cement

Table 3.1 *Central Avenue Americanization School Students, 1920–1935*

	Average Daily Attendance	No. of Teachers	Eighth Grade Graduates	Entered High School	Graduated from High School
1920–21	73	3	0	0	0
1921–22	65	3	0	0	0
1922–23	89	4	0	0	0
1923–24	130	4	0	0	0
1924–25	140	4	0	0	0
1925–26	157	7	9	6	2*
1926–27	165	7	0	0	0
1927–28	225	9	7	5	4
1928–29	212	9	6	5	4
1929–30	214	9	10	6	6
1930–31	192	8	6	5	3
1931–32	194	6	0	0	0
1932–33	196	7	0	0	0
1933–34	218	7	16	11	0
1934–35	214	7	12	7	0
TOTAL			66	45	19

*It appears that the number of Mexican students who graduated from high school includes some who attended Hudson School before Central Avenue was built.
(Source: Lucas n.d., 7)

Unlike Puente grammar schools, two separate high schools did not exist. Nevertheless, as was common among "integrated schools" throughout the Southwest, the educational experiences of Mexican and White students were often distinct and unequal at this level as well. As Leticia Mendoza explains, few Mexican students attended high school, and those who did often encountered institutional and individual forms of racism:

> Very few went to high school at that time . . . Carlos and I and maybe about four more went to high school, and all the rest went to pick oranges.

The Mendozas remember hostile high school officials who mistreated Mexican-origin students and maintained stereotyped expectations about what students of Mexican descent should be doing. Leticia explains:

> When we went to high school, we had a school principal that did not want us Mexicans coming in. He would tell, if any of the boys got in trouble, "What you ought to do is just get out and go pick oranges because that's all you're going to amount to anyway. You have no business wasting my time here." He'd throw them out of school, and they'd go pick oranges.

Though students from Central Avenue and Hudson School became schoolmates at Puente Union High, a former student of Hudson School recalled that "there was no mixing" between the White and Mexican students in high school. The two groups of student remained apart. Within this climate, Carlos and Leticia were two of the few students from their neighborhood to complete high school. They graduated from Puente Union in the early 1940s. They attribute the low high school completion rate of Mexican students to racist school officials and to agriculturalists who relied on the labor of Mexicans in the fields.

The Mendozas also recall that institutional discrimination in the forms of segregation and exclusion existed in other public facilities and leisure activities in the Puente area:

> LETICIA: When we were in the barrio, we could not go to uptown La Puente and get our hair done or get a haircut. In the pool hall in the barrio, they had a barber for all of the Mexicans. There was a girl there that did our hair.
> CARLOS: We couldn't go swimming anywhere . . . We couldn't go to a theater.
> LETICIA: We had one little section to sit when we went to the movies. In one theater, they had a section for Mexicans to sit in. Sundays, we all liked to go to the movies. We'd go and sit there in that one section only.

The Mendozas remember the Catholic church, Guadalupe Chapel, which served the barrio. Built in 1886 and originally used by various denominations, the church was dedicated in 1908 as a Catholic church—Saint Joseph. After a new Saint Joseph Church was built outside of the barrio in 1928, the original church became Chapel of Nuestra Senora de Guadalupe. According to the *History of La Puente Valley California* (1960), "The old church at Central and Stimson was turned over to the Mexicans as a place of worship and became known as the Guadalupe Chapel" (12). The Guadalupe Chapel was the church where the Mendozas were married in 1946.[11]

After graduating from high school, Carlos Mendoza left Puente and became a petty officer in the Navy during World War II.[12] However, returning home as a Navy veteran, he encountered what other Mexican American veterans experienced. He found that pre-war discrimination and segregation in jobs, many public accommodations, schooling, and housing persisted (see McLemore and Romo 1985). Carlos Mendoza was excluded from the occupations of his choice:

> CARLOS: When I came out of the war, I thought I was in my prime. I did real well in the war because I studied. I was twenty-one years old, 190 pounds. I applied for the highway patrol, the fire department, plumbing. I wanted to be an electrician. They said, "You're Mexican. Get out of here." I could've been a fireman. I had a friend who in no time was a captain, but he was a gringo or whatever you want to call them. I could've excelled because I excelled in sports all my life. I was twenty-one years old and in perfect shape . . . We couldn't get a job.
>
> LETICIA: Only picking oranges.
>
> CARLOS: Could only pick oranges, or go out into the fields and pick strawberries. When I came out I didn't want to be a barber, but I had to. I wanted to be a highway patrolman. I wanted to be an electrician. They make good money. They have a trade. I wanted to be a fireman, but they would tell me, "You're Mexican. We don't take Mexicans. Get out of here." What could I do? There was nobody that we could turn to.

Marrying three months after the war, the Mendozas wanted to purchase a home outside of Puente's barrio. However, residential segregation made it nearly impossible to buy their home, and they were forced to rely on the assistance of a third party. Carlos explains:

> Before, we couldn't, but, when we bought here, we did it deviously. A high school friend of mine owned a lot, and I asked him, "Why don't you sell me that lot?" He said, "I can't. I don't want to insult you, but they don't want Mexicans there." But his father-in-law was a Spaniard, and I went to talk to him . . . I said, "Tell your son-in-law to sell me that lot." We talked, and he said, "I'll get it for you." So, this man gave the lot to his father-in-law, and he in change sold it to me. Otherwise, we couldn't have bought it. Then when we went to move over here, they said we were going to downgrade this area.

In Los Angeles such racially exclusionary housing practices increased between 1920 and 1950 (Camarillo 1979). The proportion of Los Angeles–area municipalities maintaining practices that prevented Mexicans and other people of color from purchasing homes rose from 20 percent in 1920 to 80 percent in 1946 (Ruiz 1998, 68).

While the Mendozas were able to circumvent the exclusionary practices they encountered when purchasing a home outside of the barrio, Leticia says they still had to contend with the hostile reception that they received from their neighbors:

> We came over here even though they didn't want us. They tried to kick us out. Had awful phone calls. People were calling us all the time telling us, "Mexicans get out of here." They gave us a bad time.

Concurring with the Mendozas, a local resident of the area quoted in Sandoval (1994) describes the racial/ethnic hierarchy of the 1940s:

> On the bottom was the Mexican race; they were considered the field-workers. Then there were the Europeans because a lot of them—but not all of them—had schooling. They were allowed to be the "foremen" [of the farms], but they also had an area where they had to live. And then we had what you could call the white collar, rich. Most of them lived in the [North Whittier] Heights. (54)

To Mexican American children in the 1940s, this racial/ethnic hierarchy manifested itself in societal messages that they should attempt to distance themselves from their indigenous and Mexican heritage by identifying as Latin or Spanish. Thus, as was common in largely White communities, Puente resident Ilene Gómez, who moved to the area as a child, described how during this period she used more Europeanized racial/ethnic labels such as "Spanish-speaking" or "Latin American" when "speaking to Anglos." [13]

> You knew by third grade that being Mexican was not the correct answer, especially when we moved out here. It was a great deal more proper and more acceptable to say that we were Spanish.

La Puente the City

During the late 1940s and the 1950s, as much of Puente's agricultural land was subdivided into housing developments, tract houses and freeways replaced the area's walnut and citrus industries. As a result, most of La

Puente's houses were built in the 1950s, during the post-World War II housing boom.[14] Sixty-two-year-old La Puente resident Silvia Bravo, who moved to the area in 1956, said, "We found an inexpensive new home. At that time, La Puente was growing. They had oodles of tract homes."

With the GI Bill providing support for World War II veterans to purchase homes, some Mexican Americans, many from East Los Angeles, moved to newly suburbanized communities such as Puente (Acuña 1988, 284). This was the case for several respondents, including sixty-five-year-old Gloria Dominguez, who moved to Puente with her husband in 1949:

> They were starting to build out here. There were homes for GIs and veterans at that time. We decided to come, look, and see. My sister-in-law bought a home over here . . . Then we got here too.

Fifty-eight-year-old Marie Rogers and her husband also purchased a home in Puente through the GI Bill. Moving from East Los Angeles in 1948, Marie remembers the demographic composition of her new neighborhood: "When we first moved here, most of the people around this area were White, and there weren't that many Mexican Americans. Now of course, it's all changed." Though many of the residents of these new tract homes were White, the historically segregated community in downtown Puente remained Mexican.

As a result of Puente's growing population, a desire to maintain local autonomy, and fear that Puente would be engulfed by neighboring cities, residents sought the incorporation of Puente as a city.[15] As was the case with similar incorporation movements in the 1950s, some favored incorporation because they hoped to exclude Puente's Mexican community from its borders (Sandoval 1994). However, the Mexican-origin population was no longer confined to the geographic area of the Mexican town or barrio.

After three incorporation attempts, La Puente became a city in 1956. It was much smaller than was originally proposed (just 3.2 square miles in comparison to its proposed 13¾ square miles), but residents were hopeful that they would be able to expand the city's geography (*History of La Puente Valley California* 1960, 3; Sandoval 1994). However, this proved to be impossible when the City of Industry incorporated in 1957, and its boundaries surrounded La Puente and enclosed most of the valuable industrial land (Sandoval 1994, 74–79). At the time of La Puente's incorporation, the city's population was 20,066 (La Puente Planning Department 1972, 10).

By the 1960s and 1970s, the period when many of the residents included in this work moved to what was often referred to as "La Poeny," the Anglicized pronunciation of La Puente, Central Avenue School had been destroyed, and the civil rights movements resulted in the passage of legislation and administrative guidelines prohibiting discrimination in public education, employment, voting, and housing.[16] Reflecting a trend in working-class communities throughout Los Angeles, the demographic composition of the nearly 25,000 La Puente residents was also becoming increasingly Mexican.

Despite such civil rights legislation and the greater presence of Mexicans in La Puente, respondents whose families moved to the city during this period continued to encounter Spanish-language repression, discrimination, and an emphasis on assimilation. Likewise, students in La Puente schools during the 1960s and 1970s remember the prejudiced attitudes and discriminatory behaviors of the primarily non-Mexican school officials:

> [My mother] said back when she first came here to talk Spanish was a sin. To say that you were Mexican was a sin. My godfather was one of those who was afraid to identify himself as Mexican American. He'd say, "No, I'm American. I don't speak Spanish. I only listen to English music." . . . My mom and dad, they said they remember they were looked at because they would speak Spanish. People would look at them very weirdly, and they didn't want to get near them.
>
> MARGARITA VILLA, twenty-nine-year-old Mexican American

> When I first came, I remember a very sad experience I had at La Puente High School in which we were very strongly discriminated by staff members of the school. I remember that some of my friends because they were Spanish speakers only were called "greasers," "taco vendors," and "wetbacks" by teachers and school staff, and that really irritated me.
>
> FRANCISCO DELGADO, forty-three-year-old Mexican immigrant[17]

As residents recall, community leaders' unfavorable attitudes toward Mexicans persisted in the 1980s. Though many critique the racism and classism within the school district, fifty-five-year-old Jane Hanson also includes a critical evaluation of the difficulties Mexicans faced in her largely White-controlled Catholic church:

> The Irish priest there was very prejudiced. At that time, there were not a lot of Mexican people, and he was against us Mexicans. I don't think he wanted us there.

Table 3.2 Racial/Ethnic Distribution of La Puente Population, 1970–2000 (by percent)

	1970	1980	1990	2000
African American	3	4	3	2
Asian/Pacific Islander	NA	NA	7	8
Latina/o	46	63	75	83
White	51	30	15	7
Total population	31,092	30,882	36,955	41,063

(Source: U.S. Bureau of the Census)

La Puente Today

The city's logo, "Where the past meets the future," captures the community's changes—from a Mexican rancho to a Latina/o city. Over the past forty years, La Puente has seen a significant increase in Latinas/os and a decrease in the percentage of Whites. As shown in Table 3.2, the Latina/o population in La Puente increased from 46 percent in 1970 to 63 percent in 1980 to 75 percent in 1990, while the White population decreased from 51 to 30 to 15 percent. In 2000 the city population was 83 percent Latina/o, 7 percent White, 8 percent Asian American/Pacific Islander, and 2 percent African American. As has always been the case, the majority of Latinas/os in the city are of Mexican descent. As Table 3.3 illustrates, in 2000 Mexicans represented 69 percent of the Latina/o residents. However, the Latina/o population in La Puente is becoming increasingly diverse, with 14 percent identifying as "other Hispanic or Latino." This shift is probably attributable to the increase in Central Americans, in particular Salvadorans, in the Los Angeles area.

The demographic shifts in La Puente are in part the result of immigration. According to the 2000 Census and as highlighted in Table 3.4, 44 percent of La Puente residents were immigrants; of the 44 percent, 66 percent were not U.S. citizens. As indicated by the 31 percent of the immigrants who moved to La Puente between 1990 and 2000, the majority of immigrants in the city have been in the United States for more than ten years (U.S. Bureau of the Census 1971, 1981, 1991, 2001). Comparing the percentage of La Puente residents who were immigrants during the 1990 Census and the 2000 Census (Table 3.4), we see that a greater percentage in 2000 were immigrants. However, a larger percentage also had lived in the United States for more than ten years.

Along with an increase in immigration, there has been an increase in suburbanization and home ownership among Latinas/os. Latinas/os are the fastest-growing group of homebuyers in the Los Angeles County real estate market, and La Puente represents one of the most popular areas in the San Gabriel Valley for Latinas/os purchasing homes (O'Neil 1994). This may be attributed to the fact that housing prices in La Puente are among the lowest in the Los Angeles County, but a reputation as a "family-oriented town" with a "strong ethnic community" is also influential (Bond 1994). The growth in townhouses and condominiums in the 1980s brought some of the newer residents to the city, including most of the respondents who had moved to La Puente in the previous fifteen years. As of the 2000 Census, 61 percent of La Puente residents owned or were buying their homes (U.S. Bureau of the Census 2001).

As well as being mainly Latina/o, most La Puente residents are of the

Table 3.3 *Latina/o La Puente Residents of Mexican Origin, 1980–2000*

	1980	1990	2000
Mexican origin (%)	89	88	69
Total Latinas/os	19,291	27,663	34,122

(Source: U.S. Bureau of the Census)

Table 3.4 *Citizenship Status of Immigrant Population in La Puente, 1990 and 2000*

1990	%	Number
Residents who were immigrants	37	13,735
Immigrants who were not citizens	78	10,713
Immigrants who arrived between 1980 and 1990	44	6,043
2000	**%**	**Number**
Residents who were immigrants	44	17,850
Immigrants who were not citizens	66	11,781
Immigrants who arrived between 1990 and 2000	31	5,534

(Source: U.S. Bureau of the Census)

working class and lower middle class. Residents in 2000 were employed in production, transportation, and material moving occupations (33 percent), in sales and office occupations (24 percent), in service occupations (17 percent), in management and professional occupations (15 percent), and in construction and maintenance occupations (11 percent) (ibid.). In 1989 the median income of all households in the city was $33,273. In Latina/o households in 1990, 34 percent made less than $24,999, and 43 percent made between $25,000 and $49,999. Fourteen percent of Latinas/os in La Puente were at the poverty level. While 60 percent of Latinas/os over twenty-five years old did not have a high school diploma or equivalent, 17 percent had attended some college, with 4 percent receiving a bachelor's degree or higher (U.S. Bureau of the Census 1991).

The working-class community and the demographic shifts that have characterized La Puente are mirrored in the businesses and stores throughout the community. Many of the banks, supermarket chains, car dealerships, family businesses, and places of entertainment that were located in the city through the 1970s have closed or relocated. This phenomenon can be attributed to several factors, including the development of middle-class bedroom communities in nearby Hacienda Heights and West Covina, coupled with the growth of multiplex movie theaters in neighboring cities and large suburban shopping malls, such as City of Industry's Puente Hills Mall. While longtime residents describe La Puente as a central hub in the eastern San Gabriel Valley through the 1960s, nearby development and changes in the economy in the 1970s and 1980s negatively impacted the working-class city that could not compete with retail chains and mass-marketing corporations. Frank Gallegos, a business owner and La Puente resident since his birth in 1944, describes the impacts that such economic changes have had on Main Street, the oldest section of the city:

> One of the primary blows to the city of La Puente was the rerouting of Valley Boulevard [away from La Puente's Main Street]. It killed a lot of this downtown business section. You had several businesses down there; they just died, literally overnight. During the 1950s, we had the advent of the supermarket. There was no way small mama-papa stores could compete. We were a small neighborhood community with an economic base for our businesses. When you had at that time a [supermarket chain] opening up at Hacienda and Amar, that killed off whatever remaining business was here. Old people passed on. Younger people took over the properties and moved out. So, now you have absentee owners in a dying socioeconomic base . . . Other communities built up around [us]. City of Industry built up. We had the homes in Hacienda Heights. West

Covina started developing residential areas. People had no real reason to stay here.

Concurring with these observations, scholar Mike Davis (1998) notes that shortly after La Puente became a city, the "economic superpredator" City of Industry since its incorporation in 1957 has been able to "monopolize most of the tax assets of the southern San Gabriel Valley, including 2,100 factories, warehouses, discount outlets as well as a world-class golf course and resort" (401–402). Designed as a nonresidential city, City of Industry has fewer than 800 residents (U.S. Bureau of the Census 2001). This "economic time bomb" or "dollar swallowing supernova" has largely relied on "tax-starved" cities such as La Puente to provide the labor force for its factories and warehouses (Davis 1998, 401–402; Valle and Torres 2000, 33). Since most workers live outside of the boundaries of City of Industry, they are excluded from local elections, and they do not receive public revenues. Instead, schools and other social services in La Puente are chronically underfunded (Valle and Torres 2000). As a community with limited tax revenues, money is spent contracting out for services such as the police and fire departments. This limits city resources and the amount of control city residents have over their community.

Though a residential suburban community, La Puente is facing some of the economic problems that central cities and other older suburban locales have encountered. As a result of power differentials, economic inequalities, the buildup of neighboring middle-class communities, and the proliferation of supermarket and warehouse chains, businesses and life in La Puente have been impacted. The flight of some clients, shoppers, and small-business owners have left places such as Main Street, the downtown section of the city, struggling. In some parts of the city, lifeless remnants of previous businesses that served a different generation of La Puente residents prevail— abandoned stores, a fenced-off bowling alley, and an empty French bakery.

Despite these negative effects to La Puente's economy, vibrant panaderías, carnicerías, discos, taquerías, and other Mexican restaurants catering to the growing Latina/o community have replaced the businesses of the past, revitalizing sections of the city. In many of these commercial areas and other public spaces, young and old can be found carrying out their activities and exchanges largely in Spanish. A Mexican "cultural revolution" is occurring in one popular neighborhood disco, A Mi Hacienda, where the 1990s quebradita fad brought together mostly young Mexican and some Chicana/o vaqueras/os (R. Martínez 1998).

Reflecting on how demographic changes and this "cultural revolution" have altered the community, the Mendozas compare the La Puente of today with their memory of the past:

> CARLOS: Before, they used to tell us, "Speak English." Now, you go to the market, and you [hear] Japanese, Chinese, Korean. See the difference? Before there was only the Latino and the gringo, so they didn't want us to talk Spanish. "Talk English." I feel like going back and telling those people, "Now what are you telling the Asians?"

While residents such as the Mendozas may appear resentful of what they perceive as a change in the prevalence of languages other than English in public spaces, they find a sense of irony and amusement in these alterations. Describing the changing perceptions of Mexican food over the past forty years, the Mendozas continue:

> CARLOS: At that time, you would never think of eating a burrito in public. They looked down on it. They would laugh at us.
> LETICIA: They would laugh at us. Now it's a delicacy.
> CARLOS: See, the trend has changed.
> LETICIA: Even in food.

While such changes have been influenced by increases in Latinas/os and by the struggles and affirmation of Mexican culture and identity of the Chicana/o Movement, these shifts can also be attributed to what Valle and Torres (2000) refer to as "multicultural commodification"—it has become popular for nouvelle chefs to create caviar-filled tamales for upscale restaurants or to market tacos for fast-food restaurants as a "run for the border." All of this is accomplished through the appropriation of Mexican recipes and the subordination of the largely Latina/o workers who constitute most of the service employees (71–88). Thus, while it may be "acceptable" to eat Mexican food or more common to hear Spanish in public, inequality and institutional and individual constraints on the Mexican-origin community remain. In La Puente, they are apparent in attempts to exclude Latina/o immigrants, in the limited services provided for Spanish speakers, and in Spanish-language repression.

Cognizant of the negative perception that non–La Puente residents may have of their working-class community and aware of the inequalities in city and social services, some residents are blaming immigrants for what they perceive as the downfall of the community and of housing prices. At La Puente city meetings in the 1990s, this scapegoating and concern about the immigrant population manifested itself in discussions over domestic animals in the city, the building of new condominiums, and the presence of street vendors. While an ordinance already restricted street vendors from the city, residents and city officials grappled with how they could restrict particular animals and limit the number of families in a house. Comments made by residents addressing the La Puente Planning Commission during meetings in 1995 are illustrative:

> I always thought that chickens were livestock, not domestic animals. I have a problem with chickens . . . Is this a barnyard community? I don't want chickens living next to me. I want my property values to stay high.

> It's funny that we can't regulate the number of people on a lot. People are more concerned about the number of people than the number of animals on a lot.[18]

> Condos are a camouflage for apartments. Multiple families live in condos . . . If we bring in new kids, all of the schools in the area will be asked to accommodate them. They are migrant people who will move in [to the condos] because condos don't sell.[19]

While rarely made explicit, coded within such comments and discussions has been the desire of some residents to reduce the number of immigrants settling in the city because of the perception that they are "bringing down the neighborhood" and crowding out the schools. Such sentiment has resulted in increased emphasis on code enforcement by city officials who canvass neighborhood streets looking for and citing "violations." For street vendors, this criminalization has resulted in citations and arrests by the County of Los Angeles Sheriff's Department, the police force contracted by the city of La Puente.[20]

As in earlier times, in the 1990s and into 2000 La Puente officials and residents debated the acceptability of the use of Spanish in community and school arenas. Perspectives on these debates were correlated with race/ethnicity, generation, and power—with Latina/o immigrants tending to favor the use of Spanish but lacking access to decision-making positions. As detailed in Chapter 7, in 1996 these differences in opinion resulted in Latina/o mobilization to preserve bilingual education. Likewise, at City Council meetings in 2001 a bilingual Mexican American council member proposed printing portions of the La Puente newsletter in both English and Spanish. Arguments in opposition to the newsletter were presented in English and tended to be based on the assimilationist model. The comment from one La Puente resident to the council captures some of this sentiment: "My husband's family comes from the Azores. When his grandparents were asked why they didn't teach my husband Portuguese, she responded, 'We live in America now.' We live in America now."[21]

Those voicing support for a bilingual newsletter were Latina/o, primarily immigrants. Their arguments focused largely on the need for services that would meet the changing demographics of the community. Quoted in Rubin (2001), one woman argued, "A lot of people are treated like dummies because they only speak Spanish . . . Money comes to the city from those who do not speak English. In a city like La Puente where the majority speak another language, it would help quite a bit [to have a bilingual newsletter]. It's time for a change." When the proposal to print sections of the newsletter was brought before council members, three of the five councilors voted against it, causing it to fail. However, a month later when bilingual and Spanish-speaking residents spoke in favor of the newsletter in front of a packed City Council meeting, the proposal was accepted by four of the five.[22] With its approval, however, came the recommendation by some city officials that the Spanish translations should focus on the city's rules and on the locations for English classes.[23] Recommendations such as these reinforce the expectation that all are to speak English. Reflecting this paradigm, community events, city meetings, and most school-based meetings also continue to be conducted in English.

In instances throughout the city, individuals speaking Spanish have been criticized, reprimanded, or ignored. During La Puente's 1994 Fourth of July celebration at the local high school, Esteban Torres, a member of the U.S. Congress, addressed the city in Spanish. A year later at a La Puente City Council meeting, this issue was still being raised by embittered residents. One White resident told the City Council: "Last year's Fourth of July celebration was messed up. Spanish should not have been spoken because we are Americans." In response to this comment, the Mexican American mayor during the 1994 celebration replied, "How does the mayor tell someone to shut up? Esteban Torres spoke Spanish at the Fourth of July because we are all Americans, and we happen to speak Spanish."[24] While in this example the mayor was in a position to counter such anti-Spanish-language sentiment, this is not always the case.

Such critiques of the use of Spanish are confirmed by a La Puente–area Mexican American student who in 2001 shared with his aunt how his White elementary teacher chided the Spanish-speaking students in the class. According to this young student, one day three students known to assist each other with the teacher's instructions by speaking Spanish were berated in front of the entire classroom for not speaking English. This particular time, the teacher yelled at them, "In this class, you will speak English. This is

America. If you want to speak Spanish, go back to where you come from."[25] While the direct targets of such English-only sentiment and an emphasis on working individually were the three children, the majority of the classroom was comprised of Latina/o students. Therefore, the message was clear to all of the students.

It is not only students who are humiliated for speaking Spanish. Participant observations at various public institutions and agencies reveal that a number of community sites lack or have few Spanish-speaking employees who can adequately provide services to city residents. In such situations, residents may be ignored, ridiculed, or scolded. For example, while conducting business in January 2001 at the local post office, I noted the following exchange between a Spanish-speaking customer and a postal worker: A Latina customer approached the front counter and placed the envelope she wanted delivered on the counter. The postal worker asked in a loud voice, "When do you want it to get there?" Several seconds elapsed, and the customer did not respond. The postal worker asked again in the same loud voice, this time seeming a bit perturbed, "When do you want it to get there?" Suspecting that the customer may not have understood the postal worker, a second Latino customer in the next aisle translated the question, and this time the female customer responded, "Una semana." Translating for the woman, the bilingual customer then turned to the worker and said, "One week." Without acknowledging this response, there was a long pause. The postal worker then yelled so loud that all those present could hear, "Huh? Oh, you don't speak English."[26]

The intonation of the postal worker's accusatory tone implied that something was wrong with the customer because she did not speak English. While interactions such as these continue to send the message that all should be or should aspire to be English-speaking, we find instances of resistance among La Puente residents.

For example, the activities that followed the interaction between the customer and the postal worker depict how some are contesting the expectation of speaking English in public places. After the Latina customer completed her transaction, she turned to her female friend, and in Spanish the two of them complained about the exchange with the postal worker. Their main complaint was that the customer could have understood the worker's question if only she would have spoken more slowly. Still speaking Spanish, the Latino customer who had offered his assistance joined in the conversation. As the only other customer in the post office, I too entered their exchange. All four of us stood in the post office speaking Spanish as the non-Spanish-speaking worker looked on.[27]

In response to the lack of Spanish-English bilingual personnel and to the postal worker's contemptuous attitude, the La Puente–area residents converted the post office into a space where speaking Spanish was acceptable, even if just for a moment. However, throughout the city and schools, power differentials persist such that the complete participation of La Puente residents is limited or prevented by top-down policies and practices (as will be described in chapters 5 and 6) and by outside control (as in the Hacienda Heights–controlled school board I will describe in Chapter 7).

This overview of the racial/ethnic and class dynamics and the various transformations of Rancho La Puente to its present-day status as a Latina/o city provide the context for understanding the narratives that follow. Depending on when they arrived in La Puente, respondents have encountered different forms of inequality and expectations for acculturation. For residents such as the Mendozas whose families moved to Puente near the turn of the century, they experienced legalized segregation and an educational system based on Americanization. As other residents moved from communities such as East Los Angeles to La Puente in the 1950s and 1960s, they often entered into neighborhoods that were primarily White and where Mexican Americans had limited control over community and school affairs. By the mid-1970s the demographic shift in the city became more apparent as Mexicans began to outnumber Whites. Nevertheless, anti-Mexican sentiment persisted in schools and other arenas.

Today, as the Mendozas so vividly indicate, it is more common and acceptable to hear the Spanish language and to enjoy Mexican food in public. However, this appearance of cultural acceptance does not spell the end of inequality or institutional and individual racism. Rather, as will be unraveled in the following chapters, community and school control continue to be unequally concentrated, and acquiring English-language skills remains the dominant expectation in many arenas. Over time, while inequality has taken different forms, it as well as the emphasis on assimilation has been consistent. Thus, the city's logo, "Where the past meets the future," fittingly captures La Puente's historical and structural continuity. Perhaps it is no wonder that at the 2001 City Council meeting on translating sections of the city newsletter into Spanish one Spanish-speaking resident so adamantly declared, "It's time for a change."

This historical and contemporary context has set the parameters for today's race/ethnic relationships. As such, it has influenced Mexican Americans' experiences, their self-perceptions, and intra-ethnic relations. However, not only is an awareness of this macroscopic context important, but we must also consider how La Puente residents are actively engaged in creating, reacting to, and challenging the environments in which they live. The following chapter illustrates such individual agency. It also begins to unravel how intra-ethnic relationships are intimately connected to experiences and self-perceptions by considering how respondents are negotiating their racial/ethnic identities and what such negotiation processes suggest for intra-ethnic relations.

Chapter 4

"This Is Who I Am": Negotiating Racial/Ethnic Constructions

> I guess Mexican American. What else can you say? Well, that's the way they labeled us anyway. A lot of my friends were not Latins, so they didn't consider me Latin. That's one thing that I used to feel kind of bad about because when they would say a remark, "Hey that's me. I'm Latin too." They would forget. Even up to now, they still do it. I just ignore it.
>
> GLORIA DOMINGUEZ, sixty-five-year-old Mexican American

> One time a teacher asked, "What does Chicano mean?" Before I could explain, this White teacher said, "Oh, it's a Mexican with an attitude." That's when, with people like her, I throw that term out because I want to confront them. I want the opportunity to set them straight.
>
> DAVID GALVEZ, twenty-seven-year-old Mexican American

The history of colonization and the enduring patterns of exploitation, racism, and discrimination outlined in the previous chapters have set the landscape for contemporary race/ethnic relations. Within the United States, this history has resulted in various paradigms of race/ethnicity. Two, in particular, have been detrimental to the Mexican-origin community. The first one, a biological approach, has existed throughout much of the history of the United States. The underlying premise of this approach was that people of color, including Mexicans, were biologically different from and inferior to Anglo Americans (Mario Barrera 1979).[1] The second approach began in the 1920s and gained popularity in the 1940s and 1950s (G. Gonzalez 1990; Omi and Winant 1994; Frankenberg 1993; Brodkin 2000). During this time period, the popular discourse on race/ethnicity was framed in terms of culture and with an emphasis on assimilation. Rather than attributing and justifying the structural inequality of the Mexican-origin population to perceived biological inferiority, this assimilationist approach has focused on presumed cultural deficiencies of Mexican Americans (Omi and Winant 1994; Frankenberg 1993). As discussed in Chapter 2, this perspective continues to be prevalent in the United States.

Combined, these paradigms have reinforced a racial/ethnic hierarchy in which light skin, the English language, European ancestry, and Anglo cultural practices, values, and norms are perceived as superior to dark skin, the Spanish language, Mexican ancestry, and Mexican cultural practices, values, and norms. Likewise, such frameworks have perpetuated narrow, static, and binary conceptualizations of Americanness and Mexicanness. While Americanness has been associated with whiteness, Anglo ancestry, speaking English, and certain positive attributes, Mexicanness has been equated with brownness, immigration, speaking Spanish, and various negative stereotypes. For Mexican Americans, this strict categorization may result in exclusion from conceptions of both "American" and "Mexican." Pat Mora (1984) captures in the following section of her poem "Legal Alien" how Mexican Americans may experience binary constructions:

American but hyphenated,
viewed by Anglos as perhaps exotic,
perhaps inferior, definitely different,
viewed by Mexicans as alien,
(their eyes say, "You may speak
Spanish but you're not like me")
an American to Mexicans
a Mexican to Americans
a handy token
sliding back and forth
between the fringes of both worlds

In the lives of La Puente residents such as Gloria Dominguez and David Galvez, whose quotes begin this chapter, these exclusionary paradigms have resulted in people's negative "remarks," in friends "forgetting" that they are Mexican, or in colleagues' stereotyped assumptions. Whether responses to such encounters include declaring "I'm Latin too" or setting people "straight," as Mexican Americans contend with such externally imposed conceptions, they are negotiating their own racial/ethnic identities and their perceptions of Mexican immigrants.

To better understand the impacts of such exclusionary and binary constructions on identity and on intra-ethnic relations, this chapter is organized into two main parts. It begins with a discussion of respondents' experiences of imposed racial/ethnic categorizations. Respondents describe how others' conceptions of them tend to be limited, static, and incomplete and are typically informed by phenotypical and cultural constructions. For example, experience has shown them that Whites may focus on color to assess Mexican

Americanness and immigrants may adopt a definition of race/ethnicity that is grounded in cultural constructions in which speaking Spanish is equated with Mexicanness.[2]

After a discussion on these imposed conceptualizations, the second part of this chapter centers the multiple ways that respondents are employing, adopting, and claiming identifications that are grounded in strategies for survival, perseverance, and resistance. In this section, we find that respondents' self-identifications are more complex than the strict phenotypical or cultural conceptions that they may encounter from others. Respondents' identities are based on multiple and at times intersecting factors, including ancestry, culture, and experiences of racism and discrimination. An awareness of shared cultural practices and familial connections, others' perceptions, and, for some, the adoption of a power-conflict perspective—which is based on an analysis of power and inequality—are significant in influencing self-identifications. While respondents' narratives illustrate the fluid, multiple, and situational nature of their identities, the social construction of categories has nonetheless circumscribed their racial/ethnic options. Thus, in comparison to the scholarship that demonstrates how for Whites, race/ethnicity may be "optional," "voluntary," or a "leisure-time activity" (Gans 1979; Waters 1990), respondents' narratives indicate how for many Mexican Americans, it continues to be imposed, required, involuntary, and everyday.

By discussing how Mexican Americans perceive themselves and how they develop these perceptions, this chapter adds to an understanding of intra-ethnic relations in three key ways. First, similar external and cultural factors are influencing respondents' racial/ethnic identities and their conceptions of immigrants. Secondly, since racial/ethnic identities are socially constructed, part of the process of identifying oneself involves delineating who one considers to be part of his or her racial/ethnic group. Thus as respondents talk about their racial/ethnic identities, they are also telling us either implicitly or explicitly how they perceive immigrants and other members of the Mexican-origin community. As Hurtado, Gurin, and Peng (1994) and Niemann et al. (1999) find, we can think of respondents' self-conceptions and their perceptions of the Mexican-origin community as interdependent. Finally, those individuals who link their racial/ethnic identities to their adoption of a power-conflict view of society are among the strongest supporters of intra-ethnic solidarity and may be the most vocal advocates for social justice for Mexican Americans and Mexican immigrants.

Externally Imposed Racial/Ethnic Categorizations

Institutionalized Constructions of Race/Ethnicity

The institutional structuring of race/ethnicity is apparent in the popular discourse on race/ethnicity, in the legacy of the "one-drop rule," and in the categories contained in the United States Census. Until recently, when race and racism have been discussed, they have been framed in a stark polarity of Black and White (Shah 1994; Sethi 1995; E. Martínez 1998). Such an approach marginalizes the experiences of Latinas/os, Native Americans, and Asian Americans. It perpetuates the normalization of whiteness, as Whites become the group with which all others tend to be compared, and it reinforces the notion that race is a biological construction.

The one-drop rule or the rule of hypodescent in the United States has been key to maintaining the belief that race is biological (Omi and Winant 1994). This rule maintains that "a person with only one drop of black blood must be classified as Black" (Ramirez 1996, 55). Originating in the antebellum South to maximize the number of slaves, this one-drop rule reinforces the notion that all individuals can be categorized into one racial group or another (56).

The U.S. Census categories foster the belief that racial groupings are static, fixed, and concrete and can be designated by simply checking a box on a government form. While scholars and some in the general public have critiqued such conceptualizations, the limiting categories of the U.S. Census consistently have failed to capture the complexity of the history and experiences of Mexican Americans.

For the Mexican-origin population, a history of conquest, colonization, and migration has resulted in a population that includes people of indigenous, African, Iberian, European, and Asian descent. Thus, the selection of just one category on many standardized forms (White, Black, American Indian, or Asian) has not captured this multiplicity of backgrounds. For example, in the 1990 census 52 percent of Latinas/os identified as White, 3 percent as Black, 1 percent as Asian, 0.7 percent as American Indian, Eskimo, or Aleut, and 43 percent as Other (U.S. Bureau of the Census 1991). These numbers reveal that many Latinas/os do not identify with any of the existing racial categories. As de la Garza et al. (1992) found in a 1989–1990 Latino National Survey, 47 percent of Mexican immigrants and 55 percent of Mexican Americans classified themselves as White, indicating that about half did not (23). It remains to be seen how the Mexican-origin community responded to the 2000 census, in which individuals could check more than one racial category.

Several respondents describe how externally imposed categories have limited their racial/ethnic identifications. Sixty-nine-year-old Pete Saldana remembers that as a child in New Mexico in the 1940s, there were no categories that captured how he perceives himself today—as Latin or Hispanic. As a result, during that era he identified as "White":

> When I was growing up, they used to say there were only three races—the Yellow race, the White race, and the Black race. There was not such a thing as Latin, Hispanic, or whatever. So we were all going to school at that time, and we were just all White.

Expanding on Pete Saldana's points, fifty-five-year-old Jane Hanson criticizes the institutionalization of racial/ethnic labels and how some people have contested her self-identification. The imposition of labels has caused respondents such as Jane anger and resentment. Jane retells a confrontation with a friend that triggered some of these emotions:

> When I was a teenager, I would get into arguments. I had a friend. She's from Arkansas, all-White woman . . . We were looking at our driver's licenses. She said, "Jane, why do you have marked that you're White? You're Brown." I had a fit. I was going to slap her and throw her on the floor. I was so angry. I said, "Look, I'm not Black and I'm not Yellow, so I'm White. Okay?" . . . She kept saying, "Well, I don't understand." I said, "You know what, shut up you White trash." I was so angry because she didn't know how I got hurt. There was a lot of resentment . . . We didn't know how to identify ourselves. Now they say, "You're Hispanic." Okay, I'm Hispanic. Mexican American, I guess that's what I choose.

Using the common three-category classification scheme of Black, White, and Asian, as a teenager in the 1950s, Jane marked the category White. Though this classification system was popular during this period, it perpetuated the belief that clear-cut racial categories exist.

Such a system inaccurately assumes that the more than six billion people in the world can be classified in just three ways (Ferrante and Brown 1999), and it does not leave space for people of Mexican descent and their experiences of racialization in the United States. Jane's reaction toward the friend who questioned her selection demonstrates the resentment that may arise from such confining categories as well as from the realization that outsiders may shape, influence, or oppose how members of the Mexican-origin community identify while at the same time, Whites' identifications may remain uncontested and unmarked.

Highlighting how particular labels continue to be institutionally imposed, Jane explains that now outsiders are saying that people of Mexican origin are Hispanic. Instituted by Nixon-administration bureaucrats in the 1970s, the term "Hispanic" has been used by the U.S. government, including the Bureau of the Census, as well as by print media, advertisers, and Mexican American political elites (Gómez 1992). It has been employed as an umbrella term to classify Mexicans, Puerto Ricans, Cubans, Central Americans, South Americans, Spaniards, and people from Spanish-speaking countries of the Caribbean. Despite the prevailing use of this state-sponsored label, however, Jane Hanson declares that she prefers to name herself Mexican American. Like Jane Hanson, scholars have critiqued the Hispanic label for being externally imposed (Goldberg 1995; Santos 1997), for its emphasis on Spanish ancestry (Santos 1997), and for camouflaging the distinct histories, class positions, and racial experiences of the more than 23 million U.S. citizens, residents, refugees, and immigrants included under this one umbrella term (Nelson and Tienda 1985; Maldonado 1991; Oboler 1995; Gimenez 1997).

These institutionalized racial/ethnic categories are reflected in and reproduced by dominant stereotypes of the Mexican-origin population as inferior, dirty, lazy, or criminal. As well as having their origins in a history of conquest and domination, such "controlling images" have been essential in reproducing power differentials and justifying inequality (Collins 1990, 67–68). They also function to perpetuate dominant myths. For example, the current stereotype that Mexican Americans are immigrants reinforces the inaccurate belief that "we are all immigrants" and that the United States is "a nation of immigrants." In this way, a history of U.S. conquest, colonization, and imperialism in relation to Mexico is camouflaged, and the role of the United States in recruiting, encouraging, and limiting immigration is hidden. Likewise, derogatory labels such as "illegal aliens" and "wetback" reinforce prejudiced beliefs and discriminatory treatment of Mexicans by criminalizing and dehumanizing immigrants.

While stereotyped images are reinforced by an educational system (as I will describe later in this chapter) that tends to ignore the history and experiences of Mexicans, they are also reproduced by under- and misrepresentation in the media. Forty-year-old Mary Marquez describes this invisibility and the influence it may have on how Whites view Mexicans:

I think that Whites will always think that they're superior, mostly because of the roles they have to follow like on TV and in politics, they're all White. So, the Whites have all these superior positions and the Mexicans don't. The few they have are who? Entertainers like Ricardo Montalban, that [Edward James] Olmos guy—which are good people to look up to, but at the same time, they don't really hold intelligent jobs in politics.

As Mary Marquez suggests, a cursory look at media images reveals how Latinas/os are generally absent. Despite the growing increase of Latinas/os in the United States since the 1950s, the percentage of Latina/o characters on prime-time television programs has actually declined. Between 1955 and 1964, Latinas/os made up 3 percent of television characters compared to 1 percent in 1992 (National Council of La Raza 1997, 24). Likewise, while in 1995 Latinas/os made up more than 12 percent of the nation's population, a study released by the National Association of Hispanic Journalists found that Latinas/os received 1 percent of coverage on the evening newscasts of ABC, NBC, and CBS (C. Rodríguez 1997, 15).[3]

When Latinas/os are depicted in the media, it is often in stereotypical ways. Mexican American women are often characterized as sexually promiscuous, as servants, and as welfare cheats, while men are portrayed as criminals, clowns, or "Latin lovers." Both men and women are depicted as lazy, stupid, and powerless (Ramírez Berg 1997). In terms of news content, a 1995 analysis of the major networks revealed that 85 percent of news stories with Latinas/os focused on crime, immigration, affirmative action, and welfare, stereotyped depictions that contribute to derogatory images of Latinas/os (C. Rodríguez 1997, 15). Also, despite the multiple racial/ethnic backgrounds of Mexicans, the U.S. media have perpetuated a normative image of Mexicans as phenotypically brown or has privileged those individuals with light skin and with facial features that are typically associated with Anglos.

A couple of respondents agree with the comments made earlier by Mary Marquez that the media can have a significant effect on shaping perspectives. For example, twenty-three-year-old Eduardo Romero describes the impact he believes that the media have in perpetuating anti-immigrant sentiment:

> The media has also bolstered that they're a threat to you economically because they're taking advantage of health care, of education. I think a lot of that's just the media manipulating people. I don't necessarily buy that at all.

Media scholars have documented that many people's views of Latinas/os are informed by what is depicted and who is not visible on television (see C. Rodríguez 1997).

Whites' stereotyped conceptualizations

These institutionalized racial/ethnic categories and "controlling images" are reflected in some Whites' everyday attitudes and interactions with Mexican Americans. In particular, respondents explain how they have encountered Whites who possess essentialist and exclusionary conceptions of both Mexican Americans and Americans. These conceptions include the equation of brown skin with Mexicanness and certain raced, classed, and gendered assumptions about normative families and Mexican women. Such static and "either/or dichotomous thinking"—in this case as either Mexican American or American—categorizes people in oppositional and unequal ways and may perpetuate the feeling of "being the other" for Mexican Americans (Collins 1990, 68–69; Madrid 1995, 10). Madrid (1995) notes:

> Being *the other* means feeling different; is awareness of being distinct; is consciousness of being dissimilar. It means being outside the game, outside the circle, outside the set. It means being on the edges, on the margins, on the periphery. Otherness means feeling excluded, closed out, precluded, of disconnectedness, of alienation (12).

Most respondents' narratives illustrate their "contradictory" or simultaneous position as "the other," where they may "stick out like a sore thumb," and they may be "invisible" (Madrid 1995, 12). Experiences such as these reveal how race/ethnicity continues to influence the lives of Mexican Americans.

When meeting new people, it is not uncommon for respondents to be asked their racial/ethnic backgrounds. However, as thirty-year-old Rosario Jones describes this, such inquiries may become more pronounced in situations when someone's physical appearances do not coincide with people's stereotyped expectations. For example, at times when Rosario lightens her hair and wears blue contact lenses, she has found that people may question her background. This is precisely what occurred when Rosario first met her current employer. Excited about this meeting, Rosario recalls how their encounter quickly turned sour when her employer called attention to her race/ethnicity and to his narrow notion of how Mexican Americans look:

> I was all happy, "I'm going to meet my boss, and he's going to hire me permanently" . . . He looked at me, and he looked at his paper again. He said, "What is your last name?" I didn't make anything of it until I sat down and said, "Oh, that's my married name. My maiden name is Hernandez." "Oh," he said, "I thought you looked like you may be Hispanic, but your blue eyes threw me."

Rosario Jones' White male employer began their meeting by publicly trying to reconcile Rosario's last name and her blue eyes with his image of Mexican Americans. She believed that her race/ethnicity was not relevant to her job and that her employer was placing limitations on what physical characteristics are associated with being "Hispanic," and this exchange upset Rosario. As Anzaldúa (1998) explains, such racial/ethnic categorizing or "marking is always 'marking down'" (264). While Whites typically escape racial/ethnic labeling, reinforcing the image that whiteness is the norm, this may not be the case for those who are believed to "deviate" from this "norm" or from fixed conceptualizations. Likewise, for Rosario, who was meeting the boss with the hopes that he would hire her, this power differential required that she respond to his inquiry, but she was not in a position to ask him a similar question.[4]

Similarly, in his occupation as a hairstylist, thirty-six-year-old John Palomares finds that he is constantly asked about his racial/ethnic background. He believes that this questioning is more common when he is among wealthy Whites, and he attributes it to their perception that he "looks different," not like Whites and not like their image of Mexican Americans. Reflecting on his interactions with his Beverly Hills clients, John recalls some of his observations:

> When I worked in Beverly Hills, everybody would ask me my nationality, and I thought that was kind of funny because nobody ever asks you except when you get into the high-class areas. They're like wondering, "What are you?" That's when I would say, "I'm Hispanic. I was born in the United States, but I'm Hispanic and Italian."

John perceived such questions to be especially preposterous because he views himself as Hispanic, is generally not asked his race/ethnicity in working-class and middle-class communities (which tend to have more people of color), and was not the only Latina/o working in Beverly Hills. In fact, most of the service workers near his place of employment were also Latina/o.

Respondents such as John Palomares find that personal inquiries about their race/ethnicity are occasionally combined with other stereotypes about Mexican Americans. For John, this includes the assumption that all people of Mexican descent reside in East Los Angeles—a working-class and primarily Mexican-origin community. When his Beverly Hills clients asked him where he lived, John would explain

> that I lived in the San Gabriel Valley, and they'd ask, "Where's that at?" I even had one client who told me that she went by my neighbor-

hood. I asked, "Where's my neighborhood?" She said, "Well, East Los Angeles."

The interactions that John Palomares describes with wealthy White clients parallel Rollins' (1985) findings in her study on the relationships of White middle- and upper-class employers with Black domestic workers. Given their class and racial/ethnic differences, Rollins (1985) found that many of the employers used domestic workers as "windows into exotica" to learn about the lives of working-class African Americans. Since most employers had limited contact with women of color or members of the working class, they relied on their relationships with Black domestic workers to "explore what they assume is a very different lifestyle" (164). Rollins speculates that by asking domestic workers questions, employers may be looking for provocative information that confirms their negative stereotypes about working-class and African American communities. As a hairstylist for wealthy clients, John's experiences may be similar.

At times, the scrutinizing eyes of some Whites—or their perceiving what Madrid (1995) describes as "sticking out like a sore thumb"—may infringe on respondents' daily activities. For example, Rosario Jones, who has a child with her White husband, has been made to feel very uncomfortable when she is in public with her son because some people have suspiciously gawked at them, believing that Rosario could not have birthed a light-skinned child. In such encounters, Rosario has had to clarify people's misconceptions:

> When my son was born, people used to look at me funny and say, "Oh gosh." They would give me a look like did I kidnap him. Ladies would come up to me and just out-right ask me. They would say, "Oh, how sweet it is of you to adopt that little White boy." I'd say, "He's mine." "Oh no, oh well, his father must be very fair." They say that instead of saying that his father must be White.

Trying to understand Rosario Jones' relation to her son, people have sought various explanations. These have included assuming that her son is adopted, that Rosario is the caregiver for a White family, or, as revealed in the following quote, that she is a traditional homemaker:

> When people see the two of us together, they're like, "Is that your baby?" He's not ashamed to say, "My mother is Mexican." I tell him, "Say I'm Mexican American." They expect me to be right there making tortillas every day, if they think I'm Mexican.

These misperceptions are a reflection of dominant images (which are perhaps linked to a history of anti-miscegenation sentiment and conceptions of racial/ethnic purity in the United States) that assume that families are racially/ethnically homogeneous and that Mexican women are domestic workers and caregivers. Believing that many equate Mexican women with an image of a traditional homemaker, Rosario Jones attempts to escape such a perception by encouraging her son to tell others that she is Mexican American, not Mexican.

Such experiences have led many respondents to challenge the imposition of racial/ethnic labels. Reacting to multiple exchanges with people who have drawn upon the stereotyped images of Mexicans to make assumptions about her family, history, and identity, fifty-five-year-old Diane Gallardo proclaims her defiance:

> As a Latin person, I hate to be labeled. I hate to be labeled as a community of Latins . . . Take a look at me, and tell me I'm such and such. You haven't found out. You don't know. I come from a family that has blue eyes, dark eyes, olive complexions, white complexions, blond hair, brown hair, black hair. They're short. They're tall. They're skinny. They're fat.

Diane's response reveals her frustration with the presumptions of labeling, with people's homogeneous perceptions of Mexicans and their generalizations of her identity.

While it was more common for respondents to recount situations when they "stuck out like a sore thumb," some retold experiences of invisibility in their interactions with Whites. For a few self-described "light" or "fair-skinned" Mexican Americans, the theme of invisibility emerged in their interviews as they discussed having to contend with Whites who—not seeing them as Mexican—have expressed blatant anti-Latina/o prejudices. Thirty-two-year-old Gary Mesa explains:

> They'll make comments about ethnic groups, about Latinos. So, I have to say, "Hey, this is who I am." So, in certain situations, even campaigning for candidates, people thinking that I look White make comments against Latino candidates. I say, "This is who I am."

In such cases, Whites who equate Mexicanness to dominant phenotypical stereotypes may overlook or render invisible the histories, experiences, perspectives, families, and racial/ethnic identifications of such individuals.

In situations when Mexican Americans are made to feel both obvious and invisible, we observe some of the most blatant exclusionary beliefs and actions. Rosario Jones describes such an experience from the 1990s when the White employees at a Salt Lake City restaurant simultaneously marked her as "different" and yet ignored her by denying her service. As Rosario reveals, this denial of fair and equal treatment has led her to realize that others may not conceive of her as an American. She recalls going with White co-workers to a restaurant where they waited for more than an hour to be served. After one co-worker finally approached the waiter, she returned to the table and explained to her colleagues,

> "He said that they're going to close in a little bit," I said. "No way." I said, "I know." There were fifteen of us. About five of us left.

Walking outside of the restaurant, Rosario was able to see through the window that five minutes later the waiter was standing at the table ready to take the remaining White co-workers' order.

> There I was crying again. I said, "God, I can't believe this." I was just all hurt. If I say, "I'm American," [they say,] "Oh, no. There's no way."

Having been warned by family members of the overt racial discrimination that they encountered while in Utah and being acutely aware that she was the only person of color in the restaurant, Rosario strongly believes that the waiter's failure to take her order was intimately linked to her race/ethnicity. Rosario reiterates a warning her cousin gave to her before she left for Utah: "They don't like Mexicans over there. They don't like Blacks. They don't like anybody. If you're not White, you're not right." For Rosario, this experience was not unique. All too often she has been confronted with the realization that she is defined as "different," not quite American.

Rosario Jones' numerous such exchanges with Whites illustrate several key themes that are expanded upon in the following sections. From her experiences, we see the double bind of being "the Other," which may constrain some Mexican Americans who are excluded from narrow constructions of "American" and "Mexican." Likewise, the manifestations of such static binaries may involve restrictive interactions and practices that infringe upon respondents' daily activities.

"They see us like gringos": Latinas'/os' restrictive conceptualizations

Similar mechanisms that reinforce some Whites' narrow and negative images of the Mexican-origin community are also limiting the views that Mexican immigrants and other Latinas/os may have of Mexican Americans. For example, while the media have been a significant force in presenting few, incomplete, and inaccurate images of Mexican Americans, many people have not had access to appropriate educational materials and accurate information on the histories, lives, and experiences of U.S.-born Mexicans. Instead, Mexican culture has typically been presented and conceived of as static and disassociated from history, power, and situational contexts (Zavella 1994). Thus, rather than conceiving of culture as interactive, fluid, and variable, what often persists are essentialized, narrow, and stereotypical conceptualizations of what constitutes "Mexican culture." As we saw in the previous section, some respondents explain that Whites may categorize Mexican Americans based on phenotype or other stereotypical notions, while in their interactions with Latina/o immigrants, several individuals find that it is cultural attributes and expectations that are more typically centered.

Perhaps unaware of the assimilating pressures and exclusionary practices Mexican Americans have encountered in the United States, Mexicanas/os have not always understood why Mexican Americans may not speak Spanish or may speak it differently than they do. As a result, some Mexicanas/os make the assumption that Mexican Americans have "consciously and willingly negated their Mexican heritage and Spanish language" (Gómez-Quiñones 1990, 204). Since the early twentieth century, this perception has led some Mexicanas/os to apply the term "pocho" to Mexican Americans (Gómez-Quiñones 1990, 203) who are perceived to be assimilated or to speak Spanish "poorly" (Acuña 1988). As the voices of the following individuals reveal, for U.S.-born Mexicans, negotiating others' perceptions may occur more than just in the company of Whites. They likewise have to contend with Latinas/os who hold stereotypical associations of what characteristics constitute Mexicanness. These include assumptions that all Mexicans speak Spanish, are born in Mexico, and have brown skin.

Twenty-three-year-old Geraldo Romero expresses a concern articulated by a number of people—that some Latinas/os expect all individuals of Mexican descent to speak Spanish:

> Being a Latino, they have certain expectations, especially being a Latino who preaches or who talks a lot about Chicanismo and talks about culture. Language goes hand and hand with that, and if you don't possess that language, you're almost a farce.

Geraldo fears that he is judged negatively by Spanish-speaking Latinas/os. He is concerned that people who possess narrow conceptions of a Chicano may judge him to be a "fake," somehow less than "real" or authentic because he is not fluent in Spanish. Such concerns of being deemed inadequate also encroach on his sense of self as a teacher, despite the fact that he teaches courses in the social sciences, not in the Spanish language:

I have fears here in La Puente teaching next year. I fear being confronted by a mother who doesn't think I am adequate to teach—one, because I am young, and two, because I can't talk to them in Spanish. Although I am not teaching Spanish, it's still a fear that I have.

Though it is not institutionalized in the ways that speaking English and the assimilationist imperative are, the image and the internalized belief that Mexican Americans are "culturally deficient" if they do not speak Spanish or they speak Spanish differently from the ways that Mexican immigrants might is an ironic twist that illustrates the double bind that some may encounter—being seen as neither American nor Mexican.

Like Geraldo, second-generation Mexican American Rosario Jones believes that other Latinas/os "look down on her" because she does not speak Spanish. Attempting to avoid negative perceptions, Rosario identifies as American when asked by Latinas/os about her background:

I usually always say I'm American because they right away want to put me into a category. If I use that term Mexican American, they want me to speak Spanish, and they say, "You're not proud of where you come from."

Rosario's experience has been such that some Latinas/os who know that she is Mexican American expect her to speak Spanish and ridicule her when she does not. As will be discussed in more detail in chapters 5 and 6, this ridicule has caused anger among some Mexican Americans who do not speak Spanish because of their family's length of time in the United States and the dominant emphasis on assimilation. However, many may be unaware of a history of Spanish-language repression, and as individuals such as Rosario recount, within the Mexican-origin community there may be "self-appointed gatekeepers" (Martha Barrera 1991, 82) who exclude those individuals who do not possess some socially constructed benchmark of Mexicanness, such as fluency in the Spanish language.

Even when Mexican Americans speak Spanish, they may still encounter Mexican immigrants who differentiate themselves because of place of birth or skin color. For example, twenty-three-year-old Mireya Pardo explains that some immigrants derogatorily consider her a "gringa" (White woman) because she was born in the United States:

They see us like gringos. We don't see them that way. We see them as another Mexican. So, they always kind of set barriers like, "Oh no, you're better than me or I'm less than you." But I don't feel that way. I feel that just because I was born here doesn't make me less Mexican than you.

Such labeling was similarly recounted by sixty-nine-year-old Pete Saldana, who has been labeled a "honky" by some Latinos/as:

> When I speak Spanish, they say that I speak very fluently Spanish and I'm White. I correct them. I say, "No, I'm not White. I'm Latin." They're kind of surprised because I speak English and my complexion's very white. They think that I'm a honky. They've told me that.

While growing up in New Mexico, Pete identified as Spanish or White. Today, however, in the largely Mexican-origin community of La Puente and with the perception that more racial/ethnic categories exist than in the past, Pete no longer feels that the way he identifies is limited to these two categories. Now, in the presence of Mexican Americans and Mexican immigrants and given his ability to communicate in Spanish, Pete is in a position to adamantly declare that he is not White. Nevertheless, Latinas/os have not always accepted Pete's assertion. Instead, some have seen him as "White" or derogatorily as a "honky." Such experiences have led some respondents to believe that there are members of the Mexican-origin and larger Latina/o community who—rather than acknowledging the vast intra-group heterogeneity—are reinforcing narrow notions of what it means to be authentically Mexican. Martha Barrera (1991) has used the term "browner than thou" to describe the attitudes that are based on narrow and static notions of Mexicanness.

La Puente residents who identify as Chicanas/os also reflect on the negative perceptions some Latinas/os have of them and their preferred identifiers. Drawing on her observations, Rita Lopez Tellez believes that some people of Mexican descent, especially older immigrants such as her father, react negatively to the term Chicana/o because they think that people who use it will experience more racism:

> I know that growing up for us, being a Chicana or Chicano was bad. That was a term that we were not allowed to use. For my dad, I think because he experienced a lot of racism, for him, it meant that if you identified that way, you were going to experience a lot of racism.

Offering a slightly different explanation, David Galvez describes how his Mexican immigrant in-laws view Chicanas/os: "To them, Chicano's a derogatory term . . . Chicano is like the lower end of society, according to the way the term is used in Mexico." Historically, "Chicano" was used as a pejorative term that was applied to the working classes (Acuña 1988), and older members of the Mexican-origin community tend to react negatively to the term because of their perception that it is associated with radical political activism (Estrada 1993, 175). Thus, just as the assumption that Mexicans speak Spanish may infringe on respondents' conceptions of selves, self-identified Chicanas/os are also grappling with others' imposed constructions.[5]

Uneasy parallels may be drawn between these contemporary racial/ethnic categorizations and stereotypes and the biological and cultural paradigms of previous generations. While the biological approach involved the adoption of a nature perspective to understand and justify group placement, the fixed conceptualization of race and the emphasis on phenotype to discern Mexicanness reproduces the perception that race is a biological construct. Likewise, the belief that there are certain authentically Mexican cultural practices camouflages the vast diversity among the Mexican-origin population as well as the salience of structural factors and ideological process in shaping experiences and life chances.

Nevertheless, a key distinction exists between a cultural determinist perspective and the assumption by some immigrants that speaking Spanish is an indicator of one's Mexicanness. This distinction is rooted in asymmetrical power relations. In the United States, preference for Anglo norms, practices, and values have been institutionalized and are apparent in dominant arenas and in the expectation of assimilation. This, however, is not the case for the Spanish language where there is a history of language repression. Some respondents are frustrated or angered by immigrants who appear to be ridiculing their language abilities, but such remarks from immigrants may be in reaction to a dominant culture that devalues speaking Spanish or to experiences with Mexican Americans who ridicule immigrants or who deny their own Mexican origins and knowledge of Spanish.

Claiming Multifaceted Racial/Ethnic Identities

Within the context of externally imposed categorizations, respondents are claiming multifaceted racial/ethnic identities. They describe a variety of ways they identify and rationales for how they identify, and many include more than one label in their self-descriptions. For example, thirty-two-year-old Gary Mesa explains, "I feel comfortable with either Mexican American, Latino, or Chicano. Those are three labels that I use interchangeably to identify myself." Some agree with thirty-six-year-old Rita Lopez Tellez on the significance of the situation and the role that audience plays in racial/ethnic identification:

> I call myself a Chicana, and I use it pretty interchangeably with Latina because I know that some people don't like the term Chicana or that it

has a negative connotation. So, I'm kind of careful about who I say that to. I don't go around saying it everywhere.

Likewise, racial/ethnic identity may be influenced by physical boundaries and geographical locations. The salience of power differentials on identification as they are linked to physical space is revealed by fifteen-year-old Mel Sandoval's revealing comment that the only time she identifies as American is when she crosses the U.S.–Mexican border.

For several respondents, such a fluidity of labels and identity may involve challenging the narrow or static conceptualizations some Latinas/os have of Mexicanness. This is exemplified by Geraldo Romero's self-described "inclusive" characterization of a Chicano identity that leaves space for multiple experiences and the use of different languages within the Mexican-origin community:

> I don't think [not speaking Spanish] takes anything away from your experiences. I think that's the beauty with Chicanos and just with people because we are so different. There isn't one person who fits the Chicano identity. It's a wide spectrum of ideas and cultures and languages that make me and make the identity.

This variation in identity and the use by many of multiple terms, oftentimes depending on the social situation, makes it difficult to present definitive categories of respondents' racial/ethnic labels.[6] Regardless of the terms that they use however, a strong sense of identity persists, revealed by the fact that most respondents refer to themselves with a term and a rationale that is linked to their national origins and to their bicultural experiences and upbringing as Mexican Americans. Overall, the most common term that respondents identify with is Mexican American, but there are at least ten different racial/ethnic labels that they use, including Chicana/o, Latina/o, Hispanic, and Mexican.

Though respondents' self-conceptions are more fluid than others' constructions, their racial/ethnic identities are not voluntary or by choice. Rather, they are negotiated within a system of inequality that fosters the very constraints and limitations described in the previous section. However, in the context of institutional and individual categorizations, respondents are negotiating imposed, static, and exclusionary conceptualizations by naming themselves, challenging stereotypes, and claiming an identity that is connected to a critical analysis of power and inequality. When asked how they identify and why, respondents articulate a complex analysis that includes an emphasis on (1) internal factors of ancestry and cultural practices and

(2) external factors such as experiences of racism and inequality. While they discuss these factors as salient in influencing identity, they also reveal that class position, community, and audience are important. Though some rationales for their racial/ethnic identifications cannot be neatly linked to solely one or the other of these factors, to illustrate respondents' conceptualizations of themselves and to begin to better understand their perceptions of immigrants, the following subsections are organized along these two emphases (internal and external factors). As will become more apparent as we move from this section to the following chapters, we will also begin to see that those individuals who emphasize the significance of external factors on their racial/ethnic identity (and in particular those who have adopted a power-conflict perspective) are also more likely to articulate a connection with Mexican immigrants, to be engaged in Mexican American-Mexican immigrant community-building, and to be challenging dominant practices and perspectives.

Linking racial/ethnic identification to ancestry and culture

Not wanting to deny their ancestors' origins is a recurring theme among respondents who emphasize ancestry and cultural practices in their discussions of racial/ethnic identity, as does thirty-two-year-old Gary Mesa:

> I'm probably the fairest-skinned of all of my brothers, yet I identify more with my ethnicity. I wouldn't just label myself as American because then I feel that I would be denying wherever my ancestors came from. So, I prefer labeling where my ancestors came from in conjunction with the fact that I'm American. I would never just say American.

As someone who is light-skinned, Gary may be accepted as an "American" by the dominant society and may be granted certain privileges by having light skin. However, realizing the historical and contemporary experiences of Mexican Americans, Gary opposes such forms of inequality by asserting that he is Mexican American.

This emphasis on claiming, rather than denying, a Mexican American identity is echoed by seventy-six-year-old Leticia Mendoza:

> I'm very proud to have my ancestors from Mexico, very proud. I never let my children ever try and deny that, and they don't. But we are Mexican Americans. We were born here.

Mel Sandoval, one of the youngest respondents, also believes that identifying as Mexican American and Mexican allows her to underscore her family origins:

I usually say Mexican American. My grandmother tells me to say, "You're Mexican American." I go, "Okay." My dad is always, "No, you're American. You were born in America. You're American." But my roots came from Mexico. So I just tell people that I'm Mexican.

Reflecting the experiences of a number of respondents, these three individuals reveal that they are challenging the ways in which their identities may be stigmatized or contested. Leticia, for example, explains that she identifies as Mexican American because she was born in the United States, but her emphasis on being proud and not denying her ancestry is rooted in her experiences and awareness that Mexicans have been subjected to a subordinate position in the United States. Mel, too, centers her Mexican heritage, and her preferred identifier combines the multiple messages she receives from her family and peers.

A couple of respondents who explain that they are proud of their racial/ethnic background nonetheless distinguish themselves from other Mexicans. For example, fifty-five-year-old Diane Gallardo is the daughter of immigrant parents, a Mexican mother and a Spanish father. Preferring to identify with both of her parents' nationalities, Diane describes herself as someone who is of Mexican and of Basque descent. While Diane explains that she understands her cultural background, she differentiates herself from other Mexicans who she believes lack her level of knowledge:

A lot of these people that call themselves Mexican don't even know what it stands for. They don't even know what the culture is. They don't know that there are regions in Mexico. They don't know what different dresses come from different regions, what the music is, what dance goes with what region, what music goes with which region. They don't even know what Cinco de Mayo is for . . . These ignorances are what bring the Mexican people down.

As Diane Gallardo's comments suggest, a few respondents may use not only a hierarchy of cultural knowledge to delineate boundaries between Mexican Americans and immigrants, but they may also highlight class differences. For Diane, this involves distinguishing herself from less established Mexicans who have moved to La Puente from Mexico and from East Los Angeles and who she perceives are not assimilating:

What was coming into the neighborhood, I'm sorry to say, were people that lived in East L.A. that came with their own ideas and didn't want to change. They don't want to mainstream . . . They bring the ghetto attitude, which I resent because a lot of them are of my background.

Diane expands her critique of Mexican immigrants who she believes are not "mainstreaming":

> They come to our country, and I feel that they should be like us. I'm not asking them to lose all of their individuality, all of their tradition, all of their background, but don't come and impose on us. That's where I feel I'm very different from them. I don't identify with them.

While the various factors and situations that might account for such intra-ethnic distinctions will be considered in detail in the following chapter, Diane's use of "us" and "them," coupled with her declarative statement, "I don't identify with them," captures how a few respondents who are proud of their background may distance themselves from immigrants and other Mexicans.

As well as emphasizing ancestry, several respondents ground their identity in particular cultural practices as Mexicans born and raised in the United States. Twenty-nine-year-old Margarita Villa is among these:

> I believe that I'm both. I'm both Mexican and American. I know the whole American concept goes with the deal that we were born in the Americas, but I consider myself very much Mexican as much as the culture here in the United States. I identify myself as both.

Respondents such as Margarita who identify as Mexican American believe that not including Mexican in their identification omits a large part of who they are and how they view themselves. For Margarita, who is the daughter of immigrants, her identity is linked to her experiences in the United States and to particular cultural practices and values transmitted by her family:

> I'm very, very close to my Latin roots and the traditions. I still speak Spanish at home anything that's very traditional in the sense of Mexico. In our Christmas, we go around the house and make tamales. We do the buñuelos [fried tortillas flavored with cinnamon sugar], the food that we eat, the music that we listen to at our family gatherings. We don't listen to the English music. All of us listen to the music that comes from the north of Mexico. It's things like that. The way I talk, my upbringing, the things I think—traditional values.

Rather than maintaining fixed, limited, or narrow conceptions of Mexican Americanness, respondents like Margarita Villa articulate a range of factors that are salient in their self-conceptions, such as language, holiday traditions, food, music, and perspectives.

Of the few individuals who specifically mentioned their multiple backgrounds, most of them also link their racial/ethnic identifications to their Mexican parents' ancestry and to cultural practices. For example, Mel Sandoval's mother, forty-three-year-old Lois Sandoval, was raised by a U.S.-born mother of Irish and Cherokee descent and a Mexican immigrant father. However, because she grew up in East Los Angeles and near her Spanish-speaking relatives, she identifies as Hispanic:

> Most of the time, I say Hispanic. I guess because my mother's family was never here, so we grew up in the Mexican tradition. We'd go to my grandmother's house every Sunday . . . We grew up with the Spanish music, Mexican music. So, we were brought up with that. I guess it would have been different if we were brought up on my mom's side. They like country, and I don't like country.

Living in largely Mexican-origin communities such as East Los Angeles and La Puente have led respondents such as Lois Sandoval and other self-identified bi/multi-racial/ethnic respondents to highlight their Mexican heritage. This finding parallels the existing scholarship that has documented that individuals of mixed parentage tend to identify with the racial/ethnic background of the parent who has a closer connection to immigration or with the group whose customs, traditions, and language they know better (Stephan and Stephan 1989; Waters 1990).[7]

Integral to the narratives of respondents who focus on ancestry and cultural practices is an objection of dichotomized and narrow conceptions that one can only be American or Mexican. As seventy-five-year-old Carlos Mendoza explains, identifying as Mexican, Mexican American, or Chicana/o, does not presuppose that Mexican Americans are not also Americans:

> I'm a Mexican. I was born in the United States. I never neglect my ethnic background.

When I asked if at times he identified as American, he replied:

> No, what would be the point in thinking like that? They know I'm Mexican. Of course, I'm a citizen, and I'm entitled to everything that's entitled to a citizen.

Sixty-nine-year-old Joe Zavala took a somewhat different approach:

> [I identify as] an American, Mexican American of Mexican descent or American of Mexican descent, whatever you want to call it. Technically,

I was born here and raised here. My father was born here. My mother was born here. My grandfather, on one side, was born here too. I mean, how far can you go?

In contrast to Carlos Mendoza's reply that others know he is Mexican, Joe Zavala's response reveals how outsiders may not consider Mexican Americans to be Americans, regardless of their family's length of time in the United States. By recounting his family's history, Joe seems to be justifying his use of the label American, which is the first term he uses to name himself. As a result of the normalization of whiteness, the false view of Whites as Americans and people of color as "foreigners," and the narrow conception of America and Americans, people of color who may not be light-skinned oftentimes do not have the option or the privilege to claim or be considered "American" (Alba 1990; Waters 1990; Frankenberg 1993; McIntosh 1995; Wildman with Davis 1997). Also, some may not wish to identify as American because of what it may leave out or "deny."

These experiences of second- and third-generation Mexican Americans challenge some of the early assimilationist models of identity formation in which the underlying belief was that over time, immigrants and their children and grandchildren would follow a series of stages until there was a merging of values, symbols, and identities with the dominant society (for examples see Park 1950; Gordon 1964). Their experiences are also distinct from Southern and Eastern European Americans whose "ethnicity matters only in voluntary ways—in celebrating holidays with a special twist, cooking a special ethnic meal (or at least calling a meal by a special ethnic name), remembering a special phrase or two in a foreign language" (Waters 1990, 147). For the Mexican-origin population, not only may generations continue to identify as Mexican American (Hurtado 1995), but even among those respondents who emphasize family ancestry and cultural traditions over experiences of racism or discrimination when describing themselves, their racial/ethnic identities are influenced by public perceptions of Mexicans and Mexican Americans, their interactions with others, the racial/ethnic demographics of their communities, the era in which they are raised, and the geographical region where they reside. For many Mexican Americans, racial/ethnic categorization persists and may influence their daily lives, opportunities, and perspectives.

Linking racial/ethnic identity to racism and inequality

As described in the first section of this chapter, respondents recount exclusionary practices and beliefs on the part of institutions as well as some Whites and Latinas/os. For many, these experiences have resulted in a sense of being different and of being treated unequally in comparison to Whites, fostering a Mexican, Mexican American, Latina/o, or Chicana/o identity.

To understand the processes resulting in identity formation as a result of hostile or unequal treatment, Portes and Rumbaut (1990) have applied the notion of "reactive ethnicity." This concept is helpful for highlighting the significance of discrimination in influencing the changing racial/ethnic identities described by a few respondents. As a fourth-generation Mexican American woman, thirty-six-year-old Deana Martinez has always considered herself "just to be American," though she explains that she is "Hispanic, technically." However, Deana's self-perception as American was recently disrupted when she moved back to her childhood city of La Puente. After a divorce, she left her middle-class and largely White community of more than ten years and returned to La Puente with her three children. As a result of class and race/ethnic mistreatment that Deana and her children encountered by Hacienda–La Puente Unified School District employees, Deana explains that her sense of self changed from feeling "American" to feeling "Mexican":

> I never felt that I was anything but American until I came to live in this school district. I never felt that I was ever discriminated against . . . until I came to live in La Puente . . . For the first time in my life, I felt like I was treated like I was Mexican.

Living in cities with differing racial/ethnic and class demographics, Deana returned to La Puente with a frame of reference from which to compare her children's' educational opportunities and school officials' perceptions of parents and students. This point of comparison allowed her to observe the disparities between school systems that she did not see as a child in La Puente. Overall, Deana's awareness of teachers' and administrators' stereotyped expectations in La Puente illustrates the impact of external factors on the development of her shared racial/ethnic and class identity with other working-class Mexicans.

While the process of "reactive ethnicity" is useful for understanding the experiences described by individuals such as Deana Martinez, this concept may not sufficiently capture the intersection of racism and individual agency. There are examples of individuals whose exposure to historical and structural analyses of Mexicans in the United States or whose participation in social movements helped to foster a framework in which they actively claim politicized racial/ethnic identities. The following narratives illustrate that as individuals become increasingly aware of the structural and ideological processes maintaining inequality, they may become more racially/ethnically conscious and motivated to impact change.

In comparison to Deana Martinez, who was one of two respondents to identify only as American, most respondents realized at an earlier age that they were treated unequally. However, this knowledge may not have manifested into what some respondents describe as "embracing" racial/ethnicity identity until later in life. For example, forty-four-year-old Diego Tellez knew by the fourth grade that he was "different from people" and that this difference (as compared to and defined by Whites) was deemed as inferior. He describes the first time that he remembers feeling the impact of this distinction:

> Some real fat White guy called another kid a dirty Mexican, and I kind of stuck up for him. I knew we were Mexican, obviously. But I guess that I didn't realize it was really that different from being Anglo.

Though respondents such as Diego describe a lifelong awareness that they are Mexican, several echo Diego's story that this was not an identity they embraced until more recently. For Diego, it was through participation in a program on inter-ethnic relations that he learned about the historical and structural factors influencing the Mexican-origin population. Subsequent to his involvement, Diego began working with Latinas/os in East Los Angeles, a community he "felt that [he] could relate to" in comparison to his previous experiences working and volunteering in an upper-middle-class city where he "never really felt like part of the community." These experiences and knowledge base influenced him such that in his late thirties he began to identity with other individuals of Mexican descent.

Diego Tellez describes this process of embracing his identity as an "awakening," and some respondents characterize their identity formation, primarily as Chicanas/os, as "a rebirth" or "an epiphany" that emerged from their increasing awareness of inequality and the knowledge and critical thinking skills that they developed through participation in the Chicano movement or in Chicana/o studies courses. Forty-six-year-old Denise Villarreal attributes her identity as a Chicana and Latina to her college experiences as a Chicano studies and Spanish double major and to her involvement in the Chicano movement of the late 1960s and early 1970s:

> When I became a Chicano studies major when I was in college, I embraced my background more . . . I didn't want to speak Spanish as a child because we grew up in that time period where it wasn't the thing to do . . . So I pretty much embraced that when I was in college.

The narratives of twenty-three-year-old Geraldo Romero and twenty-seven-year-old David Galvez best illustrate the processes that lead some to identify as Chicanos as well as the role of schools in identity formation. Growing up in La Puente in the 1970s and 1980s, Geraldo and David vividly remember the intense pressures to assimilate. In an attempt to conform to such expectations, Geraldo was known throughout his school years as Gerald. He attributes this name change to the assimilating pressures in school, the absence of Latinos in the course curriculum, and the lack of discussion of race/ethnicity and class while he attended school in La Puente:

> I don't remember having teachers who really talked about identity and about just being Latino in a predominantly Latino community. Working class, [I] never had an idea of what it was, growing up.

Criticizing his schooling experiences, Geraldo faults the administrators: "Their focus isn't on tending to the needs of the constituents, of the people who go to the schools."

Likewise while he was a La Puente student, David Galvez did not want to speak Spanish, to listen to Mexican music, or to eat Mexican food:

> I remember those middle school years, early high school, and maybe elementary years where I didn't want to speak Spanish. Now, I think about it, "Ah, I'm so ashamed." I pretended I didn't know Spanish. I didn't want to speak Spanish to my dad, especially in front of other people. The whole pronunciation of my last name was different. That was a pretty serious identity issue I went through those years.

These experiences and observations of prejudicial comments and discriminatory practices led David to undergo what he describes as a "rebirth in terms of identity" in high school. During his last year in high school, David began to critically assess the attitudes and actions of some of his bigoted teachers, leading him to proclaim a Chicano identity:

> "Chicano" was the term I started using in high school when I had these teachers that are pretty conservative. I started realizing certain comments they made and how condescending they were toward Latinos, and then I adopted that term.

For David, adopting a Chicano identity was one way to confront some of his teachers' perceptions by affirming what they saw as negative—being Mexican. He remembers how he was then labeled "a troublemaker" because of this new sense of identity:

I remember comments from several teachers. So, I kind of turned it into something that brought me satisfaction to throw it in their face. If they want to present being Mexican, being Chicano, as something negative, then I threw it in their face. "Well, you may perceive it as negative, but I see it as something that I'm proud of." So, it got me into trouble in high school. They started to look at me as disrespectful. "He doesn't do what he's told." Basically, I was just voicing my opinion. I wasn't going to be this little kid that just sat there and listened to all that they had to say.

Like David, Geraldo Romero describes the formation of his Chicano identity as a "rebirth, an epiphany" that emerged from his experiences of exclusion and his exposure to Chicana/o history. In particular, Geraldo attributes his "rebirth" to the experiences and knowledge that he acquired while a college student:

It was a litany of different things. It was being there, being away from the predominantly Latino community, and having to challenge the ideas that others had of me. It was being around people who were political and who were talking about stuff that I had never heard about. It was engaging in conversations and challenging myself. It was an incredible time for me, and I really found a niche for myself in academia. That was like my birth right there.

As with David, part of Geraldo's Chicano consciousness stemmed from his experiences with people who had stereotyped expectations of him because of his position as a working-class Mexican American male. Geraldo's college courses were also instrumental in his becoming Chicano. He remembers how his politicizing experiences in college provided him with the skills and a point of comparison to criticize the public school education in La Puente for its exclusion of Mexican Americans in the course curriculum:

I didn't learn anything. You learn basic arithmetic and other skills, but as far as learning and connecting ideas and challenging concepts, I learned that at UCLA . . . UCLA was the space for me to learn about my culture and to learn about myself. It's almost like an oxymoron because UCLA is an ivory tower, but now I'm actually learning about myself. Instead, I should have probably been learning about myself in a place like La Puente.

For Geraldo, it is ironic that he had to leave La Puente and attend school at an elite institution in order to acquire the history and knowledge of Mexicans that were instrumental in the formation of his Chicano identity.[8]

As college students in the 1990s, both David and Geraldo became active in the Chicana/o student movement for some of the same reasons articulated by a generation before them. Geraldo recounted how he participated in campus demonstrations and student organizations that advocated increasing the number of working-class students of color in colleges and universities. David worked with students, faculty, and community organizers in an attempt to create a core Chicano studies department at UCLA with its own tenure-track faculty.[9] David said participation in such protests and in the Chicana/o student group Movimiento Estudiantil Chicanos de Aztlán (MEChA) "really affirmed a lot of my beliefs."

While the experiences of Geraldo Romero and David Galvez magnify some of the processes that fostered their oppositional identities, nearly one-quarter of all of the respondents discuss their identity formation as a process of becoming increasingly aware of inequality and of leading to a perspective that involves challenging the status quo, presenting an anti-assimilationist critique of society, and advocating for social justice. As Morris (1992) notes, such an oppositional consciousness involves

> that set of insurgent ideas and beliefs constructed and developed by an
> oppressed group for the purpose of guiding its struggle to undermine, re-
> form, or overthrow a system of domination. Oppositional consciousness
> is usually a reactive force, given that it is developed to battle a hegemonic
> consciousness utilized by ruling groups to repress potentially empower-
> ing beliefs and behaviors of an oppressed constituency. (363)

This consciousness is intimately linked to the adoption of a power-conflict perspective that emphasizes the unequal historical events, structural factors, and ideological processes that continue to influence the lives of Mexicans in the United States. As we will see in chapters 6 and 7, this power-conflict perspective has implications for the formation of a collective Mexican American–Mexican immigrant identity.

Though not all of the respondents who adopt a power-conflict perspective identify as Chicana/o, many do. On average among the respondents, individuals like Geraldo Romero and David Galvez who claim a Chicana/o identity and advocate for social justice tend to be younger and to have more years of education than other respondents. These patterns parallel older quantitative studies that documented how Chicana/o identifiers were more common among individuals thirty years of age or less and with higher educational levels (Grebler, Moore, and Guzman 1970; Garcia 1981). Respondents' narratives also support work illustrating the positive relationships of contact with the dominant society (in this case, through place of residence, location of work, and college education), political identity, and an orientation to social change (Gurin, Hurtado, and Peng 1994). Such studies have found that while contact with the dominant society is important for allowing inter-group comparisons (as we saw in the example provided by Deana Martinez), frequent intra-group contact is also necessary for fostering political consciousness and motivating collective action (Rodriguez and Gurin 1990; Gurin, Hurtado, and Peng 1994).

Conclusion

Respondents' experiences reveal how racial/ethnic identities are socially constructed through interactions between self and society. In particular, we see how cultural and external factors may intersect with individual and group agency to influence racial/ethnic identities. While the labels respondents use to refer to themselves are often multiple, situational, and varied, contrary to the experiences of Whites (see Waters 1990), Mexican Americans' identities are usually marked by limited choices. Institutions, ideologies, and individuals may structure, limit, and constrain Mexican Americans' life chances such that their identities often are not optional, not voluntary, and not temporary. Within these constraints, however, respondents are negotiating fixed racial/ethnic constructs by challenging stereotypes, naming themselves, and claiming a Chicana/o identity that is linked to political awareness, collective identity, and the struggle for social justice.

Since respondents' identities may be multiple and fluid, it is difficult to make definitive statements about the relationships between identity and intra-ethnic relations. However, several connections emerged that will be unraveled in more detail in the upcoming chapters. First of all, similar factors and processes that are influencing respondents' identities are also shaping intra-ethnic relations. Secondly, respondents are actively engaged in defining and creating relationships with Mexican immigrants in ways that are not distinct from their constructions of selves. Thirdly, just as those individuals who articulate cultural and familial connections with immigrants may demonstrate patterns of intra-ethnic identity and cooperation, many of the respondents who are fostering inclusive spaces and engaging in political activism for social justice are emphasizing the external factors that are influencing the Mexican-origin community and have adopted a power-conflict perspective. Finally, while several respondents reflect on the significance of teachers and course curriculum on identity formation, in additional ways schools prove to play critical roles in intra-ethnic relations.

To better understand why some Mexican Americans delineate clear boundaries between themselves and Mexican immigrants and the role that schools might play in this process, the next chapter considers in more detail the structuring of intra-ethnic conflict.

Chapter 5

"Between a Rock and a Hard Place, with No Easy Answers": Structuring Conflict

Sixty-two-year-old Silvia Bravo smiles warmly as she invites me into her home. She escorts me to her kitchen table and offers me a drink. As she walks toward the refrigerator, she gestures to the neatly arranged papers at one end of the table and says she is coordinating a large donation project at the church. I soon learn that she is very involved in the local Catholic church and parochial school. Detailing her involvement in this project, she returns to the table with two glasses of water, sits down, and begins to describe herself and La Puente.

Silvia Bravo is the daughter of Mexican parents who migrated to Texas, the state where she was born and completed high school. Her first language was Spanish, and it was in elementary school that she learned English. Silvia remembers her schooling experiences as "very hard," saying the teachers were "always getting after me in school to speak English because they wanted me to learn it correctly." She now says she speaks Spanish "well, but not very well because it's mostly the slang type of Spanish."

After she married a third-generation Mexican American, the couple moved to Los Angeles in the 1950s. Three years later, they purchased their first home, and it was in La Puente. Having spent most of her life in the city, Silvia fondly recounts learning to drive, raising her children, and participating in the Catholic church and school in La Puente. She is taking care of two of her grandchildren and has enrolled them in the same Catholic school that her own children attended.

Silvia has been actively involved with the Catholic church and vividly remembers her early participation when the church was being built:

> They were building the church when we first moved . . . There was just the frame, and then they finished the building. There were no pews when

they first started mass. We were sitting on the painters' cans. The boards on top of the painters' cans, and that's all we would sit on. helped build that church from the very beginning. Now we're ready to build another hall, so we've pledged to build a hall.

As one of the original members of the Catholic school's Women's Council, she continues to raise money for the newly founded Parents Association.

Over the years, Silvia has noticed the growing number of Latinas/os and immigrants who are attending church services:

There's oodles of them. Some of them aren't even from La Puente. They come from all over, but they come to our church.

As someone who has worked hard to build the church, she is concerned that immigrants appear unaware of the congregation's history and the longtime involvement of Whites and Mexican Americans who feel that they are being "shunned or pushed to the side" by immigrants. Silvia is also critical of what she perceives as a growing inclusion of the Spanish language in the Catholic school:

The teachers are forever speaking in Spanish, and she's got to sing the songs in Spanish. She's got to read in Spanish. So everything [is in Spanish]. I can see where the children need to get started, but I think that the parents need to study the English language. If they come here, they should pick up the customs.

Silvia Bravo attended school at a time when learning and speaking English in public arenas were the dominant expectations, and she believes that while she acculturated without any support, recent Mexican immigrants are being privileged and are experiencing a United States where there is greater individual and institutional acceptance of the Spanish language. As will become apparent in this chapter, Silvia's sentiments are echoed by other La Puente residents who argue that they have "played by the rules" by acquiring the English language. Thus, they criticize immigrants who are perceived to not be adopting the language, norms, and values of the dominant society, and they are frustrated with the use of Spanish and the rising number of immigrants in their local schools, churches, and other neighborhood sites.

While some, like Silvia Bravo, express beliefs that may suggest intraethnic conflict and others articulate ideas that illustrate unity, these attitudes among respondents tend not to be static or mutually exclusive. Listening to their narratives, one senses that what individuals express in the comfort of their kitchens or family rooms about immigrants may differ from the attitudes and actions that they demonstrate when interacting with others. Just as respondents' racial/ethnic identities are varied, multifaceted, and oftentimes context-specific, so too are their attitudes toward and interactions with Mexican immigrants. Individually and collectively, their attitudes and interactions can be placed along a continuum of conflict and solidarity and include intra-ethnic antagonism, a shared connection, and collective political mobilization. Since their beliefs and behaviors may be simultaneous and situational, respondents' attitudes cannot be used to categorize or typologize individuals. Thus, to best illustrate their oftentimes fluid perspectives and the range of their overall views, this chapter and the two that follow it are organized around a conflict-solidarity continuum.

This chapter focuses on one end of this continuum—the factors and situations that are influencing respondents' unfavorable or ambivalent attitudes toward and interactions with Mexican immigrants. Though negative sentiments are the least common attitudes described by respondents, their appearance in nearly half of the interviews warrants discussion. Such sentiments or concerns vary, but four recurring and at times overlapping themes emerge in respondents' narratives: (1) that immigrants are catered to more than U.S.-born Mexicans; (2) that immigrants are imposing their culture on U.S. citizens; (3) that immigrants expect Mexican Americans to possess a shared sense of identity, and (4) that immigrants are ridiculing Mexican Americans.

Underlying such concerns is a perception that expectations for acculturation have changed. Respondents say they have noticed a shift from earlier eras when they were ridiculed and reprimanded for speaking Spanish in schools, churches, and supermarkets. They resent what they perceive as the growing acceptance of the Spanish language and the economic advantages that may now accrue to bilingual individuals. Raised during the period of Americanization or with strict expectations to assimilate, some support the belief that the English language, along with Anglo and middle-class values and traditions, should be standard in public spaces. They also may have accepted the dominant conceptualization that defines Americans as individuals in the United States (as opposed to North, South, and Central Americans) and Americanness as speaking English. Some may adopt these conceptualizations to distinguish themselves from immigrants.

With limited power in community institutions and having been influenced by dominant ideologies, some La Puente residents believe that not only do seemingly unacculturated immigrants threaten their position but that immigrants are being held to different, easier expectations for integration. In this context, respondents are reconciling their experiences of language repression with their observations of the growing presence of Mexican immigrants and the public use of the Spanish language.

Given the structure of institutions and the location of Mexican Americans in the racial/ethnic hierarchy, in many ways respondents find themselves as mediators, buffers, or, as one individual describes it "between a rock and a hard place," that is, between Mexican immigrants and Whites. In this position, some support and reinforce dominant practices and assimilationist ideologies, though simultaneously these very practices and ideologies can work to their own detriment.

To better convey some of their conflicting sentiments toward immigrants and the changing demographics, this chapter is organized around three intersecting factors that influence Mexican American–Mexican immigrant relations: the structure of institutions, the dominant expectation of acculturation, and the location of Mexican Americans on the racial/ethnic hierarchy. While these structural factors, ideological processes, and racial/ethnic categories intersect and may foster simultaneous and situational attitudes and behaviors, for purposes of elaboration they are each discussed here separately. The analysis also reveals how respondents are negotiating these factors and processes that influence intra-ethnic relations.

"We're divided, the office people and the plant people": Institutions Structuring Relationships

The hierarchical structuring of institutions is shaping and constraining relationships between established residents and immigrants (Lamphere 1992, 4). In La Puente, institutions influence the amount and type of contact between Mexican Americans and Mexican immigrants. On average, the more limited their informal and personal exchanges, the more likely Mexican American respondents are to express antagonism toward immigrants. When asked what their experiences have been with immigrants, many begin their descriptions with something like "I don't have any personal experiences." They then proceed to describe their experiences in general ways, focusing on language and customs in public arenas.

While limited personal interactions between Mexican Americans and immigrants may result from a conscious attempt at avoidance, institutions also constrain their relationships. For example, within the city, many Mexican Americans are homeowners, while new immigrants are more likely to live in apartment complexes with other immigrants. This physical distance tends to limit formal and informal interaction. The experiences of Miriam Flores, a thirty-six-year-old woman who migrated to the United States in 1990, are illustrative. She explains that about 90 percent of the residents in her La Puente apartment complex are immigrants. Thus, she interacts daily with other immigrants and has little contact with Mexican Americans except during her weekly grocery shopping, and even then she has few opportunities to speak with Mexican Americans.

In the workplace, respondents generally possess different types of jobs than immigrants or work in distinct areas within the same company.[1] Mary Marquez, a forty-year-old purchasing clerk, attributes the limited interactions at her place of employment to a division of labor:

> Most of the plant people are Mexican [immigrants]. Most of the management is White. It seems like most of the middle people are Mexican [American] like me. It seems like all the middle people are Mexican but speak English, where the people in the back speak Spanish, and that's the labor . . . It's kind of like we're divided, the office people and the plant people.

Besides performing different jobs, Mexican Americans and immigrants may be assigned to different locations within the company. As Mary explains: "Immigrants tend to work in the back of the company as plant workers." This class- and language-based occupational segregation reproduces these differences and hinders intergenerational interactions.

This pattern of occupational differentiation between Mexican Americans and Mexican immigrants is also documented by Ortiz (1996). In the Los Angeles region, she finds Mexican Americans were more occupationally isolated from immigrants in the 1990s than they were in the 1970s. In 1970 Mexican Americans were more likely to be employed in occupations that they shared with immigrants, such as manufacturing, construction, and gardening. In recent years, a decline in well-paid jobs in the manufacturing of steel, automobiles, and rubber and an increase in low-wage jobs in light manufacturing of goods such as garments and plastics have resulted in the employment of Mexican American men in trucking and as police officers, mail carriers, and heavy-equipment operators. In contrast, employers have typically targeted Mexican immigrants to fill low-wage jobs in light manufacturing and in the service sector. The contemporary occupations of Mexican American women in the Los Angeles area mirror those held by several of the La Puente respondents. They are employed in a range of low-skilled white-collar professions, as receptionists and typists and in other forms of clerical work (Ortiz 1996, 260–261).

Table 5.1 Racial/Ethnic Demographics of Hacienda–La Puente Unified School District, 1995–1996

	White (%)	Latina/o (%)
Teachers	73	13
Classified Staff	33	56
Students	12	67

(Source: California Department of Education)

At the La Puente school where sixty-two-year-old Erica Handel is an instructional aide, Mexican American–Mexican immigrant relations are also influenced by a racialized and nationalized division of labor in which established residents tend to hold positions of power relative to recent immigrants, and most contact occurs in formal situations.[2] This division of labor is noticeable in Erica's assessment that the majority of teachers and administrators at her school are Whites who live outside of La Puente, and most of the instructional aides are Mexican Americans who reside in the city. In contrast, the students and their parents are predominantly Latina/o, with individuals of Mexican descent and immigrants representing a substantial population. As illustrated in Table 5.1, Erica's observations of these racial/ethnic differences mirror the school district's demographics at the time of her interview.[3] Similar racial/ethnic gaps are apparent in public schools throughout the nation where in disproportion to the student population, Whites are overrepresented as school board members and teachers (deMarrais and LeCompte 1999). In 1995, for example, 91 percent of teachers of kindergarten through twelfth grade in the United States were White, while students of color constituted 35 percent of the student population (Galguera 1998, 411). In California, nearly 80 percent of teachers were White, and about 60 percent of the student population was of color (ibid., 412).

At Erica Handel's school, administrators, teachers, aides, and parents usually interact in formal situations across power differentials. White teachers and administrators are largely responsible for determining school and classroom policies, and Mexican American instructional aides typically hold intermediary positions in which they are expected to implement the policies. In this intermediary position, Mexican American instructional aides may be placed in buffering or gatekeeping positions, having to negotiate between school officials and parents. As instructional aides, they may be expected to support school policies, even if they and the Mexican-origin population that is being served do not endorse them. Moreover, as with Erica Handel, Mexican immigrants may look to Spanish-speaking Mexican American aides to ensure that the desires and the needs of the community are being met. To the extent of any gap in their interests, these competing pressures of serving the expectations of school officials and those of their fellow community members may result in conflictual relations or may reinforce prevailing beliefs about immigrants, especially if this is one of the few sites of cross-generational interactions.

As a bilingual instructional aide, Erica seems to be influenced by these factors in her perceptions of and contacts with immigrant parents. Erica's few interactions with immigrants have been in her intermediary position as a school employee between school officials and parents and largely between Whites and Mexican immigrants. Erica shares that this mediating position has often frustrated her. At the time of our interview, Erica had just returned home from a day of administering standardized tests. She was upset from watching frustrated third-graders complete these tests. Trying to understand why the students were having such a difficult time, Erica faults state policies that require tests, school officials who advance unprepared students, and parents who "don't seem to care" about their children:

> Half [of Latina/o immigrant parents] are just using the schools as baby-sitters, and they don't care what their children learn or if they learn at all. It's frustrating. Right now, we're testing, and oh, you come home with a headache. You come home tired, and then you want to talk to the parents. I'm in third grade right now. We still have a couple of kids that don't know the alphabet. [They] can't read. They are having problems still writing their names. They shouldn't even let them go, but the parents don't care. A lot of these parents, the negative ones, are not from around here. They've emigrated from Mexico, and we have a few from Nicaragua and a few other little places. They just don't seem to care.

While Erica expresses dissatisfaction with standardized tests and an administration that promotes students who cannot read, she directs most of her anger toward immigrant parents. This anger stems in part from Erica's interactions with parents who expect her, as a fellow Mexican, to assist and to ally with immigrants because of a shared racial/ethnic background. However, several generations away from immigration and as a school employee, Erica holds views that tend to differ from the views of the Mexican immigrant parents she meets.

Describing encounters she has had with parents regarding their divergent beliefs on bilingual education, Erica becomes more frustrated:

They want to know why we're not talking Spanish to them. First of all, we are using the English language there so the other kids, for example, in our class, can pick up English faster. If they hear it more often, they will pick it up faster. They want to know why we're not teaching it a hundred percent. Well, because that is not an all-Spanish school. It's bilingual. Bilingual means two, but they don't know that.[4]

As a bilingual instructional aide, Erica's interactions with Spanish-speaking parents have revolved around the school site, where regulations and roles for instructional aides and parents are clearly defined. Oftentimes, these regulations and roles conflict, and parents and instructional aides may have limited decision-making power over school policies and practices.

Erica favors the elementary school's bilingual education program that emphasizes learning English quickly through English immersion. Part of her support may stem from her own experiences and upbringing when English-language acquisition was emphasized over Spanish-language maintenance. In comparison, the Spanish-speaking parents whom Erica encounters endorse an additive bilingual education program that focuses on preserving the Spanish language while still learning English.

Because of a shared ability to speak Spanish and a perceived common background, immigrant parents may hold accountable those bilingual Mexican Americans with whom they have contact. However, the same type of pressure may not be placed on the mainly White teachers, administrators, and school district officials to change their policies on bilingual education. As a school employee, Erica is placed in a contradictory position in which she may find fault with administrators who practice social promotion, yet she endorses the school's emphasis on English immersion and criticizes the parents for not understanding this approach. She is also resentful of some immigrants' assumption and expectation that she and other Mexican American school officials should support the teaching and speaking of Spanish within the school. Arguing that English should be taught at school and Spanish can be the language used within the home, Erica describes a situation in which her opinion and the school's practices clashed with the perspective of a Mexican immigrant parent of a student at the school:

She wanted to know how come he wasn't learning Spanish in class. Well, he's in a Spanish class, but we're tutoring him in English because he has to learn the English too. She wants to know, "He has to learn all Spanish." Well, he's supposed to be learning Spanish at home. Well, he is not learning the correct Spanish, but that's her problem—not ours. We're pushing English.

Erica's oftentimes strained interactions with parents become evident in the school's front office. Since Erica supports the use of the English language in the office, she disagrees with Mexican-origin parents who expect her to speak in Spanish:

> You try to be nice to them, and they're civil to you, but once you start treating them like everybody else, like maybe you're working with some Black people here, Orientals here, they want to be taken care of right away because after all, "We're Mexican too. Take care of them later. They're not Mexican." It doesn't work that way. They figure, "Hey, she's Mexican." They then refuse to speak English. They'll tell you, "Why should I speak English? I'm Mexican. You're not proud because you won't speak Spanish." I say, "No, we're in the office now." They usually call you in to translate. The only time that we will speak Spanish is if you definitely can't speak English. It's hard. It's hard. You're juggling them.

While one of Erica's roles is to translate for Spanish-speaking parents, she—unlike many of the Mexican-origin parents she comes into contact with—believes that she should not speak Spanish in the school office. These disparate perspectives and unequal power relations seem to contribute to Erica's frustration and to generate conflict. It is such exchanges that have led Erica to conclude that Mexican immigrants "demand things and they add, 'Well, just because you're so and so, you forget that you're Mexican.' We don't forget anything. It's just that we're what we are, and that's it."

Erica Handel's experiences as an instructional aide underscore a number of important points. Similar to most who describe intra-ethnic antagonism, she has had little informal and personal interaction with immigrants. Most of her exchanges have been as an instructional aide, in an intermediary or gatekeeping position. Although some parents may initially see Erica as an ally, her support for English immersion and her belief that English should be spoken in the school office may lead Mexican parents to see her as a representative of the school and may act in ways that confirm Erica's perception that immigrants are "demanding." As a result of their difficult position, individuals in jobs such as Erica's may be more prone to conflictual relationships with immigrants.

Within the school system, not only are relationships between Mexican American and Mexican immigrant adults often strained, but also teachers' attitudes and the educational structure may limit intra-ethnic interactions and may even serve to reproduce divisions among students. Such divisions often result from the system of curriculum tracking, in which students are placed into classes depending on their language skills and perceived abilities or levels of motivation. When racial and class stereotypes as well as perceptions of English-language skills are used to determine track placement, racial/ethnic, class, and generational segregation and divisions among students crystallize (Oakes 1985; Valenzuela 1999; Mendoza-Denton 1999). The experiences of fifteen-year-old Mel Sandoval reveal the institutional structuring of such relationships. She explains how as a high school honors student, she has minimal contact with Spanish-speaking students enrolled in English Language Development (ELD) courses:

> All these three years, I've been exposed to honors kids, and we all follow each other. Those are the only people I know. I don't know people that are in regular classes. And then there's other people who are Mexicans who mostly speak Spanish, and they're on the verge of coming into English. I don't really talk to them. I have nothing to do with them. There's no way I interact with them. I have no reason to talk to them.

Mendoza-Denton (1999) also describes how divisions between Mexican American and Mexican immigrant students are reproduced within schools. In her study of a Northern California school, she finds that inflexible school policies requiring students to pass state competency exams, to score within a certain percentile on the school's standardized test, to maintain passing grades, and to be "functioning" in school make it nearly impossible for students to switch curriculum tracks. Thus, students whose first language is English and those who are learning English remain apart (47).

Curriculum tracking may not only isolate Spanish-speaking students from their English-speaking peers, but such separation, in combination with dominant expectations of assimilation, may reproduce a racial/ethnic hierarchy in which more acculturated and light-skinned students are also designated the popular students in school. This is the phenomenon that Mel Sandoval recounts at her high school, where popularity is connected to one's generation in the United States and to skin color:

> G.L.O.: The popular, "cool" people, do they tend to be from one particular ethnic or racial background, or is the group a mixture?
> MEL: Actually, Mexicans, maybe not dark Mexicans—maybe light. Like maybe my color.
> G.L.O.: They tend to have been born in the U.S. or in Mexico?
> MEL: In the U.S.
> G.L.O.: But you said lighter?
> MEL: Yeah, probably lighter, and they don't really look like they came straight from Mexico . . . If they migrated to America, then I think

I'd be able to tell. They have sort of a look. I'm not saying that they all look the same, but I think that I could totally tell.

Continuing, Mel expands on what she means by "a look" that immigrants have and how the popular students disparage such students:

> MEL: At school, you can tell if you're really Mexican. They call them chunties. They are like really dark. They're real dark, and they like soccer.
> G.L.O.: Who's the "they" that calls them "chunties"?
> MEL: The popular people. They look down on them. They're just there; they're in their own little world. They call them chunties or wetbacks . . . They say it in a bad way. Like my friend will ask me, "Oh, who's that guy with?" "Oh, he's with some chuntie girl." To put her down, they say, "Yeah, she's ugly. She's some chuntie."

At times, the institutional distance (through separate classrooms that often manifest into distinct friendship groups) and the social distance between Mexican American and Mexican immigrant students are reinforced by teachers' derogatory comments about Spanish-speaking students. Thirty-six-year-old Deana Marquez describes how exposure to his teacher's stereotyped views led her twelve-year-old son to also denigrate Mexican immigrant students:

> My son's sixth-grade teacher was one teacher who would have these children transition. The children would come in maybe twice or three times a week. He would assist them for an hour. Meanwhile, the other kids in his regular classroom, he'd give them whatever to work on — math or something to work on so he could help these children. After these children would leave his class, he'd tell his main class, "You know, I really don't like doing this. I don't even know why they have me doing this." He would talk about these children and put them down. One day my son came home and told me, "You know, Mom, these Mexican kids that are in these classrooms, they can't speak English. It's terrible; they should learn how to speak the language."

Emphasizing how such practices "pit kids against kids," Deana continues:

> Right away, my kid was like, "I don't like that kid because they don't speak English." It's wrong. It's creating a prejudice within children. This is the type of teacher they employ continuously.

To the extent that institutions structure and constrain intergenerational interactions, communication, and awareness, such prejudice and stereotypes may develop and persist. The result may be a cyclical relationship in which some Mexican Americans may then consciously avoid contact with immigrants, reinforcing their limited interaction, lack of knowledge, and possible misunderstanding (see Valenzuela 1999, 191).

Finally, the changing structure of the economy and limited institutional resources may be fueling Mexican American antagonism toward immigrants. Such scapegoating was apparent in the narratives of several respondents who believe that immigrants are "pushing" Mexican Americans out by receiving greater access to public resources and social services. Repeating some of the popular conceptions surrounding the 1994 "Save Our State" initiative, a couple of individuals blame state agencies for differentially treating immigrants and Mexican Americans. For example, seventy-year-old Cristina Saldana complains that "a lot of people that are really citizens here in California that need a lot of help from the state don't get it as much as other people coming from Mexico or other places." She expands:

> Friends that we know that have asked for help, and they have rejected them for some reason. Then comes people from other places and they go and because they have two or three kids, they just give them the help . . . you just kind of wonder why some people get help and some people don't.

Forty-three-year-old Lois Sandoval also believes that Mexican immigrants are being assisted to the detriment of Mexican Americans:

> They come here, and it seems that they focus more on them than they do our own people. They should focus more on us than people that try to come into the state. They just come over, and it seems like they rule everything, and they leave us aside. It seems like they cherish more the people that are coming in than they do the ones that are actually here, that have been here for years. It's just not fair.

Rosario Jones concurs, adding that she resents immigrants who she believes prefer receiving assistance from White social workers than from Mexican American residents. Compared to other racial/ethnic groups,

> Mexican Americans make more effort to be hospitable to the immigrants that come. We want to help them, but when they don't accept the help, they want everything for free. They just want to come here, and "Here's a silver platter with everything on it." When you try to help them along, I think they're more resistant. They want to go to the White social worker who's going to say, "Okay, here's your check for the month, and you can live in this housing."

To the extent that institutions have limited resources to aid U.S. residents, the misplaced frustration of some Mexican Americans onto Mexican immigrants will persist, especially during periods of economic downturns, with increased anti-immigrant sentiment, and in light of the massive decline in high-wage, stable, and largely unionized manufacturing jobs that has hindered the progress of Mexican Americans. While respondents' narratives suggest that the structure of institutions may play a critical role in limiting interactions and in fostering divisions, as expanded upon in the following section, their interviews also reveal the salience of the assimilationist ideology and the resulting practices on Mexican Americans' experiences, perspectives, and relationships with immigrants.

"They have to learn how to be American":
Expectations of Cultural Assimilation

> My grandparents were able to become contributing, productive members of our society because they learned English and because the public schools taught English to their children. That was the traditional American way—the melting pot, assimilation, and a united America containing a single people with the English language uniting our nation. We must return to that America!
>
> RON UNZ 1997[5]

At the time I was conducting research for this book, the United States—and California in particular—were ensnared in debates over English-only education, bilingual education, and national identity. While debates over language and the emphasis on assimilation are not new, the 1980s and 1990s saw an unprecedented wave of English-only activism. In 1981 U.S. Senator S. I. Hayakawa of California ushered in the first of many legislative campaigns to establish English as the official language in the United States (Crawford 2000). This proposed amendment to the U.S. Constitution called for governmental business, including the administering of social services, to be conducted in English and to prohibit federal and state laws, ordinances, regulations, orders, programs, and policies from requiring the use of other languages (Crawford 1992, 1; see also Tse 2001). Though Senator Hayakawa's proposed amendment did not pass Congress, it effectively fostered a climate of anti-bilingualism and established a precedent for additional legislation. Currently, twenty-three states have adopted measures that make English the official language (Crawford 2000, 4), including California, where 73 percent of voters in 1986 supported a constitutional amendment designating English as the official state language (Schmid 1992, 202).

U.S. politicians and voters who support English-language amendments do so for various reasons. The above quote from a letter by millionaire software entrepreneur Ron Unz, who proposed and financed the 1998 anti-bilingual California initiative "English Language Education for Children in Public Schools," captures some of these beliefs: that the English language unites Americans and America; that immigrants should learn English and assimilate; and that in comparison to previous generations, recent immigrants refuse to learn English and are receiving "special language accommodations" (Crawford 2000; Tse 2001, 3).

In Unz' words, what is at stake with bilingualism and bilingual education is "the traditional American way." While his comments were specifically targeting bilingual education, the ideas underlying them—support for assimilation and the belief that not speaking English "disunites America"— have been common sentiments throughout the United States. As described in Chapter 2, some of these assimilationist ideologies have guided Americanization programs and the emphasis on learning English.

As La Puente residents negotiate their relationships with immigrants, individuals who support such dominant ideologies and worldviews also advocate for immigrant acculturation. For example, outspoken supporters of acculturation Diane Gallardo, along with her husband, stresses English-language acquisition and "mainstreaming" for immigrants:

We respect anybody that comes to this country and speaks English or tries to learn . . . It's the ones that don't want to mainstream, that want to keep speaking Spanish only, that don't want to adopt a lot of the thinking of our country that creates an imbalance.

Diane is adamant in her beliefs, and she is not alone. Forty-seven-year-old Roberta Zavala also supports acculturation:

People came because they wanted to immigrate for whatever reason. I have no problem as long as they maintain our values. You want to assimilate. We don't want to bring the nation down. You have to come in . . . with an attitude, "I come here to work. I come here to follow the rules. I come here to be a good citizen, respecting the country, respecting my neighbors, respecting myself, get a job to do what's good for my children."

Sixty-nine-year-old Pete Saldana and twenty-nine-year-old Shirley Garcia concur:

ᴇ: Immigration is all right, if they left their habits there. If they come
ere with their habits, like they're doing now, it's no good . . . If they
ome from the south, from Mexico, once they're here, they should
orget their Pancho Villa style. They should speak their English and
.orget. Be bilingual instead of just speaking Spanish . . .

sʜɪʀʟᴇʏ: They complain about our government, about the gangs, about
this and that. I think that if they really want to do something about
it become citizens, so they can speak their voice. You can't live here,
reap all the benefits of California, the United States. You didn't vote
for what's happening, so don't complain about it.

These narratives reveal how the acceptance of assimilationist ideologies and
the structures that maintain them may foster negative perceptions of Mexican immigrants who are believed to not be acculturating.

For a few individuals, supporting acculturation includes disapproving of
the use of Spanish in public. This objection stems from a perception that immigrants are "imposing" the Spanish language. Diane Gallardo's comments
are illustrative:

They come here, impose their language on us, impose their attitudes.
They don't keep it within their home. They spread them around so that
you can't walk into a store and make a purchase without being spoken
to in Spanish where we're in America.

Agreeing with Diane's depiction of immigrants, a few believe that immigrants "don't seem to follow the customs here." In fact, thirty-year-old
Rosario Jones and her sister feel so strongly about what they have observed
that they submitted an editorial to the local newspaper expressing their
contention that Mexican immigrants should "learn American ways." Their
article begins:

I know we welcome Mexican immigrants to our country and go out of
our way for them, but who is going to teach these people manners and
the American way? Who can teach them that we don't spread laundry
out on the chain link fence in the front yard?[6]

The belief in Anglo cultural superiority may underline the push for assimilation that is apparent in Americanization programs and English-only
movements, including Ron Unz' support for the elimination of bilingual
education. In her community study, Menchaca (1995) found that due to
the ranking of cultures, which places Anglo culture over Mexican culture,
Mexican Americans may consider Mexican immigrants to be "backward" if

immigrants are unfamiliar with or have not assimilated Anglo norms, practices, and values (206–207). Thus, some individuals of color have accepted this racial/ethnic hierarchy and may judge themselves and other people of color by an Anglo-constructed norm or standard.[7] This acceptance is apparent among a couple of La Puente respondents who explain that they support assimilation or "mainstreaming" because they believe that "the Anglo world" is a better world. Diane Gallardo explains:

> They're always reaching up for this higher level of superiority, of excellence, of position, and there's a lot of discipline in that. I notice that there isn't that discipline amongst the Latin community. The Anglo world keeps striving for more. They keep striving for something better. They're never satisfied with the mediocre. I find that the Mexican people accept the mediocre.

Though most respondents do not articulate this overt belief in Anglo superiority, by supporting acculturation some endorse "Anglo conformity"—the ideology that the English language and English-oriented cultural patterns should be maintained as dominant and standard in the United States (Gordon 1961).[8]

As the preceding quotes illustrate, most respondents, including those who advocate for assimilation, are not opposed to immigration. In fact, this is one key area where such respondents diverge from many supporters of English only. Researchers have documented that California residents who supported the 1986 official English measure were likely to also endorse the 1994 proposition designed to eliminate undocumented immigration (see Crawford 2000, 24). However, rather than oppose immigration, it was more common for respondents to support acculturation and the assumption that if immigrants do not acquire the English language and U.S. values and rules they will destroy California and the United States.

Generally, individuals who believe that not learning English and not adopting mainstream values are detrimental have themselves adopted prevailing images of Los Angeles and the Southwest. Conceiving of the region as English-speaking, they neglect the historical context of a Los Angeles where the Mexican population predates the Anglo presence. Los Angeles was founded in 1781 as a Mexican pueblo, and even when Los Angeles and the rest of the Southwest were forcefully incorporated by the United States in 1848, cultural rights were to be protected under the Treaty of Guadalupe Hidalgo. As Vigil (1980) notes, "Mexican cultural customs and patterns were to be given equal consideration with Anglo culture; this meant recognition and accommodation of the Spanish language and Catholic religion" (127). California's first state constitution was written bilingually, in Spanish and English (Pitt 1966; Vigil 1980). By overlooking this history and the contemporary scene in which Latinas/os have numerically surpassed the White population in La Puente and constitute more than 40 percent in Los Angeles County, some accept an image of Los Angeles and California not as Latina/o and Spanish-speaking or as multiracial and multilingual but as White and English-speaking.

Likewise, some individuals who advocate learning American customs or being American do not describe what they mean. Rather, they criticize the behavior of immigrants and label American customs as the antithesis of what they perceive to be immigrant behaviors or "Mexican customs." Some say that being American includes living in the United States (as opposed to living in all of the Americas), speaking English, maintaining a job, following rules, respecting others and self, becoming a citizen, and voting. Thus, some respondents accept dichotomized and stereotypical notions of Mexicanness and Americanness, perpetuating the belief that there are national values that U.S. citizens possess and that immigrants may lack.

Due to real and perceived differences, a few Mexican Americans consciously maintain social distance from immigrants. They attempt to limit their contact by declining invitations to parties, by frequenting stores outside of La Puente, or by not attending Spanish-language masses. Silvia Bravo describes why she and her husband maintain minimal interaction with their immigrant neighbors:

> My husband and I stick with each other. We don't visit them. They have invited us to their little gatherings, but we feel out of place because we don't know their friends. They're all Mexican immigrants, and their customs are very different than ours, really. They've invited us two or three times, but we've gone once. But like I said, I do feel out of place even though we can communicate with the language. But it's very different.

While Silvia does not specifically describe what she means by her neighbors "having different customs," she explains:

> I can't relate to the people next door. I see the chickens out in the front yard. I hear roosters around, and they all come from these Mexicans. They leave their trash out in front, and they gather all their junk out in front, their broken cars.

Believing that Mexican Americans and Mexican immigrants observe different customs, Rosario Jones also prefers to minimize her contact with immigrants—leading her to use public facilities and spaces that are outside of La Puente. To maintain social distance, Rosario shops in a more middle-class and less Latina/o city "to get away from those darn Mexicans over there" at a La Puente supermarket. Rosario's desire to avoid immigrants is echoed in the editorial she and her sister submitted:

> I now shop in a neighboring market because I have been made so uncomfortable by constant ogling, whistling, and calls of "Hey, mamacita" by some of these men. Never mind that their wives are standing next to them along with their children.

Much of respondents' negative sentiment stems from their perception that while they and their families were raised with the pressure to acculturate, the same expectations do not exist for Mexican immigrants. As products of Americanization or as a result of the emphasis on acculturation, respondents recount being raised with the dominant expectation of speaking English, and some have accepted and endorse this expectation. Thus, while they remember having to acquire the English language, respondents who advocate acculturation compare their experiences with their belief that recent immigrants are being catered to in today's institutions and public spaces. This sentiment was more common among older respondents, as seen in the next subsection.

Experiencing/Perceiving the Transition from Acculturation to Spanish-Language Maintenance: Centering the Voices of the "Mexican American Generation"

Support for immigrant acculturation emerges primarily from the narratives of older respondents, the cohort described as the "Mexican American Generation"[9] because of their unique "collective consciousness" that resulted from their similar socialization processes (R. Alvarez 1973, 920) and their position as the first generation of Mexicans born in the United States (M. García 1985). More important than the age cohort of this Mexican American generation is the political climate that influences their shared experiences, a climate in which acceptance and cultural integration into the United States were stressed (ibid.).

In general, the individuals within this generation moved to La Puente in the 1960s and 1970s, and their move tended to signify their social mobility. As was the case with Silvia Bravo, whose narrative began this chapter, they came of age during a period when the dominant ideology and practices was assimilation, and they entered into a La Puente that was primarily White and, as Diane Gallardo describes it was referred to as "La Poeny," the Anglicized pronunciation. And compared to today's demographic context, in which two-thirds of the Mexican-origin population in California are the children of immigrants, in the 1960s most Mexican Americans in California were at least third-generation (Lopez and Stanton-Salazar 2001, 59). Within this climate, some residents followed a pattern that was common among upwardly mobile groups of color—"being American" (see Horton 1995, 191). In comparison to previous generations, this generation became more committed to the United States and to acculturation, leading some to self-identify as Americans of Mexican descent and to question their immigrant parents' attachment to Mexico (R. Alvarez 1973; M. García 1989; Horton 1995). For many, their loyalty to the United States was strengthened by the participation of a large number of Mexican American youth in World War II and to the economic prosperity that followed the war (Alvarez 1973).

Illustrating a shared consciousness that has become associated with members of the Mexican American Generation, several respondents of this era contrast their educational experiences with their perceptions of the experiences of recent immigrants. Key among these comparisons is that speaking Spanish was explicitly discouraged when they went to school. Fifty-two-year-old Delia Centeno remembers the assimilating pressures she encountered as a student in Texas:

> Spanish was spoken in the household, but when we were in school during that time, it was discouraged that we would speak any Spanish, and so you quit that. You try dropping the Spanish-speaking, and so you put a block on that area of your life.

Raised in Southern California, fifty-five-year-old Jane Hanson has a similar recollection:

> In El Monte or wherever I lived, everybody was so prejudiced. When I was in school, we weren't allowed to speak Spanish in California . . . where I was living, we were told, "At home you speak Spanish. At school you speak English."

These experiences of language repression were common (see Wollenberg 1976; G. Gonzalez 1990; Menchaca 1995). As we saw in La Puente's Central Avenue School, through the 1940s Mexican-origin students attended segregated schools or were placed in "Mexican classes," where the focus was on Americanizing Mexican students. Underlying the emphasis on Americanization was patriotism, citizenship, and a belief in the superiority of the English language (G. Gonzalez 1990). A common sentiment among Whites, as expressed by a Texas school district superintendent, was that a Mexican child "is foreign in his thinking and attitude until he learns to think and talk in English" (quoted in G. Gonzalez 1990, 41). In 1923 a school superintendent in Los Angeles addressed district principals by describing his desire for Americanization. He stated, "We have these [Mexican] immigrants to live with, and if we can Americanize them, we can live with them" (quoted in G. Gonzalez 1990, 36).

Americanization programs significantly shaped the schooling experiences of students of Mexican descent. Gilbert Gonzalez (1990) illustrates how this happened:

> Through the program of Americanization, the Mexican child was taught that his family, community, and culture were obstacles to schooling success. The assumption that Mexican culture was meager and deficient implied that the child came to the classroom with meager and deficient tools with which to learn. This implication was quite consciously woven into the methodology and content of instruction. (45)

Thus this period of Americanization during approximately the first half of the twentieth century marks the schooling experiences of many older Mexican Americans.

While some respondents attended school at a time when Americanization was an explicit goal, Mexican Americans who were in school between 1950 and 1965 still encountered school policies and practices that emphasized assimilation. During this time, educational policy was informed by the concept of cultural deprivation, in which Mexican culture was seen as a factor in impeding Mexican American adaptation to Anglo culture (G. Gonzalez 1990, 14). Solorzano (1995) describes the ideas behind such a cultural deprivation model, which contends

> that since Chicano parents fail to assimilate and embrace the educational values of the dominant group, and continue to transmit or socialize their children with values that inhibit educational mobility, then the low educational attainment will continue into succeeding generations. (43)

Thus, the underlying premise during this period was that Mexican American parents and their culture were to blame for the educational outcomes of students.

Comparing their schooling to the experiences of today's students, some older Mexican Americans believe that schools are now more accommodating toward immigrants and the Spanish language. For example, Silvia Bravo believes that immigrants and their children are receiving services "geared to them":

> Everything has to be translated for them. I can see translate, but when they want everything to suit them, they want to bring their customs here instead of getting used to our customs. All this bilingual education, they have to have a teacher. I didn't speak English when I started kindergarten. Our teachers didn't speak Spanish, so we got by.

Silvia's use of the pronouns "they" and "our" reveals the distinctions that she makes between immigrant and dominant customs, describing her customs as dominant, despite the fact that similar to many Mexican immigrant children, she too entered the school system speaking Spanish. Arguing that she was able to adjust without bilingual education programs when she attended school in the 1930s and 1940s, Silvia opposes such programs and asserts: "If they're going to be here, they should learn the language and not have everything geared to them in Spanish."

As a result of the hardships they faced and hoping to facilitate their children's integration into the school system, several individuals decided not to teach their children Spanish. Delia Centero explains:

> I think the reason for that was that I didn't want them to be hampered like where we were not allowed to speak Spanish in school. I didn't want them hampered in that way.

Raising her children in the late 1960s and throughout the 1970s, Delia says she thought she was doing what was "proper" by teaching them English:

> At that point of time, you would have never thought Spanish was going to come back ever, and now look at what's happening.

Comparing the current generation of students with her generation, Mary Marquez reiterates Delia's point:

> I just think that the generation now is more geared towards speaking Spanish than when I was growing up. When I was growing up, it was English. That was it. In school, it was just English.

Mary provides another example of how previous generations were explicitly discouraged from speaking Spanish while today's youth seem to have a closer connection to the language:

My nephew is in his first year of confirmation at Saint Joseph, and he asked me to be his godmother. So, I went to the first meeting last week, and the man speaking was older . . . he looked Mexican down to his black mustache, the black hair, the dark color, and he didn't speak Spanish. He said, "You know, people look at me and they say, 'What's wrong with you?' " At his time, they were actually discouraged from speaking Spanish. So a lot of our generation I think lost out on that, where a lot of my kids' friends . . . have that connection to speaking Spanish.

Given the emphasis on assimilation and the racial/ethnic demographics of the period, individuals of this generation believed that they were aiding their children by not teaching them Spanish. Now, in light of the growth of Latinas/os and a resurgence of the Spanish language, some reflect on their child-rearing practices and are remorseful for not having taught their children Spanish. Delia bemoans that her children cannot speak Spanish and says Spanish "was one thing I would have loved to have gone back to, but it was too easy to speak English." In comparison, Silvia Bravo, like others, is angry that "people criticize me for not having taught them Spanish." This anger stems largely from Silvia's belief that recent immigrants are unaware of the historical experiences of Mexican Americans and from her perception that it is easier to maintain the Spanish language today than it was in the past because immigrants are receiving services that are "geared to them."

In addition to highlighting perceived differences in schooling experiences and Spanish-language emphases over time, older individuals were more likely than younger ones to criticize church services that they think are assisting Mexican immigrants at the expense of Mexican Americans. Having spent the past twenty-two years participating in her local Catholic church, fifty-five-year-old Diane Gallardo resents the increase in Spanish-language masses for this reason:

It's becoming more Latin. They had to take away our eight o'clock mass where we were used to going because they changed it to a Spanish mass. Where there was only one Spanish mass, now there's three or four.

Involved in various church committees, Silvia Bravo complains of the growing number of immigrants at the church. She animatedly describes this growth in immigrant participation during special masses such as Ash Wednesday:

You should see it on Ash Wednesday. They come from all over, and it's all Latin American immigrants. People from the parish don't even go anymore to get ashes, or they go early in the morning because the Latins, they come running with five to twelve children, running, running because they think it's a sin or that they're going to die if they don't get ashes. It's an experience for anybody to see on Ash Wednesday.

Reflecting on an experience at a Spanish-language mass, Jane Hanson says immigrants are literally "pushing me out" of church:

I go to the White masses. If I wouldn't have been strong with my faith, I think I would have been long gone. I went to a Spanish mass . . . We sat down . . . this lady was pushing me out of my seat . . . If I wouldn't have been Catholic, I think I would have gone to another religion because this lady was pushing and pushing.[10]

Such reflections on immigrant participation in the church capture some of the tension occurring in community spaces. This tension, however, may be a reflection of the larger issues affecting Mexican Americans and Mexican immigrants and described in more detail in the following chapter—that both groups may have little power within the Catholic Church. As Cadena and Medina (1996) have documented, while Latinas/os constitute a growing percentage of the laity, about 35 percent in 1990 (see Chapter 6), they are underrepresented among the Catholic leadership in the United States. About 3 percent of the 54,000 Catholic priests and 5 percent of the Catholic bishops were Latino in the 1980s (Cadena and Medina 1996, 100).

Within La Puente, as Jane Hanson shares in Chapter 3, until fairly recently most of the Catholic priests in the local churches likewise have not been of Mexican descent. For example, volunteers of one area church compiled a list of the seventeen priests who had served the church since its inception in 1955 and reported that five of these priests had Spanish surnames.[11] According to a few respondents, at times La Puente–area priests have expressed stereotyped perceptions of the city's Mexican-origin and working-class residents. Among the few occasions when individuals laud La Puente–area priests for their work to include the Mexican-origin community, residents have found that the priest has often been moved to another church outside of the area. Studies have indicated that active engagement of priests and nuns with community residents may result in situations where churches "represent a strategic place to do collective work" (Pardo 1998, 230). Likewise, as will be discussed in Chapter 6, church officials who are disconnected from community members and hierarchical structures that result in top-down policies may hinder community building and foster cross-generational scapegoating and conflict.

The narratives of older Mexican Americans highlight the significance of generation and historical context on beliefs about acculturation. Their general support for acculturation may be attributed to the era in which they were raised, their experiences with the Spanish language, and the period in which many entered La Puente. Interwoven within these generational experiences, however, are the larger patterns that emerge among respondents across age and experience. These include the significance of prevailing ideologies, the ways that institutions may shape relationships, and Mexican Americans' position within the U.S. racial/ethnic structure.

"I think Mexican Americans are in a position where you have loyalties to both": Negotiating between Dominant Society and Mexican Immigrants

As a racialized group in the United States, Mexican Americans are oftentimes in an intermediary position between the dominant society and Mexican immigrants. As is apparent in their articulations of race/ethnicity recounted in the previous chapter, respondents may be perceived or treated as "the other" by Whites, and Mexican immigrants may not include them in their conceptions of "Mexican."

While some La Puente residents describe their racial/ethnic identities with an awareness of this position, trying to meet seemingly conflicting demands and expectations from Whites and from Mexican immigrants may be a source of tension and result in anger and ambivalence. For some, this anger may stem from their awareness that while Whites may be perceived as individuals, people of color are often seen as "representatives" of their perceived community. As a result of racial/ethnic lumping or the perception that "all Mexicans are the same," respondents may fear that the behavior of immigrants will reflect poorly on them, giving all people of Mexican descent a "bad reputation." This perception fuels attempts by some to distance themselves from immigrants. Rosario Jones explains, "I have such a hard time being Mexican American when I see the things that some of these people do." Forty-year-old Mary Marquez expresses a similar sentiment:

What I don't like is how dirty a lot of them are. There's dirty diapers in the parking lots, and it's just like they have "This is not my country, so I don't care." It just gives all Mexicans a bad reputation, like "Oh, she's Mexican. Marquez, she's Mexican. She must be dirty or not care."

Though this is not a concern for thirty-two-year-old Gary Mesa, it is for his mother, a New Mexican woman whose family has lived in the Southwest since before the U.S. conquest. Gary discloses his mother's frustration at being perceived by Whites as an immigrant:

> She argues with me, "Well, you don't have a problem. They're not going to confuse you" . . . There's times when she's been driving, they don't like the way she's driving, "Move, you f***ing wetback."

Expanding on why individuals like his mother might maintain negative perceptions of Mexican immigrants, Gary continues:

> I think it frustrates people when you know you have the same ethnic connection or national origin. There's resentment, not that they come, but they're not willing to show any pride in their property or the laws.

Menchaca (1995) also has found that some Mexican Americans are embarrassed by immigrants and attempt to disassociate themselves from them (207). She finds that the embarrassment stems from some immigrants' display of "mejicanismo," which included speaking Spanish and playing Mexican music in public (206–207).[12]

Some respondents have found that immigrants assume that Mexican Americans speak Spanish. This too has caused animosity, especially if immigrants mock Mexican Americans' Spanish-language abilities or do not know of Mexican Americans' historical experiences of language repression. Illustrating the experiences of ridicule shared by several respondents, Diane Gallardo recounts episodes at the supermarket where her husband has been derided because he does not speak Spanish:

> When we go to the market, they start speaking to my husband in Spanish. He doesn't answer because he doesn't speak the language. He knows very little of it, and they'll give him the cross-eye. I think that's wrong. They're in our country, and they give us the cross-eye.

Diane says the attitudes that most infuriate her are those such as: "You better speak to me in Spanish. You're Latin, why can't you speak to me in Spanish?"

Sixty-five-year-old Gloria Dominguez also expresses resentment on this point:

> Some people laugh at some of the words I might say. I say, "Hey, I don't do that to you when you mispronounce words in English." They shouldn't do that to us because of the fact that we spoke most of the

time in English. I mean, when we went to school, we didn't have what you have now. During my time you didn't have bilingual.

Erica Handel also describes being mocked: "They have a very low opinion of what I think they call 'the pochos' because we don't know their language as it is."

Delia Centeno has had similar experiences:

> The ones from over there will see the ones from over here as pochos, and they think that you're just not at their level. It's a little put-down, if you speak your Spanish in the way you speak it. It's like a little tear-down because it's not the proper Spanish. It's not going to be proper here. You pick up a lot of other things.

Navigating the expectations of both the dominant society and Mexican immigrants may place Mexican Americans in complex and at times contradictory positions in the United States. Forty-four-year-old Diego Tellez captures this complexity:

> I think Mexican Americans are in a position where you have loyalties to both . . . you have this national loyalty to other Americans, and then you have the cultural loyalty to Latinos. Between a rock and hard place, with no easy answers.

"Outsiders Within" Adopting Both/And Perspectives: Assimilationist and Power-Conflict

It is precisely the position "between a rock and a hard place" that may account for respondents' complex attitudes toward immigrants. In fact, rather than expressing attitudes that fall only along the conflict end of the continuum, it was more common for respondents to articulate multifaceted attitudes. For example, fifty-two-year-old Delia Centeno's perspectives on language and immigration are illustrative. Initially, she feels that immigrants need to speak English:

> They say that you go someplace to make it better, and then you make it what you had. It doesn't make sense. A lot of them won't even try speaking the language to even assist the kids.

However, she retracts some of her animosity as she reflects on the difficulties encountered by Spanish-speaking individuals. Delia ponders how a racial/ethnic hierarchy that denigrates the Spanish language and accent may deter immigrants from speaking English:

It takes a lot to speak it because who's going to want to be teased or anything. Where other languages are accepted, Spanish isn't. They'll laugh at the way you speak it, while French is totally acceptable, as are English and Irish.

Such multiple attitudes may be a reflection of respondents' perspectives and experiences as "outsiders within" dominant institutions and in the context of prevailing assimilationist expectations (see Collins 1990).

Discussing the relationship between social location and perspective among African American women, Collins (1990) explains how, because of historical and contemporary experiences of exclusion, African American women may have a unique angle of vision that enables them to see the contradictions and complications in the practices and ideologies perpetuated in dominant arenas and institutions. For example, as outsiders within academia, African American women may have a unique perspective of higher education and the construction of knowledge (Collins 1990). As a result of their experiences, Mexican Americans may have a similar angle of vision that may be complicated when considering their relationships with Mexican immigrants, a group they may be both similar to and distinct from. Perhaps arising from their unique vantage points in society, some respondents rather than articulating an assimilationist or a power-conflict perspective have instead adopted a "both-and conceptual framework" (see Collins 1990); they may articulate the prevailing expectations of assimilation as well as some of the ideas apparent in the power-conflict paradigm of race/ethnicity.

Respondents' multifaceted attitudes regarding Mexican immigration illustrate how some are negotiating between support for assimilation and their experiences and observations of exclusion and inequality. Rather than endorsing comprehensive restrictive immigration policies, the attitudes toward immigration that fall along the conflict end of the continuum were much more likely to illustrate respondents' multiple perspectives. For example, some supported free entry into the United States but believed that immigrants should assimilate. Forty-seven-year-old Roberta Zavala's comments exemplify this:

Immigration, I'm so torn. I feel that everyone has a right to come to the United States. That's why it is what it is. People came because they wanted to immigrate for whatever reason. I have no problem as long as they maintain our values. You want to assimilate.

Delia Centeno's descriptions of immigration are similar. She argues, "My God, if over there they're starving to death, who's going to deny them? Who has that right to deny them that?"[13]

Despite Delia's perception of immigrants and her open-border perspective on immigration, she differentiates between earlier waves of Mexican immigrants, whom she characterizes as "humble," and more recent immigrants, whom she labels as "too aggressive":

> I don't have a problem with them whether they're immigrants from Mexico. To me, I have a special place in my heart for them . . . I am not from over there, but my parents were them, and some are very, very different from what you'd see in the parents. They're much more aggressive than what I saw in my parents. I guess they were more humble.

Delia continues:

> They're aggressive. Mostly it would have been in the schools or you go to the store, and you're waiting in line. It's like, "You're unimportant, and I'm important." It's like push and "Out of the way."

Delia's perception parallels some of the earlier comments by those who believe that Mexican Americans are being "pushed to the side" by immigrants who are making inappropriate demands and "want everything to suit them." However, her sentiment of "I have a special place in my heart" depicts her sense of connection and identity with immigrants.

Other individuals endorse seemingly contradictory perspectives such as support for monitoring immigration in general but a greater reluctance or ambivalence to restrict migration from Mexico. Sixty-year-old Ray Sanchez expresses this sentiment:

> You just can't have wide open, just an invasion of people coming, whether they come from the south or whether they come from the north. They should not be allowed to stay because they should honor our rights as a country to enforce the regulations of these people coming into this country, but those things are hard to enforce. . . . It wasn't their problem that certain events happened that changed things. So, it's been a tradition for these people to come up here. All they want to do is better themselves. They are not here to cause a burden on the country. A lot of them pay taxes when they start working. They pay taxes, and they don't get any benefits from that.

Though Ray begins by arguing for the regulation of the United States' borders, when discussing Mexican migration he alludes to the U.S. conquest of northern Mexico, the construction of the border, and restrictionist policies that have sought to limit or exclude the movement of Mexicans into the United States. In addition, Ray challenges the perception that immigrants are "a burden on the country." Thus, his historical and economic analysis of Mexican migration leads him to lessen his original comments about immigrant restriction and "an invasion of people coming."

Similar attitudes toward immigration were also evident in several respondents' reflections on Proposition 187. Sixty-nine-year-old Joe Zavala explains that voting on Proposition 187 was difficult for him as an individual of Mexican descent because he empathizes with Mexican immigrants and their search for more opportunities. Nevertheless, he has a difficult time reconciling his sense of shared experience with his opposition to "breaking the rules and regulations":

> But it's illegal to cross the border because it's against the rules and regulations, but what are you going to do? You going to shoot them down? Kill them if they cross over? You can't. They're human beings. So, it's a two-way thing. I can't say that I'm for it or against it . . . That 187 did a lot, but yet it didn't solve anything. We, everybody, voted for it. It passed, but it didn't help anything. It didn't solve any problems. It's just that I feel sorry for everybody. I feel sorry because I know what it was like in the Depression when we were young. Well, it's still like that in these countries.

Unsure about the best course of action when it comes to immigration, Joe voted for Proposition 187, though he believes that the proposition itself did not solve anything. Poverty, inequality, and immigration persist. Joe's comment "It's just that I feel sorry for everybody" captures the competing and complex sentiments that some have. Such respondents seem to be "torn," demonstrating an understanding and connection with immigrants while at the same time believing that immigrants must "follow the rules." Overall, as described in more detail in the following chapter, Mexican Americans' experiences, generation, and racial/ethnic and class positions may enable them to understand not only some of the factors and processes that may lead individuals and families to leave Mexico but also the opinions and concerns of immigration opponents.

Scholars attempting to understand the multiple and seemingly contradictory attitudes shared by some Mexican Americans have also described these competing perspectives (Gutiérrez 1995; Miller, Polinard, and Wrinkle 1984; J. Garcia 1981). For example, Miller, Polinard, and Wrinkle (1984) describe Mexican Americans' attitudes toward undocumented workers as "a certain play of tension between the positive feelings of ethnic and cultural kinship and ethnic identity and the negative feelings of direct and indirect economic fears" (483). Gutiérrez (1995) finds that some Mexican Americans recognize the historical, cultural, and kinship ties that bind Mexican Americans and immigrants but still believe that unrestricted immigration has reduced their life chances by increasing economic competition and contributing to the reinforcement of unfavorable racial and cultural stereotypes about the Mexican-origin population (1995, 4–5). While most La Puente respondents do not describe fears of economic competition with immigrants, some nevertheless exemplify this tension between a similar history and background coupled with their support for cultural assimilation and their concern that the presence of immigrants may fuel stereotyped perceptions of all Mexicans.

Conclusion

An analysis of the factors and situations that may foster intra-ethnic conflict sheds light on the complexity of Mexican American–Mexican immigrant relations. We find that the hierarchical structure of institutions limit and constrain exchanges with immigrants to the extent that Mexican Americans who express the most resentment also tend to describe the least personal or informal interaction. This pattern illustrates the significance of the unequal distribution of power (as demonstrated by one's location within institutions such as schools) on race/ethnic relations. It also confirms the scholarship on contact hypothesis that contends that the more frequent the interaction, the less likely the conflict (Hood and Morris 1997). Despite their limited contact or perhaps because of it, respondents have much to say about immigrants and language usage, a great deal of it paralleling the pervasive discourse on race/ethnic relations—the assimilationist perspective.

As reflected in many of the respondents' narratives, the educational institution is one of the primary sites where we can discern the salience of assimilationist ideologies and institutional practices on intra-ethnic relations. Respondents remember attending schools that taught the dominant values and where speaking English and "becoming American" were emphasized through segregation, the implementation of no-Spanish rules, or by punishment. As products of such an educational system that elevated the English language over the Spanish language and often ignored the Mexican origins and presence in the Southwest, some have accepted prevailing expectations such that they now endorse immigrant acculturation.

Looking specifically at the individuals whose attitudes tend to fall along the conflict-end of the continuum, age, racial/ethnic identity, and gender are all salient. While there is variation, as quantitative scholars have documented, older individuals tend to express the most resentment toward Mexican immigrants (Hoskin and Mishler 1983; Binder, Polinard, and Wrinkle 1997) and toward the public use of the Spanish language (see Schmid 1992).[14] This seems to be especially apparent for respondents born and raised in the United States between the 1930s and 1950s. It is perhaps their experiences of Americanization programs, the overall pressure to assimilate, and their longtime involvement in La Puente that account for their strong support for immigrant acculturation. Likewise, when placed in the era during which they were raised, older respondents who support the ideology of assimilation may implicitly be challenging biological-determinist beliefs that assumed that non-Anglos were inherently inferior. Such beliefs still prevailed in the 1920s and 1930s (see Omi and Winant 1994).

Remembering their experiences, some older respondents characterize their efforts to learn English and to acquiesce to other dominant expectations as individual and familial endeavors. Explaining how they have "played by the rules" by acculturating and working to strengthen community arenas, they are resentful for both the level of institutional support that they presume immigrants are receiving and for the growing use of Spanish. This has led to anger or frustration on the part of a few who believe that immigrants are being catered to, that they are imposing the Spanish language on Mexican Americans, and that they expect Mexican Americans to speak Spanish.

Some Mexican Americans believe that what they have worked hard at establishing for themselves and for their families could be jeopardized by recent immigrants. Realizing that members of the dominant society may not differentiate among the heterogeneous Mexican-origin community, some individuals express concern that no matter how much they have acculturated they are perceived as immigrants. For respondents who may not approve of the activities of immigrants, others' homogenizing perceptions of the Mexican-origin community may be especially disconcerting, leading them to distance themselves spatially, socially, and culturally from immigrants.

Suggesting the salience of gender on intra-ethnic relations, only a few respondents and a smaller percentage of women than men cited economic competition as a source of conflict. Likewise, the workplace was not a location on which respondents focused when reflecting on their interactions with immigrants. This is contrary to previous studies that have found economic competition to be a cause of tension between Mexican Americans and Mexican immigrants (see Miller, Polinard, and Wrinkle 1984; Gutiérrez 1995; Rodriguez and Nuñez 1986). Rather than focusing on the labor market, interactions in multiple public sites and in traditional women's spheres are brought to the forefront as respondents center their discussions on their exchanges in schools, in churches, in supermarkets, and in the neighborhood. As others describe it, women, whose prescribed gender-role responsibilities often bring them into these community arenas, are more likely to engage in neighborhood activities that result in closer contact with immigrants (Lamphere 1992; Goode and Schneider 1994). Such gender divisions of labor and the greater percentage of women included in this current work might account for the tendency for respondents to discuss interactions within community sites. In addition, this chapter suggests that Mexican American–Mexican immigrant occupational differentiation may explain the general silence among most respondents on the relationships of immigration, the economy, and labor-market competition. This occupational differentiation may be further highlighted because nearly all of the respondents have completed high school, providing them with greater access to jobs that require this level of education.

Overall, understanding the conflictual attitudes of some respondents involves considering their location and experiences in the United States' racial/ethnic hierarchy as a racialized group oftentimes in intermediary and conflicting positions. Having been raised in the United States, Mexican Americans have been subjected to the prevailing ideologies and practices of Americanization and assimilation. Regardless of the extent to which they may have acculturated, however, Mexican Americans may not be distinguished from immigrants and may not be accepted by the dominant society. Because of the narrow constructions of a cultural, national, and racial identity as defined as Anglo and White, Mexican Americans may be seen as "foreigners" and "not Americans." Those individuals who have assimilated to the Anglo norms, practices, and values may believe that in public arenas immigrants should also speak English or learn "American customs." Despite the fact that assimilation has been the dominant ideology, some respondents find that immigrants expect them to speak Spanish. Therefore, the seemingly competing expectations of either acculturating or speaking Spanish may explain some resentment.

As the demographic composition of La Puente and communities throughout California continue to change, respondents are attempting to reconcile their experiences of and support for acculturation with the increasing public presence of the Spanish language. Within this process, they have little control over the institutions of power and the dominant ideologies that may be shaped and influenced by individuals and organizations outside of the city.

While much of this chapter focuses on Mexican American's attitudes and interactions that fall more along the conflict end of the continuum, we also get a glimpse of the simultaneous, multiple, and situational attitudes that some respondents hold. The following chapter provides additional insight into these varied attitudes by considering the factors and situations that may foster Mexican American–Mexican immigrant solidarity.

Chapter 6

"We Can't Forget Our Roots": Building Solidarity

Sitting behind her desk, forty-six-year-old Denise Villarreal unwraps her sandwich and motions to me to begin the interview. She is a gregarious woman, and her jovial demeanor creates an inviting atmosphere. Between phone calls, knocks on her office door, and her lunch, she reclines in her chair and talks about her life and her experiences as a La Puente resident and a local school principal.

Denise is the granddaughter of Mexican immigrants. She was raised twenty minutes from La Puente in an area where even today her family members "are still the only Mexicans on the block." As a result of this experience, she remembers, "We were real Mexican at home, but not when I walked out that door." Growing up, Denise didn't want to speak Spanish; she didn't want anybody to know that she was Mexican.

Denise's perspectives on the Spanish language and her racial/ethnic identity have changed. She now describes being fluent in Spanish, appreciating music in Spanish, and identifying as both Latina and Chicana. She attributes this transformation to the Chicano movement and to her college experiences in the early 1970s as a double major in Chicano studies and Spanish. Upon learning about the history and experiences of Mexican Americans, Denise explains that she started to "embrace my background more."

In the 1980s she moved to La Puente, and after several years Denise began familiarizing herself with the schools in the Hacienda–La Puente United School District (HLPUSD). She met educators in the district and attended a bilingual advisory committee meeting. Such experiences began to suggest to her what she describes as the "mistreatment" of La Puente community members by school officials. She remembers the dynamics at one district bilingual advisory committee meeting that fueled this perception:

It was a school district employee who was yelling at parents at this meeting . . . I said, "Man, those people need help, those poor parents. All they're doing is asking for what the children are really entitled to by law, by federal law."

Hoping to get involved with the parents and the bilingual advisory committee, she remembers approaching a school principal to inquire about volunteering in the school. Denise recalls how her assistance was refused:

She says, "Why?" I said, "Because I'm going to have children who are going to end up going to your school. I'd like to get involved and help out." I said, "I can sell tacos at a fund-raiser or something." She said, "If you don't have children, you can't participate." I said, "Excuse me. I'm a taxpayer in this community. I live in your attendance area. If I want to run for your PTA, I'm entitled to it." Well, she basically told me off.

While working as a bilingual teacher in a neighboring city, Denise applied for and was hired as a La Puente school principal in the HLPUSD. In this new capacity, she has improved her Spanish-language vocabulary to better communicate with immigrant children and parents. She supports bilingual education, encourages parent participation, has sought to hire teachers who are community-centered, and has attempted to create a school climate that is inclusive of English and Spanish speakers.

Denise has maintained such philosophies and practices even when she has been accused by some school officials and parents of being "too compromising" or "too immigrant-identified." She explains:

I have one parent in this community here who says that she's a third- or fourth-generation Californian, and she's "an American" and that "this school is going to the wetbacks" and that I'm the head wetback. She yells at me on the phone and cusses me out all of the time. She does not want me to ever put her child in a bilingual classroom. She has a Hispanic surname. All of her children's names can be translated into Spanish, and God bless them—they have skin color pretty much the same as mine.

Denise Villarreal's narrative is an example of how some Mexican Americans are aligning with immigrants and engaging in community-building activities. Despite the institutional and ideological structuring of conflict described in the previous chapter, there are multiple examples of how Mexican Americans are working to create inclusive spaces for the growing immigrant community and are trying to build bridges between Mexican Americans and

Mexican immigrants. Among the La Puente respondents, such demonstrations of unity are evident individually when Mexican Americans express an alliance with immigrants and at a group level when Mexican American and Mexican immigrant parents mobilize in support of bilingual education.

While parent organizing is centered in the next chapter, this chapter focuses on respondents' individual forms of solidarity by considering (1) the factors and processes fostering solidarity and (2) community-building activities. This chapter suggests that for those respondents whose attitudes span the conflict-solidarity continuum, it is in the context of anti-Mexican and anti-immigrant sentiment that they most highlight the connections that they may share with immigrants. In comparison, individuals such as Denise Villarreal who possess a power-conflict perspective of race/ethnic relations are the most likely but not the only ones to express beliefs that fall along the solidarity end of the continuum. They typically draw parallels between the macrostructural factors that influence the lives of immigrants and their own lives. Similar to Denise Villarreal, who majored in Chicano studies, several respondents describe access to an education that offered a critical analysis of power and inequality as an important element in fostering both a power-conflict perspective and a sense of connectedness with Mexican immigrants.

Following a discussion of those factors that foster solidarity, this chapter then focuses on how respondents align with immigrants and engage in community-building activities. Of particular importance in this chapter are schools as sites of intra-ethnic relations and the influence of school policies and school officials on intra-ethnic attitudes and interactions. Overall, the findings suggest how restructuring institutions and adopting more inclusive ideologies may enhance race/ethnic relations.

Factors and Processes Fostering Solidarity

While the institutional practices and prevailing ideologies described in the previous chapter may negatively influence race/ethnic relations, respondents' narratives suggest a number of explanations for why some Mexican Americans may be challenging such practices and beliefs as they connect with immigrants and build bridges. These explanations include an awareness of similar cultural, familial, historical, and class connections and shared experiences of prejudice and discrimination.

As well as illustrating the factors influencing intra-ethnic relationships, respondents' narratives also demonstrate the processes fostering the adoption of a power-conflict worldview over an assimilationist perspective. This power-conflict worldview that considers the significance of external factors and ideological processes on the Mexican-origin community seems to enhance the potential for Mexican American–Mexican immigrant solidarity.

"We're all one": Making Connections

As has been the case historically (see overview in Chapter 2) and revealed in their descriptions of race/ethnic identities (discussed in Chapter 4), for some Mexican Americans a shared identification with Mexican immigrants emerges from an awareness of cultural similarities, a common history of conquest and colonization, familial experiences of migration, and poor or working-class backgrounds. The comments by third-generation Mexican American Leticia Mendoza are illustrative of a few respondents' sentiment about the significance of cultural similarities on intra-ethnic identity: "I just feel they're my, our culture, our people. I feel that we are them. They are us. We're all one." This perspective is seconded by fifty-eight-year-old Marie Rogers, who believes that "all Mexican Americans were descendants from immigrants. We can't forget our roots. That's where our parents came from."

Some respondents identify the nineteenth-century U.S. military conquest of northern Mexico as a shared history. For example, as illustrated in Chapter 2, Denise Villarreal distinguishes between the unequal historical experiences of European immigrants and Mexicans, highlighting the fact that California was once part of Mexico: The United States has "always accepted people as long as we are European. My father will tell you that this is occupied Mexico." Sixty-year-old Ray Sanchez provides a similar interpretation of immigration and of the history of the Southwest:

> The Mexican people for a long time have been coming here. Since day one they have always had access to the United States that was part of the country. All of the Southwest was part of Mexico from day one; it wasn't their problem that certain events happened that things changed. A lot of them, of course, basically the Mexicans and the Spanish, were here when there was the landing on the east coast and had the missions, twenty-one missions up and down the California coast. So, it's been a tradition for these people to come up here. That's why when they come up here, they feel at home, because I'd say 90 percent of the names are Hispanic—La Puente, Ventura, San Francisco, Los Angeles, San Gabriel, San Diego. All over, the streets are all Spanish names. So to them, it's part of them.

Such historical differences between European immigrants and the Mexican-origin community have been recounted by numerous scholars employing a power-conflict framework (Mario Barrera 1979; Blauner 1972; Almaguer 1994). Blauner, for example, argues that the initial form of incorporation of the United States distinguishes the experiences of Mexican Americans and European immigrants. While Mexicans were conquered militarily and forcefully incorporated into the United States, Europeans immigrated individually and relatively voluntarily. Both Blauner's theory and the perspective offered by some respondents directly challenge traditional perspectives that equate the experiences of European immigrants with the racism directed against Mexicans and other groups of color.

By providing a historical overview of the United States' treatment of immigrants and the incorporation of northern Mexico into the southwestern United States, a number of respondents connect their family's migration and current immigration with the historical and contemporary relationships between the United States and Mexico. Illustrating both the differential treatment between Europeans and Mexicans and this unequal relationship between the United States and Mexico, Denise Villarreal describes how her family, which migrated to the Los Angeles area in 1912, was part of the waves of mass deportations of Mexican immigrants and their Mexican American children. In particular, Denise's family was divided by the deportations of the 1930s:

> There was that time when my mother was repatriated to Mexico . . . That was that whole period of the thirties and everybody was unemployed, so my grandfather went back to Mexico. Pobrecito, he didn't read, and so they marked his passport "Deported." So my mother was never able to get him back into this country.

Margarita Villa's perspective on immigrants and immigration is similar. However, her view is influenced by more recent familial connections with Mexican nationals who have been denied entrance to the United States. Observing restrictionist U.S. policies, Margarita is a strong advocate for the elimination of borders:

> I'm one of those people that believes that we shouldn't have any borders . . . I think that people should be able to come and enter because my family is in Mexico. I can't see half of them because I have to visit them because I can go wherever I want. They can't come and visit me. We were trying to get a visa for my grandfather. Because he was retired, they would not let him come and visit over here because he didn't have the government papers saying that he had a job to come back to.

Providing a structural analysis of immigration, Gary Mesa builds on some of these ideas. In particular, he understands immigration as a process that has been instigated and controlled by the United States. In Gary's estimation, such influences include U.S. involvement in Mexico in the form of export processing zones and through the establishment of U.S. corporations:

> In some of the cases, American corporations have gone into these countries, raped these countries. We've given nothing back to them, taken what we've needed and what we wanted out of those places for ourselves. I think part of it is our government and our companies are why people are coming here.

Connected with an awareness of a shared history of incorporation, migration, and U.S. domination, some respondents say that because of their own poor or working-class origins, they can relate to Mexican immigrants' aspirations and struggles to improve their lives. Consequently, some identify with immigrants because of a belief that they share similar class origins or work experiences. For example, Joe Zavala, a third-generation Mexican American man, says he understands immigrants' motivations to improve their living conditions. He believes that his own experiences as a poor child born and raised in La Puente provide him with the insight to relate to Mexican immigrants' desires to migrate:

> The living conditions are awful. I don't want to stay in this little wooden box or cardboard house all my life and have no electricity, have no water, have nothing. You can't even take a bath. These are the old days when we were young. When we were young, we used to make a fire on Saturdays. Take one bath, once a week, and bring the water inside. We had no hot water. We had cold water, and that was it. We had no electricity. I remember that. We used to use those Coleman lanterns. This is the way they still live. I feel that they're in the same situation that we were in when we were young. You don't want to live that way all of your life. You want to better yourself. So, if you look at it that way, they have just as much right as anybody else because they're human beings.

Like Joe, Ray Sanchez also believes that he can empathize with some of the struggles Mexican immigrants confront because of his experiences working on a ranch:

> I used to work with the braceros picking lemons, and it's no picnic, but that's the way it was. I needed some extra money, but things haven't changed. There is no way that you are going to stop them from coming.

A number of race and ethnic relations researchers illustrate how such a shared history strengthens group identity (Saito and Horton 1994; Gutiérrez 1995). For example, focusing on Monterey Park, California, Saito and

Horton (1994) argue that a shared history of discrimination is one factor that can unite Asian Americans, whose shared history includes exclusionary immigration laws and anti-Asian activities (Saito and Horton 1994). Centering the experiences of the Mexican-origin community, Gutiérrez (1995) finds that though Mexican Americans' perceptions of immigrants vary, many recognize the historical ties that bind the Mexican-origin community.

"I think they'll always look down on us": Awareness of Prejudice and Discrimination

A sense of group identity within the Mexican-origin community may also emerge from individuals' experiences of prejudice and discrimination in their everyday encounters—sometimes with family members and friends as well as with strangers. For example, Rosario Jones is acutely aware of the unequal treatment that individuals of Mexican descent may encounter. It is this awareness and her experiences that lead her to see the commonalities that she shares with Mexican immigrants. Rosario recounted numerous occasions when she was forced to contend with people's negative perceptions of her as a Mexican American woman who lives in a working-class community. In fact, her husband's White family members have not always accepted her because of her racial/ethnic background:

> When he first brought me home, they looked at me like, "Okay, she's just his girlfriend. He's going to get rid of her one of these days." Then, we ended up getting married. They were not too happy, my mother-in-law, I think, more than my father-in-law because for years he had another girlfriend that she really, really liked. She was Anglo, and then he comes home with me. She just didn't care for me.

The anti-Mexican response Rosario received from her husband's uncle was even more blatant than from his parents:

> My husband's all, "Hi, Uncle Bob. This is my wife." He turns around and looked right at me, and then he looked a little further beyond and looked right at my husband, and he said, "Where? Don't tell me that is your wife?" He pointed right at me. He said, "Don't tell me that this is her?" I said, "Excuse me. I'm Rosario. I'm Brad's wife. I've spoken to you on the phone several times." He just nodded. I extended my hand, and he wouldn't shake my hand. He wouldn't touch my hand, and I said some nasty words to him. I turned around, I got in my car, and I left.

In addition to their experiences of prejudice from friends and relatives, several respondents describe the low opinions that some Whites maintain of any member of the Mexican-origin community who speaks Spanish. Jane Hanson, a third-generation Mexican American and an instructional aide at a La Puente elementary school, elaborates:

> I think they'll always look down on us. There was this sign at one of the schools—"If you know two languages, you're counted as two people." It was in Spanish, so the Whites didn't know what was on the wall. That's the way I feel. We know two languages, we're counted as two people. We're not dumb. We're not dumb.

Jane reveals a shared experience and identity with Mexican Americans and Mexican immigrants through her use of "us" in reflecting on the bigotry some Whites display. She also connects the persisting negative assumptions with her experience of being regarded as "dumb" by some people outside the Mexican-origin community. She has encountered such sentiment both as an adult and as a child who was "belittled all of the time" and who was "kept way down" by racist teachers. As Jane describes the sign in the school's office, she affirms the significance of being bilingual. She further hints at the irony behind such negative stereotypes about the Mexican-origin community when she explains that many Whites may not understand the sign because they cannot read Spanish.

Jane's opinions and experiences are shared by twenty-nine-year-old Shirley Garcia. Shirley, however, focuses on some Whites' apparent perceptions of those who speak English with a Spanish-language accent: "If they know that you're more Americanized, they're like, 'Oh, you blend in.' If you have a little accent, they right away think that you don't know anything. They think that you're dumb or that you don't know what's going on."

Another example of prejudice that may also explain why many respondents demonstrate unity with immigrants is the stereotyped perception that all Mexicans are immigrants. In fact, several respondents describe the processes that led to their realization that some Whites may not distinguish between Mexican Americans and immigrants. Thirty-two-year-old Gary Mesa explains:

> People see these brown faces . . . I think if it's a white-faced person, they're not going to assume, "Oh, you're an illegal immigrant." They're not going to look at a White person and say that or an African American. They see a brown face, people think, "Is this person illegal?"

Expanding on what this means for people like his mother, Gary continues:

> She's darker than I am, and I don't see other individuals, especially Anglos, differentiating her brown skin from someone who might come

here illegally . . . It scares me to think if they're trying to persecute recent immigrants or illegal immigrants, where will it stop? I don't necessarily think that they differentiate this person.

In describing her spouse's attitudes toward immigrants, Rosario Jones expresses the reality that, to some, including to her husband, she may be seen as an immigrant:

I think too many Anglos, once they've heard things about Mexicans, they think that we're all the same. My husband does the same thing. When he's driving home from work, "God darn it. All I see are those darn Mexicans up and down the street, selling oranges, selling bananas, selling this. Why don't they go back to where they come from?" He's like that in general. A lot of Anglos don't accept Mexicans whether they're immigrants, or maybe they can't differentiate. If this White person came in right now, for all they know, I could have just gotten off the boat.

As Rosario describes the perceptions "too many Anglos" have of Mexicans, the intonation in her voice changes. Initially Rosario's tone appears direct, almost matter of fact, as though she is sharing something that she has heard her husband say often or that she has recited to others. However, as she says "or maybe they can't differentiate," it is as though she is exposing her awareness that it is not just some Whites who maintain negative feelings toward Mexicans and possibly toward her—but even her own husband among them.

Similarly, Shirley Garcia describes her recognition that despite the fact that her spouse was born in the United States, he might be seen as an immigrant:

We're driving along, and someone will cut us off . . . He does his little cursing thing, you know, and that other person . . . if it's a White person, they've even called him a wetback. My husband, because of the way he looks. He looks Mexican. They'll call him a wetback in the process of their arguing. I don't think of him that way. I think of him as an American . . . Why'd they call him a wetback? Why? He's from here. Just because of his looks.

Labeling all people who appear to be Mexican into the category of "immigrant" or "wetback" perpetuates the belief that Mexicans are "foreigners" and not "Americans." Just as such labeling dehumanizes and criminalizes Mexicans (by assuming that all crossed the border without documents), it also ignores the historical and macroscopic factors that shape immigration—including the role of the U.S. government and corporations.

The stereotypical categorization described by Shirley Garcia is also recounted by thirty-six-year-old Deana Martinez, who finds that regardless of generation, people assume that she and her children are immigrants. She details how school officials believed that her fifth-generation daughter was Spanish-speaking because of her last name:

> I went into the principal's office, and I asked that my daughter be transferred out of the bilingual class and into a straight English class. The principal says to me, "It's better for her because she's being explained the lesson twice, and that's wonderful for her. So, that way she'll get it. It will assist her in understanding the information." I said, "It would, if she spoke Spanish."

While Deana supports bilingual education, she criticizes the school principal for believing that he knew what was best for her daughter, for not looking at her daughter's file, and for assuming that she is Spanish-speaking because of her race/ethnicity. Deana attributes the demeaning encounters she and her children have had with school personnel to paternalistic attitudes and stereotypical views that many of the district's principals, teachers, and school board members hold with regard toward the parents and the students of La Puente.

For several individuals, the awareness of others' racial/ethnic lumping of all Mexicans (and possibly all Latinas/os) as immigrants was heightened in the context of the 1994 California State Proposition 187. The public and statewide displays of anti-immigrant and anti-Mexican sentiment as well as the resistance movements that Proposition 187 engendered led some respondents to reevaluate their own views on immigration and their connections with Mexican immigrants. Much of this reevaluation stemmed from an enhanced awareness of how the passage of such a proposition could infringe on the civil rights of not only undocumented immigrants but also on the rights of Mexican Americans.

Thirty-six-year-old Rita Lopez Tellez explains how the process of racial/ethnic lumping in the context of Proposition 187 led her to reevaluate her own views on Mexican immigrants:

> I went through a period where I really internalized a lot of the stereotypes that people have about immigrants . . . And it was because of this whole immigrant-bashing that started and just hearing about immigrants and how they come here, and they all pee on the streets, they're all dirty . . . I started to feel like I was being identified with that group, and so I really wanted to push away from them. I hated them. I really did. I hated that people were going to think I'm an immigrant.

As Proposition 187 emerged, Rita started to understand that what she was feeling was a "kind of internalized racism and self-hatred." She began to reflect on her own status as part of the group that the proposition targeted—and on the fact that her own parents were immigrants. This growing awareness resulted in her shift in identity: "[Immigration] is part of my identity. It might not be an immediate part, but that's where I came from. I can't cut that out." She was also motivated to get politically involved in the movement to fight the proposition:

[Proposition 187] really made it very personal, and it was like, "If I don't get involved now, when will I get involved? And how can I expect other people to get involved if I'm not?" So, it really galvanized a lot of things for me, and I think it's probably right at that time that I really started to call myself a Chicana and to care much more about the community.

Confirming the significant impact that Proposition 187 had on the Mexican-origin community, twenty-seven-year-old David Galvez observed some Mexicans who began to publicly challenge assimilationist imperatives and to unite across generations:

D.G.: I sensed that after [Proposition 187], people took more pride in being Mexican. That's when the popularity of quebradita, and you saw teenagers wearing cowboy hats and cowboy boots. You never saw that in the eighties . . . Now, today you see Mexican Pride stickers everywhere.

G.L.O.: Why do you think Prop. 187 had such an effect?

D.G.: It unified a lot of Mexicans, whether you were an immigrant or you were children of immigrants. I think that it brought a lot of people together. It motivated people. It stirred up some feelings in people. Although a lot of Mexican Americans supported it, I think that in large part it just brought out a lot of pride, a lot of resentment that they would go ahead and pass such a law. You saw high school students protesting. [During the big anti-187 demonstration in] downtown L.A., I was there, and there were so many people, something that just really made people feel good.

The demonstration and the pride David describes manifested across the state. Students throughout California—more than 10,000 in Los Angeles alone—walked out of schools in opposition to Proposition 187 (Acuña 1996, 159). La Puente students and parents also expressed their outrage against this proposition. During a 1996 interview with me, a high school principal in La Puente at the time of the proposition recalls the activism:

It was an issue that kids were very concerned about. In any high school, I think some of the kids are very politically active and politically aware . . . There were kids who were actually going into Los Angeles and picketing and protesting and marching on the weekend and who actually knew the issue. So, during those couple of days when students were walking out, kids were walking out at schools throughout the district.

As well as politicizing some of the students, the impending vote on the proposition prompted La Puente residents to organize a march to protest and to demand that city officials make a public statement against Proposition 187. Such protests against Proposition 187 occurred throughout the state; the largest, organized by a La Puente resident, drew 100,000 demonstrators in Los Angeles two weeks before the elections of December 8, 1994 (Acuña 1996, 158). Scholars have found that the proposition and the campaign against it served as a catalyst to unite large numbers of Mexican Americans and Mexican immigrants who realized that the Mexican-origin community as a whole would suffer from implementation of the policies and practices it set forth (Valle and Torres 2000).

Since the anti-immigrant fervor surrounding Proposition 187 targeted Latina/o immigrants and relied upon race/ethnicity, such nativism highlighted the similar racial/ethnic barriers Latinas/os may encounter regardless of class position or generation. California Governor Pete Wilson, who endorsed Proposition 187, became the Latina/o community's "number one enemy" and as such has been credited with mobilizing Latina/o voters (Valle and Torres 2000, 183). Roberto Delgado, a La Puente resident who immigrated to the United States as a teenager, explains:

> R.D.: The Mexican-origin community has come together more, and I have worked with people I've never did before, especially at La Puente High School, and they are Mexican Americans . . . I think it's a new generation that is coming, and they are getting to know and accept each other better.
>
> G.L.O.: Why do you think this is?
>
> R.D.: Because there is more awareness, more Hispanic awareness, and the way that the government and especially Pete Wilson targeted the Mexicans. He singled out one particular group, our group . . . Proposition 187 really shook everyone up, saying, "Hey, get yourself together. Get your citizenship and vote." I think thousands of people have become citizens since 187. I think Pete Wilson, more than doing harm, did good for us because a lot of people woke up. They are denigrating our people, and here we are sitting on our butts.

These examples of racial/ethnic lumping and the concerns about Proposition 187's potential effects on Mexican Americans along with Mexican immigrants highlight that Latinas/os across generations may face similar barriers. This treatment and categorization of the heterogeneous Mexican-origin community in a homogeneous way is an example of how external factors can lead to group identity and cooperation. Scholars of race and ethnic relations document similar patterns. For example, Gutiérrez (1995) finds that some Mexican Americans see themselves reflected in recent immigrants because some U.S. residents discriminate against Mexicans regardless of generation or citizenship status (5). Likewise, Saito and Horton (1994) find that the treatment of all Asians as immigrants rather than as Americans has resulted in a shared barrier for Asian Americans to challenge. Studying panethnicity, Lopez and Espiritu (1990) argue that racial/ethnic lumping in outsiders' perceptions that "they all look alike" has often been an effective force for unity because prejudice and discrimination affect all members of a particular group and require organization at a panethnic level.

"Everybody still thinks La Puente's a gang-infested, run-down city": Geographical Inequality

Geographical concentration may also lead to a sense of solidarity, especially when groups share material status and interests (Lopez and Espiritu 1990). Living in a largely working-class Mexican-origin community, many La Puente residents are aware of outsiders' disparaging views of their city. In the words of forty-two-year-old Alberto Perez, "Everybody still thinks La Puente's a gang-infested, run-down city. It's not. It's a good working-class community." Such misperceptions of the city and its residents are oftentimes based on stereotypes rooted in race/ethnicity and class position. Rosario Jones illustrates the way some outsiders regard the city as she recounts the time some members of the La Puente parish went to the funeral of the pastor's mother; there she discovered the attitudes of her pastor:

> It was in Newport Beach. It was all ritzy titzy. All of his family was there, and they're doctors and lawyers and everything fancy. They had this big fancy reception at the country club. When Father was standing behind a tree, this woman with blonde hair and big gold earrings said, "Where are you now?" He said, "Well, you might not know where it's at. It's in La Puente." She said, "La Puente? Oh my God, over there?" He said, "You know, I have to deal with a lot of Mexicans." He was whispering that name, so after that I said, "I don't like you."

Rosario encounters similar sentiment from her husband, whom she has "to force" to stay in La Puente because "he thinks it's a bad thing for my son to be around." Despite such degraded perceptions of La Puente and of Mexicans, however, Rosario is determined to remain in the city where she and her father were raised.

Residents in the same community observe the unequal facilities and resources that affect almost everyone in La Puente, regardless of generation and immigration status. While a few respondents mention inequalities within the church and within the city in general, most focus on the unequal school resources, unfair school policies, and biased teacher expectations. Focusing on the education that La Puente–area students receive, former elementary instructional aide Delia Centeno complains, "You see what one district has compared to another, and you see the discrepancies there. Say the other school district will have the latest in computers. It's a handicap." She continues:

> I worked as an instructional aide for seventeen years in the school system, and I saw, compared to other districts, how little our kids had or how ill-prepared some of them are to compete with others in other school systems.

Such dynamics have an impact on La Puente students, Delia laments:

> I have seen not only my kids struggle through [the school system], I have seen my neighbors' kids that were college-bound really have to struggle to make it. They're not the only kids.

These observations have led Delia to speculate that such "discrepancies" among school districts have been designed "to cause Mexicans to fail."

La Puente residents also detect discrepancies among schools within the district. The Hacienda–La Puente Unified School District serves the majority of La Puente residents as well as residents of largely middle-class Hacienda Heights, an unincorporated area of Los Angeles County. Many describe differences in the educational facilities of the schools in these two communities. Fifty-year-old Susan Hernandez-Riley recounts what she has discovered in her own comparison of schools:

> There are chairs over here that are full of splinters, and the floors are missing tiles, and the tiles on the roof are falling down, and the books are full of graffiti and very, very, old. I went over there, and everything was new and spotless. They had carpet, air-conditioning. It was different.

Lourdes Fernandez, a school principal in La Puente, confirms Susan's observations by describing the condition of the school where she is employed:

> We had a bungalow here, a leaning bungalow. First of all, they should've just replaced it. Well, they just cleaned it up. The wood was rotten and the smell was bad. Sometimes I think, gee, I wonder if we were in Hacienda Heights, would they have replaced these portables already? They probably would have. So we had a leaning portable, and we had a smell to it like something dead was under there. When they lifted the portable, of course all the bugs came out, and the teachers were getting bitten.

While such perceptions of the facilities and supplies in La Puente and Hacienda Heights schools are considered in more detail in the following chapter, they shed light on how an awareness of shared material status and interests as a result of living in the same community may translate into a collective identity.

Within La Puente schools, residents also critique the poor treatment of children and parents by school officials. Former La Puente instructional aide Delia Centeno remembers some teachers' racial/ethnic and class stereotypes of La Puente students:

> I know that they are overworked, but there was a lot of "I don't care" type of attitude on the part of teachers. Some are good, but you've got a lot of them that think, "They are not going to do anything with their life anyway, so what's the point?"

Comparing her children's current educational experiences in La Puente with their previous schooling in a neighboring middle-class school district, Deana Martinez has this to say about La Puente–area schools and the treatment of their students:

> The schools here are terrible. It's the worst school district my kids have ever been in . . . Children are being suspended for outrageous things to where they're becoming desensitized. My child because they were starting to suspend him so many times, and he was only in the first and second grade, he became desensitized to the whole issue. So I started doing some investigation of my own in regards to the manner in which they treat the children. What I've found is that they're being screamed at, they're not treated with respect, and the parents are always blamed for anything that happens.

Deana says everyone of Mexican origin in La Puente may be subjected to such mistreatment. As she states in Chapter 4, it is precisely these experiences and this realization that have led her feel more "Mexican" than "American."

As will be illustrated in further detail in the following chapter, experiences of inequality at both the individual and institutional levels may explain why many Mexican Americans align themselves with Mexican immigrants. This explanation is consistent with research on race/ethnic relations that demonstrates how external forces such as exclusion and mistreatment may strengthen group identity (Padilla 1985; Portes and Rumbaut 1990; Espiritu 1992; Zavella 1994). For example, researching Latinas/os in Chicago, Padilla (1985) finds that the disadvantaged political and economic status imposed on Puerto Ricans and Mexican Americans can lead to a panethnic Latina/o identity. Focusing on Chicanas, Zavella (1994) also argues that structural conditions, though they are experienced differently depending on one's social location, often lead to a shared identity because certain social forces often have similar impacts on Chicanas' lives.

Acquiring an Empowering Education and a Power-Conflict Perspective

As Denise Villarreal's narrative at the beginning of this chapter suggests, access to what Shor (1992) has referred to as an "empowering education" or a "critical-democratic pedagogy for self and social change" (15) may facilitate the process of making cross-generational links. Approaches to empowering or liberatory education include critical analyses and reformulations of power, domination, and knowledge as well as opportunities to devise strategies and to engage in activities that may foster change (Freire 1970; Shor 1992; Solorzano 1997; Ochoa and Ochoa forthcoming). Such forms of education challenge Eurocentric curricula and the traditional "banking method of education" in which the teacher is the conveyor of knowledge and students passively receive information (Freire 1970). An empowering education is based on an interactive and cooperative environment that relies on multicultural approaches and curricula that emphasize the connections between personal lives and public issues (Freire 1970; Shor 1992; hooks 1994). With their origins in student, community, and faculty struggles of the 1960s and 1970s, courses in women's studies and ethnic studies are often examples of such liberatory education. Premised on the underlying tenets of *El Plan de Santa Barbara,* a document that emerged from a 1969 conference at the University of California, Santa Barbara, that outlined the objectives of Chicano studies (Muñoz 1989), many Chicana/o studies classes offer anti-assimilationist critiques of society and emphasize political activism and social change.

Some La Puente residents explicitly ground their understandings of race/

ethnic relations and immigration in their participation in courses that encouraged critical thinking, offered an analysis of power and inequality, exposed them to macrostructural approaches to understanding society, and provided material on the history and contemporary experiences of Mexicans in the United States. As was described in Chapter 4, it is this knowledge and understanding that have been helpful in developing among Chicana/o-identified respondents a power-conflict approach to understanding the structural factors and ideological processes that constrain the lives of Mexican Americans and Mexican immigrants. Such individuals have gone through a process of affirmation, reclamation, and connection with the Mexican-origin community. It is as a result of this emerging power-conflict perspective that a few respondents have experienced what twenty-three-year-old Geraldo Romero describes as "a rebirth" or "an epiphany." Geraldo attributes much of this "rebirth" to college classes on politics and inequality and to reading Paulo Freire's widely acclaimed *Pedagogy of the Oppressed*, a book Geraldo characterizes as "revolutionary." In this 1970 book, Freire interrogates systems of domination and articulates a pedagogy of liberation in which the teaching and learning process involves reflection and action for social transformation.

We heard briefly from Denise Villarreal how her enrollment in Chicana/o studies courses influenced the transformation of her identity and perspectives, and twenty-seven-year-old David Galvez describes a similar process. As he recounts, while growing up in La Puente he ridiculed immigrants and was embarrassed by his working-class Mexican-origin community:

> I'm ashamed, but I remember using the term "wetback" back then, referring to recent immigrants who stood out because of the clothing that they wore, the way they cut their hair. All they spoke was Spanish.

> Growing up, I don't think I was very proud of living in La Puente. I remember when people would ask me where I was from, a lot of times I would say West Covina [a more middle-class and racially/ethnically diverse city]. When I left and went to college, that is where for some reason I became proud of being from La Puente. I think that a lot of it goes hand in hand with the fact that I was no longer ashamed of being from a minority community or working-class area. After my experiences in college, it became something that I could be proud of. There was nothing wrong with being working-class or being part of a community such as La Puente.

As David states in Chapter 4, his interactions with high school teachers who had stereotyped perceptions of the Mexican-origin community, his political activism in college, and his college courses (in political science and Chicano studies) helped him to rethink the assimilationist perspectives that he had previously accepted. He explains, "[High school was] where I began to notice a lot of the ideologies of our teachers and how they were really in conflict with what our community stood for and was all about."

Engagement in college courses that encouraged critical thinking and that provided a larger framework from which to analyze his observations led David to reassess his original attitudes and to become a self-described "advocate" for immigrants. He is now "proud" of his La Puente origins. Illustrating how his views have changed, David decided to teach in La Puente with the intent of counteracting the attitudes and practices of some of the prejudiced teachers he encountered as a student:

> I just look back at my experiences with a lot of my teachers, and I realize that a lot of those experiences were negative. I was a pretty strong student. You could tell me that I wasn't going to succeed, and I was going to use that as motivation. But I realize that a lot of students aren't that way. When they're told that, they sometimes believe it. So I just knew there were a lot of teachers like that here, and I wondered how many students they had held back by their comments or sometimes not even their comments, but their way of teaching . . . I just realized, "You know what, I want to go back and hopefully try to counterbalance what's going on with a lot of those teachers."

While being interviewed for a teaching position, David came into contact with one of these prejudiced individuals who hoped to prevent the inclusion of Chicana/o studies in the courses David would be teaching:

> The guy that hired me, the department chair, who was one of my teachers who told me that I wouldn't make it at UCLA, he actually wanted to hire me. One of the comments he told me when he told me he would hire me was, "Well, just don't bring that Chicano crap here."

Thinking about his new position, David laughs: "He doesn't know what he's going to get next year."

Respondents such as David Galvez are making historical, structural, and cultural connections with their immigrant neighbors. As described in more detail in the following section, within institutions such as schools, these individuals may be strategically positioned to challenge assimilating forces and exclusionary practices by using counter-hegemonic discourse and activities to create a politicized and united Mexican-origin, Latina/o, and working-class community. However, they are not alone in this community-building process. Other respondents are also making connections with immigrants and engaging in everyday activities that are facilitating intra-ethnic relations.

Building Community

When asked to describe her neighbors, fifty-five-year-old Ilene Gómez beams. She begins, "They're wonderful, but they've changed." In 1973 her family was just the second Latino family to move into her neighborhood. Now everyone on her street is Latina/o. Thinking about the observations she had made while watering her front lawn the night before our meeting, she continues:

> The couple across the street was having a birthday party . . . I was watering and people were parking their cars. "Hi, señora Gómez, como está?" I'd take off my glasses and think, "Oh, it's somebody else that belongs to the PTA at Sparks Middle and Sparks Elementary." Then, I'd reply, "Oh, como está, señora? Muy bien."

Ilene Gomez's rendition of her community captures what for her is so "comfortable"—the Latina/o presence, her familiarity and the history that she has developed with her neighbors.

While we learned in the previous chapter that some Mexican Americans are conflicted over the increase of Mexican immigrants in La Puente, as with Ilene Gómez, a substantial number are embracing and adapting to the changes that have accompanied these demographic shifts, including the growing public presence of the Spanish language and Spanish-language music. These cooperative adjustments are transpiring despite a societal emphasis on linguistic assimilation and recurring patterns of Spanish-language repression.

Just as Mexican immigration may be influencing the beliefs and practices of Mexican Americans, the everyday activities of many respondents may be facilitating the integration of Mexican immigrants into La Puente and improving intra-ethnic relations. As scholars have documented, many Mexican immigrants face hardships and difficulties in their transition to the United States (Melville 1978; Ainslie 1998). As immigrants adjust to a new environment and language, they may experience stress, loneliness, or mourning caused by separation from family and support networks, familiar neighbors, home, and well-known cultural surroundings (ibid.). Therefore, settlement in a community with members from similar racial/ethnic backgrounds has the potential to reduce the stress and to ease immigrant adjustment (Massey et al. 1987; Portes and Rumbaut 1990; Pardo 1991). As the following examples illustrate, Mexican Americans can play critical roles as "buffers," "cultural brokers," or bridges between the dominant society and Mexican immigrants (Portes and Rumbaut 1990; M. D. Gonzales 1999; Ochoa 1999). They are doing so in their homes, neighborhoods, churches, and schools.

Building Community in Homes and Neighborhood Spaces

> That day that she was born, my husband said, "This baby's going to speak English." I said, "This baby's going to speak what I teach her because you're going to be at work, and I'm the mother, and she's learning what I want her to learn."
>
> JANE HANSON, fifty-five-year-old Mexican American

As described in previous chapters, Spanish-language repression and English-language preference have taken many forms, from de jure segregation and Americanization programs to the English-only amendments and movements against bilingual education in the 1980s and 1990s. While these movements have targeted the public use of languages other than English, as Jane Hanson's quote suggests, they have also manifested in homes and communities.

Just as Jane Hanson had to contend with Spanish-language repression and assimilationist ideologies as she taught her daughter Spanish, the impacts of similar pressures are evident in the lives of Mexican Americans who may not have been taught Spanish because their parents hoped that they could shield them from the language discrimination that they had experienced. This was the case for thirty-year-old Rosario Jones:

> G.L.O.: What language(s) was spoken in your household while you were growing up?
> ROSARIO: English, only English . . . My dad wanted us to be American. He said, "You're in America. You speak English, and that's what we're going to teach you." They wanted us to learn how to speak it well, and I think we did.
> G.L.O.: Why do you think he felt that way?
> ROSARIO: I think he saw his family how they struggled a lot, how they were segregated from other people because they spoke Spanish. So he didn't want us to have to go through that.

In spite of the emphasis and pressures to speak English, respondents such as Jane Hanson and Rosario Jones are learning, improving, or maintaining Spanish for themselves or for their children. Within their homes and in other neighborhood spaces, they are engaged in community-building activities by (re)claiming the Spanish language, appreciating the growth in Spanish-language music, countering anti-Mexican sentiment, and assisting their neighbors.

Many respondents are motivated to strengthen their Spanish-language skills because of the growing immigrant population and the public presence of Spanish in La Puente. Geraldo Romero's comments highlight how this motivation is often linked to a desire to communicate with community residents and with family members. He wants to learn Spanish for practical reasons:

I think I'd be a more functional person in this area. You walk into grocery stores, or just being a teacher, I want to be able to provide service to my students and to their families. The best way of doing this is by speaking to them in their native tongue, their language. Secondly, I'd be closer to my roots. There's awkwardness with my family when I go to Mexico to try to talk to them and [they] see me struggle with the language, and I don't want that.

Forty-year-old Mary Marquez also wishes that she could speak Spanish:

I wish I knew Spanish that well to be able to talk to people. Even at work, the majority of the plant employees speak Spanish, and so I feel frowned on because I don't say "Hello" to them.

In particular, Mary believes that because of the shifting demographics, speaking Spanish would increase her level of "comfort" in La Puente:

I notice that in this neighborhood, if you are Spanish-speaking, you would get along a lot better and just feel more comfortable. I feel uncomfortable because of that. The only reason I feel comfortable is because I've lived here all my life, and I feel like, "Hey, this is my place." If I just moved here and I spoke English, I'd probably feel a little bit more self-conscious or afraid of my neighbors.

A few people also link their desires to speak Spanish to remorse, embarrassment, or guilt for not being "fluent" in the language. For example, Rosario Jones feels "badly" that she cannot better assist Spanish-speaking clients at work. She also laments her inability to order food at Mexican restaurants in Spanish: "Even when I go to a Mexican restaurant, I feel so stupid that I have to sit there and say, 'I'll have an enchilada.'" Such experiences have led her to proclaim, "I really want to know how to speak Spanish. In my heart I know that I should know it, so my mom and dad see now that I want to learn. So they're working with me to help me." The discomfort that Rosario experiences in Mexican restaurants is similar to the sentiment that sixty-five-year-old Gloria Dominguez describes:

> I find myself apologizing to a lot of these Latin people that are not from here because they know that I don't speak as well as they do in Spanish. I feel embarrassed, though I took Spanish in school, but still not enough. I'm sorry that I didn't.

As respondents shared in previous chapters, part of this embarrassment is linked to others' expectations that all individuals of Mexican descent speak Spanish.

To improve their Spanish, some La Puente residents are taking Spanish classes, attending Spanish-language masses, and practicing Spanish with friends and relatives. Several took Spanish in high school or in college. Growing up in a Spanish-speaking household, Geraldo Romero understands Spanish but is accustomed to responding to his parents in English. To improve his Spanish-speaking skills, he sought out courses in college:

> I realized that I should learn more Spanish. I should learn more about my culture. That's what I was doing . . . My parents' dominant language is Spanish. My mom, she's really good at both languages, but while I was growing up, they would talk to me in Spanish, and I responded in English. Now I regret that. I should have answered in Spanish.

Also wanting to learn the language, forty-seven-year-old Roberta Zavala majored in Spanish and is now the principal at a La Puente school where a large number of parents and students speak Spanish. Her decision to study Spanish was based on her desire to understand her grandparents:

> Being born here, English was my first language. I had to learn Spanish. I didn't have to, but my grandparents on my mom's side when they would speak to me they always spoke in Spanish, and I would say, "What did they say?" So my grandfather, as I got older, says, "Mi'ja, you need to learn Spanish." So, with my grandfather in mind, I said, "Okay, I'll take Spanish. This ought to be a cinch." I did. I took it in high school and college, and I mastered Spanish.

As a school principal, Roberta petitioned for the school where she is employed to become an academy. Part of this move entailed altering the bilingual program at the school. This included teaching Spanish-speaking children language arts, reading, and math in English. Thus, despite the fact that Roberta's focus in college was Spanish, she favors an education program that emphasizes English-language immersion. With her attitudes, we observe the multiplicity of beliefs articulated by some. In this case, Roberta supports English-language acquisition within the schools, perhaps at the expense of not retaining or improving Spanish-language skills.[1]

Since it takes from five to seven years to acquire average levels of proficiency in a language and it is more difficult to learn a language after childhood (Cummins 1996), a couple of respondents explain how challenging it has been to learn Spanish as an adult. For example, thirty-two-year-old Gary Mesa, who has enrolled in Spanish-language classes, has not been able to acquire the language. He explains, "I've gotten lazy. I tried to make it a point that I wanted to eventually learn on my own, but I just never really did. I tried taking classes. I'd just get frustrated."

While a significant number of respondents lament their Spanish-language abilities, this is not the case for all. A few say they speak Spanish "fluently," and a couple resist narrow conceptions of what constitutes "fluent" Spanish. For example, given the experiences of Mexican Americans in the United States, the history of language repression, and illustrating how culture is dynamic, a few individuals dispute the idea that code-switching, the integration and alternation of Spanish and English within and between sentences, is incorrect and instead highlight that they speak two languages. Jane Hanson explains:

> The day that she was born, my husband said "You know what you people do? You rattle on, rattle on, and you're speaking Spanish, speaking English, and you mix it." I said, "You know what? Who cares?" I go, "We understand two languages, so what?" He said, "This baby's going to learn English completely." [I said,] "Shut up."

While Jane explicitly challenged her White husband's criticisms of her Spanish and English skills, a few other respondents explain how they disregard Mexican immigrants who may believe that Mexican Americans are "ruining the Spanish language." Anzaldúa (1987) finds that although what has been referred to as Chicano Spanish has often been thought of as "a mutilation of Spanish," it is a "living language" that emerged out of "Chicanos' need to identify ourselves as a distinct people . . . who are neither Spanish nor live in a country in which Spanish is the first language . . . who are not Anglo . . . who cannot entirely identify with either standard (formal, Castilian Spanish nor standard English)" (55).

Just as those respondents who are learning Spanish are better able to interact with Spanish-speaking community members, recent research illustrates how code-switching may also foster interaction between different groups of people. In her study of a New Mexican community, María Dolores Gonzales (1999) describes how code-switching may be a "linguistic strategy" that enables its users to effectively communicate with English- and Spanish-speakers across generations and ages (35).

For many of the same reasons and intra-ethnic benefits that respondents give for improving their Spanish-language skills, some individuals decided to teach their children Spanish. Their rationales for raising bilingual children parallel the sentiment described in other studies on Mexican Americans and language, including wanting their children to be able to communicate with Spanish-speaking relatives and because of the intimate connections they perceive between language and culture (Hurtado 1995; Niemann et al. 1999). These two reasons have motivated David Galvez to teach his children Spanish, despite his own childhood rejection of the Spanish language:

> I think the language is the most important thing because when you lose the language, you kind of lose hopes of retaining anything. If you have the language then everything else is out there for you to grasp onto, like food. My son loves Spanish music. So the language is really important for me. If he maintains it, he can seek out everything else and communicate amongst Mexicans when he grows up.

Reflecting on their child-rearing experiences, several older La Puente residents express remorse for not having taught their children Spanish, especially in light of the changing demographics and economy. Remembering the intense language discrimination that they experienced when they entered La Puente schools in the late 1920s, Carlos and Leticia Mendoza spoke only English to their children because it came "naturally" and because "there was still some racism." However, the Mendozas and their adult children now regret this decision:

> CARLOS: They're doing all right, but they feel that they're a little bit . . .
> LETICIA: They get embarrassed now because they don't speak a fluent Spanish. They all went to college. They're all graduates, and they all have good jobs. But they wish, especially my nurse; she's the worst. I have two girls that speak pretty well.

As well as feeling embarrassed because they do not meet the assumption or expectation that Mexican Americans speak Spanish, the Mendozas' children are not benefiting from what is now seen as an advantage in the job market—speaking Spanish. Leticia Mendoza hints at the unfairness of this phenomenon as she connects this contemporary pattern with a history of workplace discrimination encountered by Mexican Americans:

> They understand Spanish, and they say a lot of words in Spanish. They really try now . . . I want them to speak Spanish. It's a great advantage now. That's an advantage for us. When we were young, we didn't have to know Spanish in order to get a job because you couldn't get a job anyway. But now, it would be for them, and it's sad. They feel very bad about not knowing Spanish.

The Mendozas wish that their children could communicate in Spanish. However, they are also aware of the double standard in which Whites may be praised for their attempts to speak Spanish, while Mexican Americans may be expected to speak Spanish and judged derogatorily if they do not.[2] Observing the social and economic benefits that may accrue to bilingual individuals, a couple of respondents such as the Mendozas describe the irony that while for Mexican Americans Spanish has been "subtracted" through assimilation efforts, punishment, or ridicule (see Valenzuela 1999), Whites who are bilingual may be benefiting.

The remorse that several respondents describe for not teaching their children Spanish suggests their support for bilingualism and perhaps reflects a common sentiment among Latinas/os in the Los Angeles area. Many in Los Angeles' Mexican-origin communities speak Spanish or are Spanish-English bilingual. The history of the Southwest, years of continual migration and interaction between Mexico and the United States, the growing prominence of Spanish-language media, and geographical proximity to Latin America have resulted in Spanish-language retention among U.S.-born Latinas/os at rates higher than among other racial/ethnic groups in the United States (Piatt 1990; Lopez 1996; J. Gonzalez 2000). The percentage of Mexicans who speak Spanish has increased in proportion to their growing population (Lopez 1996). In 1990 in the Los Angeles region, 81 percent of all Latinas/os reported speaking Spanish at home, including 63 percent of U.S.-born Latinas/os (ibid., 149). Thus, after English, the Spanish language was used thirteen times more than the next most popular language (ibid., 141). In 2000, 70 percent of individuals in Los Angeles County who spoke a language other than English in their homes spoke Spanish (Hillburg 2001). Sixty-nine percent of all La Puente residents five years of age and over speak Spanish at home (U.S. Bureau of the Census 2001). Jane Hanson's bilingual daughter captures some of this support for speaking Spanish when commenting on her non-Spanish-speaking cousins when she exclaims that "they don't know Spanish. Well, they better hurry up. They're in California. They better learn."

Just as affirming the Spanish language in their own lives and homes may foster an inclusive perspective and enhance intra-generational communication, respondents who enjoy and advocate Spanish-language music are also creating a welcoming environment in their neighborhoods. Several respondents say they appreciate the growth of Spanish-language music that has accompanied the demographic shifts. For example, fifty-eight-year-old Marie Rogers says that while her children ridicule the increase in Mexican music and derogatorily refer to La Puente as "Little TJ" (Tijuana), she enjoys the change:

> I remember the time when the music for one thing. The loud music was rock and roll, and the [shift] from rock and roll to skinhead music or the heavy metal. Now it sounds like Mexican. My kids say it sounds like TJ. Little TJ, my kids call it. I enjoy it. I think it's better than heavy metal or skinhead music. I'm comfortable with it.

Given Marie Rogers' labeling of the popular music heard in 1970s La Puente as "skinhead music," it appears that Marie is not only "comfortable" with Mexican music, but she may also be more comfortable with her current neighborhood and community.

Such enjoyment and acceptance of the changing music in La Puente is best exemplified by fifty-five-year-old Ilene Gómez, who literally invites the Spanish-language music into her home, as she leaves her windows open at night to thoroughly enjoy the sounds of her community:

> On Saturday nights, not often—but you do have the parties here, and the music is on . . . I enjoy that at night . . . Now we've got a lot of people complaining, but it doesn't bother me. I keep my bedroom window open when I go to bed, and I say, "Let me just salsa."

Public displays of mejicanismo or latinidad are refreshing for some individuals who remember childhood pressures to assimilate by listening to music in the English language. Thirty-five-year-old Irene Renteria-Salazar explains: "There was that time, that peer pressure, when at school all you listened to was American music. Eventually, I took a stand and I said, 'Well, I like Spanish music, and no one is going to make me change.'" Twenty-seven-year-old David Galvez shares Irene's sentiment and her changing perspective on music:

Like, growing up, Mexican music was, "Turn it down. Turn it down." Now, today some of the most popular music is coming from Latin American artists. I'm actually going to a concert today, Mark Anthony. So I listen to a lot of Spanish music of different types—salsa, rancheras, mariachi.

As with David Galvez, some respondents sense more acceptance of Mexican and other Latina/o musical forms because of the increase in the number of Spanish-language radio stations and the greater recognition of Latina/o musicians and singers. With the growing popularity of and access to Mexican music, Rosario Jones listens to Spanish-language music to improve her Spanish and to acquire a better sense of her family origins. She does this in spite of the flack that she gets from her White husband:

I listen to Spanish music a lot. I have Spanish in my car. My husband gets mad at me. He says, "You know, honey, this is America. Why do you want to be like that? Why don't you go to Mexico and live if you want to be Mexican?" I won't go that far, but I want to know where my father came from and my mother's parents.

As we learned in the previous chapter, Rosario is one individual who advocates that immigrants learn American customs. However, in her life she emphasizes the importance of acquiring the Spanish language despite others' perceptions. Rosario Jones' multiple beliefs and actions are an example of the mix of attitudes that some individuals may articulate regarding immigrants and assimilation.

As some recent scholarship has demonstrated, speaking Spanish in public arenas, listening to merengues, cumbias, and banda music, and organizing cultural manifestations are among the diverse ways that Latinas/os are claiming public spaces (Rocco 1997; Rosaldo and Flores 1997; Ainslie 1998; Valle and Torres 2000). These public displays may be challenges to the dominant culture and forms of resistance against expectations of "appropriate" English-language, middle-class, and Anglo-centered public decorum (Rocco 1997; Ochoa 1999). As a result, they are examples not of acculturation but of what Gutiérrez (1998) describes as "cultural reinvigoration" (311). Such cultural reinvigoration among Mexican-origin communities, especially along the U.S.-Mexico border, is also noticeable in the growing popularity of Los Angeles' major Spanish-language newspaper, *La Opinión*; the popularity of Mexican music, epitomized in top-ranking Mexican music stations; the outselling in grocery stores of salsa picante over ketchup; and in the public use of the Spanish language (Lopez 1996;

Gutiérrez 1998). Just as this cultural reinvigoration may be influencing the activities and preferences of Mexican Americans, to the extent that established residents welcome the languages and music of their immigrant neighbors, both Mexican Americans and Mexican immigrants may be orchestrating the sounds of La Puente.

Part of the process of aiding immigrants in their integration into La Puente and of creating inclusive neighborhoods is challenging anti-Mexican and anti-Spanish-language sentiment. When Mexican Americans challenge xenophobic or racist comments, they align themselves with immigrants and convey that such derogatory ideas and exclusionary practices will not be tolerated. Respondents describe their objections to such expressions in churches and schools and their disapproval of anti-Mexican comments made by their neighbors. Fifty-two-year-old Frank Gallegos says that because he is often seen as White, some members of the Mexican American community are more apt to reveal to him their negative views of immigrants. He criticizes what he describes as "bitterness" or "animosity" on the part of some Mexican Americans regarding these demographic shifts:

As you can see, I'm probably too white to be considered Latino, and people who would look down, "We have nothing against those people." Just the use of the words, certain words, inflections tell you that there's something more than the words that you hear. Too often we get to the point that we want to be confrontational or enter into a superior-inferior relationship. "I'm going to dazzle you with how important I am." You would have one minority kill another minority.

Frank adamantly disagrees with such anti-immigrant sentiment and maintains his own positive image of immigrants:

I welcome any and all. I really do. I still have first cousins that are Mexican citizens living in Mexico, and I would welcome them to come over here and try and participate in fulfilling their dream because as long as you try and you go out of your way to try and help others to get what they want, eventually you will get what you want. It's just a different play on "What goes around, comes around." Try and help people. Mexican immigrants are very hard workers. They really are. The economy, the socioeconomic condition of Southern California is really becoming very dependent on them.

La Puente residents also enact a form of solidarity with immigrants when they use their monetary resources to assist the incorporation process. For example, sixty-five-year-old Gloria Dominguez recounts an incident when she provided a neighbor with food and money:

I know some of them have a lot of kids, and if I have a lot of food, I take it to them. There was this one man that would pass by my house . . . he had a big family . . . and that man ended up with a tumor in his head. Before he had passed away, [his spouse] told me, "I'm having a hard time because there's not any income coming in. Whatever they can give, I take it, but it's hard." So I felt sorry for her, and he was nice to me. So I went and bought a lot of groceries, and I took them over. When he passed away, I gave her a donation. What I could, I gave. I did it because I knew these people needed help and they weren't from here.

Like Gloria, Carlos Mendoza has also provided support to his immigrant neighbors, as Leticia Mendoza recalls:

There were a couple of men that came from Mexico, and Carlos having a barber shop, he was able to help them out a lot. He helped them when they went to buy a house, helped them when they went to buy their car, helped them when they went into business.

Such examples of economic assistance illustrate how Mexican Americans may play key roles in facilitating the transition of immigrants into La Puente. Their roles may be especially critical when there is limited institutional support for immigrants and when immigrants may be unable to provide financial aid to family, friends, and other compatriots once they are in the United States.[3] Thus, by proving such economic assistance, Mexican Americans may not only diminish the risks and costs of migration and settlement for Mexican immigrants (see Massey et al. 1987), in the process they may also be solidifying a sense of community.

Much of what motivates these individuals who are improving their Spanish-language skills, challenging anti-immigrant sentiment, and providing assistance to immigrants is a desire to better interact with family members, neighbors, and co-workers and stems from the connections that they believe they share with Mexican immigrants. It appears that those individuals who are Spanish-English bilinguals (including those who code-switch, speak Spanglish, or other variations of Spanish and English) are able to do what María Dolores Gonzales (1999) has described of other bilingual Mexican American individuals — "cross social, cultural, and linguistic borders to enter new social networks" (35). The formation of such social networks may be mutually beneficial to Mexican Americans and Mexican immigrants by providing them with the support, advice, assistance, and knowledge that may accompany these connections.

There are ways that institutions can build upon the desire of respondents to improve their Spanish-language skills and their interactions with Spanish-speakers. To the extent that institutions move away from assimilationist and hierarchical practices by adopting more collaborative practices that respect the cultural integrity of Latinas/os and build upon the knowledge and language bases of individuals, groups, and communities, they can enhance intra-ethnic and cross-racial/ethnic relations. The following two subsections on the ways respondents engage in community-building in their churches and schools offer some possibilities for change.

Building Community in/through the Catholic Church

Given the large percentage of Mexican Americans and Mexican immigrants who identify as Catholic and participate in their churches, church practices and activities have the potential for fostering a community space that eases the transition of immigrants and brings together immigrants and established residents (Lopez and Espiritu 1990; Goode and Schneider 1994; Pardo 1998). As Pardo (1998) discusses in her work on Mothers of East Los Angeles, members of working-class communities may perceive their church as one of the few accessible and trusted institutions. As such, the church may serve as a bridge for other institutions and may be a location where women in particular are actively engaged in working for the betterment of their communities. In their analysis of panethnicity, Lopez and Espiritu (1990) also describe how Catholicism, particularly when individuals and groups attend the same church, may bring Latinas/os together. Likewise, the everyday actions of the church laity may be critical in this community-building or unifying process. While in the previous chapter a few La Puente respondents expressed concern about the rise in immigrant and Spanish-speaking parishioners and the changes in the church that have stemmed from these demographic shifts, many individuals are welcoming the greater inclusion of community residents. They are doing so by challenging others' opposition to Spanish-language masses, conceiving of the Catholic Church as an arena that should foster a sense of community, and advocating for more progressive perspectives and policies in the Church. These actions and beliefs may simultaneously enhance intra-ethnic relations and help to shift the unequal distribution of power within the Church.

Recent scholarship indicates that 75 percent of the Mexican-origin population in the United States—73 percent of Mexican Americans and 82 percent of Mexican immigrants—are Catholic (Cadena and Medina 1996, 100). This percentage is substantially higher among the La Puente respondents, nearly 90 percent of whom identify as Catholic. Many respondents attend church at least once a month, several are involved in church groups, lead classes, and volunteer in the church, and a few describe themselves as "non-practicing Catholics" or "Catholic by culture, not religion."

Reflecting the demographic shifts over the past twenty years, the percentage of Latinas/os who constitute the Catholic laity in the United States has increased, as Cadena and Medina (1996) note:

> Within the Catholic Church, Chicanos and Latinos comprised about 28 percent of the Catholic Church in 1980 and about 35 percent in 1990. Soon after the turn of the next century, Latinos will be about one-half of the Catholic laity. More than a dozen (arch)dioceses are over 51 percent Latino and over twenty-seven (arch)dioceses are between 25 and 50 percent (100).

Latinas/os comprise 65 percent of the Los Angeles archdiocese (Cadena and Medina 1996, 100), which includes the two Catholic churches in La Puente —Saint Joseph and Saint Louis of France. Many of the longtime parishioners of La Puente's Catholic churches say they have noticed the growing proportion of Latinas/os and in particular of immigrants who are attending church services.

As the Latina/o population and the percentage of residents who speak Spanish as their primary language has risen, respondents explain that due to demand, the churches are offering more Spanish-language masses than they did before. For example, at Saint Louis of France, the first Spanish mass was started in 1970, and now three of the seven weekend masses are in Spanish.[4] Considering the city's two Catholic Churches, about a third of the weekend masses are conducted in Spanish.

Though some La Puente residents may disapprove of these changes, the alliance that Mexican Americans share with immigrants is evident in situations where they counter others' opposition. The comments by twenty-nine-year-old Shirley Garcia are illustrative:

> There was this one White lady, and she was making comments about how she doesn't understand why they changed the masses to every other mass in Spanish. The majority that go to mass speak Spanish, so why should we have to conform with a thing like religion? . . . I guess she didn't like it because all this time it was geared towards her kind, and all of a sudden it was being changed for Mexican people . . . It's positive for our community. It brings more people to church now. Before, they would go to church in [a nearby city] because all the masses over there are in Spanish . . . They wouldn't even participate or couldn't partici-

pate because of that, which is ridiculous. So now we have that change. It made a big difference in the positive.

While in the previous chapter Shirley argues that Mexican immigrants should Americanize, here—when a White woman complains about the addition of Spanish-language masses, Shirley asks: "Why do we have to conform with a thing like religion?" She argues that "when you have a community [where] everybody in that area speaks that language or can understand the signs, why not" speak the most common language? So in spite of her support otherwise for assimilation, when exposed to anti-Spanish-language comments and in the context of the changing community, she aligns herself with immigrants by advocating for changing institutions such as the Catholic Church to best serve community residents.

Though as we heard earlier Rosario Jones' attempts to distance herself from Mexican immigrants by shopping outside of La Puente, she too is supportive of Spanish-language masses. She describes how some of the changes at her church have been regarded:

> We had to arrange our whole mass schedule to accommodate three Spanish masses versus the two that we had, so that was a big thing. A lot of the Whites in the parish, they were, "Oh God, another one." They didn't like the fact that instead of having an English bulletin, it was bilingual. A lot of our major masses like Thanksgiving and Christmas, it's a bilingual mass, so everybody can join in. There are a lot of people that don't like that. I like it simply because I think everybody should have a chance to participate in a special mass.

In addition to aligning themselves with immigrants when confronted with complaints about adding more Spanish masses, several respondents say the increase has raised the level of unity within the Mexican-origin community. Thirty-one-year-old Sylvia Espinosa, who early in her interview argued that immigrants "are not in Mexico anymore, and the way I see it is—if you're coming here, you're going to have to become Americanized," changes her tune when she realizes that Spanish-language masses are under attack. In this situation she argues, "You have a lot of Mexican and Mexican American people that all they speak is Spanish. They need their services in Spanish. So, I think more unity is what I've seen."

Part of this unity may be attributed not only to the increased opportunities for Spanish-speakers to participate in the church but also to the number of Mexican Americans who may be joining immigrants by attending church services in Spanish. In fact, a few respondents are attending Spanish-language masses to improve their language skills. For example,

David Galvez sought out a church where the services are conducted in Spanish to provide additional opportunities for his "kids to be exposed to Spanish."

While some parishioners are speaking out on the benefits of Spanish-language masses, some also are advocating for additional changes in the Catholic Church. Key among these changes is the replacement of what a few individuals describe as "conservative," "traditional," and "old-fashioned" priests. A couple of women say that to the extent that such replacements have occurred, they have noticed opportunities for the increased involvement of community residents. For example, over the past seven years, thirty-one-year-old Sylvia Espinosa has attended Sunday mass at her local church. However, her level of activity and others' participation was minimal until a new pastor was brought into the church. In her opinion, this pastor has been receptive to the parishioners by making changes in the church "wherever the demand is. He's trying to fill that demand." She expands:

> They have more involvement with the layperson, you know the common person. My husband and I are Eucharistic ministers, where before we would have thought, "Oh, no, that's for some holy person to do." Now, it's more focused on the layperson. I've seen that a big change has been to involve the layperson more in the celebration of the mass.

Twenty-nine-year-old Shirley Garcia concurs with Sylvia Espinosa about the positive influences of the church's new priest. Reflecting on experiences in her childhood, when she believed that the church was not sufficiently serving all of La Puente residents, she credits this new priest with listening to the Mexican-origin community and with designing programs that have led to their greater inclusion:

> I noticed that when I first started getting involved with the church as a child, most of the programs they had there were more geared to the English language. They weren't geared to the Mexican people at all, but the Mexican people were the majority. The programs weren't geared to them. I don't know if that had to do with the priest, or maybe no one ever realized it. I don't know what the deal was, but all of a sudden now the change I've noticed is we got this new priest in our parish. He's been taking surveys. He's been taking a look at our parish, and he realized that we are mostly Mexican. He realized none of the programs were geared to Mexican people. He's been making a lot of changes.

Shirley's sentiment that the restructuring of religious programs and the addition of community-wide activities is overdue is not unique. As others have documented, the Mexican-origin community has typically not been involved and not been encouraged to participate in the Catholic Church (Cadena and Medina 1996). The exclusion of the Mexican-origin population by limiting programs maintains the unequal distribution of power and control over decision making and is not conducive for community-building.

For a couple of respondents, part of ensuring the active involvement of the Mexican-origin community in church events is to increase the number of priests who are committed to and knowledgeable about the constraints and experiences of working-class Latinas/os. Cadena and Medina (1996) note that many Latinas/os have found the Catholic Church in the United States lacking in its embrace of Latina/o cultures and traditions. Margarita Villa's experiences with uncaring Whites and concerned Latinos suggest that Latino priests may be better able than their Anglo counterparts to begin to address such a deficiency:

> The monsignor, I didn't think he really cared for our area. He came from Palos Verdes from the rich area, and he got put in our area. I only had a short time with him, but from what everyone tells me, he was more money, money, money. His contract was over, and he moved to the Pacific Palisades. He's up there where he's probably happy. Our two priests that we have now are great. They're both Latinos. They both speak Spanish. They're just more with the community. They're easier to get along with. You feel more comfortable with them. I adore both of them. I think they're the two best priests I've seen.

Finally, in the words of forty-year-old Art Marquez, part of building community in and through the church involves teaching "tolerance":

> I think that the churches are probably one of the main contributing factors to helping the social, economic, or social understanding of our community because I think that people that live here are religious people. I think that the church is playing a greater role in trying to have community cohesiveness and tolerance and is also trying to educate our young to be tolerant of other people and have understanding and trying to make decisions that relate to being socially responsible.

However, not all respondents agree that this awareness and appreciation of diversity and heterogeneity is occurring within the Catholic Church. Forty-two-year-old Alberto Perez is among these:

> I'm Catholic, but I don't practice it as well as I should because I'm at odds with the Catholic Church and a lot of its political stances . . . I believe in a woman's right to abortion, and I believe in a woman's right for divorce, but the Church is still saying no to divorce and no to abortion.

Alberto adds that he is at odds with Church doctrine also in that he is "open-minded about gays." Just as the implementation of religious practices and activities that include the Mexican-origin and Spanish-speaking community in La Puente may be unifying, as Alberto Perez alludes to, these more conservative perspectives are divisive.

In the same ways that Mexican Americans are building community in their everyday lives by advocating for Spanish masses and other adaptations, church officials can also enhance unity. As respondents suggest, increasing the active participation of the laity, responding to community demands, and adopting more progressive beliefs are just a few of the strategies that may foster opportunities for community-building and may shift some of the unequal power dynamics within the Catholic Church.

Building Community in/through Public Schools

As with Catholic churches, schools are a critical site where Mexican Americans and Mexican immigrants may interact. However, school policies may result in the situations described previously in which both groups are in the same school but are physically apart. As instructional aide Erica Handel's experiences illustrate, the structure of schools may minimize the contact between school officials and parents and between Mexican Americans and Mexican immigrants. Likewise, high school student Mel Sandoval says a system of curriculum tracking isolates her from Spanish-speaking students. This separation, in combination with dominant expectations of language assimilation, may foster the internalization of a racial/ethnic hierarchy in which Mexican American students may distance themselves from their immigrant or Spanish-speaking schoolmates and refer to them derogatorily (see Valenzuela 1999).

Schools have long been sites of Spanish-language repression where the objective has been to "transform the Mexican community into an English-speaking and American-thinking community" (G. Gonzalez 1990, 36). Studies indicate that decades after the Americanization programs encountered by older Mexican Americans, some students still are punished or embarrassed for speaking Spanish (Acuña 1988; Valencia 1991). Through the early 1970s, "No Spanish" rules were common (Valenzuela 1999). Students who violated such rules were often reprimanded by teachers or punished by having their "mouths washed out with soap" (Vigil 1997, 3). During this same period, the U.S. Civil Rights Commission found that nearly 14 percent of elementary schools in California and 66 percent in Texas discouraged the use of Spanish (Acuña 1988, 387).

More recently, schools attended by Mexican-origin students continue to emphasize learning and speaking English. They tend to be guided by the assimilationist paradigm, evidenced by the values, traditions, knowledge, and language that are often given priority in the school structure, course curriculum, and school policies and practices. As Valenzuela (1999) illustrates in her Texas-based study, schools emphasize assimilation and minimize the Spanish language, subtracting and undermining the social and cultural resources many students of Mexican descent bring to school. Such assimilating pressures in school, combined with similar messages in the popular youth culture of the 1980s and 1990s, led twenty-seven-year-old David Galvez, who entered La Puente schools as a Spanish-speaker, to denigrate the language:

> I don't know when I began to consciously not want to speak Spanish. I don't know when that happened, but I just know that influences from TV and what was the cool thing, and the cool thing was speaking English, being American, and all that.

The experiences of individuals such as David Galvez are echoed in current research on youths' attitudes toward the Spanish language. Such studies indicate that by fifth grade bilingual students often have internalized the prestige given to the English language, leading them to prefer speaking English over their home language (Orellana, Ek, and Hernández 2000). School practices and individual experiences such as these may stifle the participation of Spanish-speaking parents in schools and limit the resources and knowledge bases with which Spanish-speaking students enter school. To the extent that students attempt to distance themselves from the Spanish language and immigration, these practices and experiences also may hinder the development of relationships between individual Mexican Americans and Mexican immigrants and may complicate Mexican American–Mexican immigrant relations more generally.

Aware of the community that La Puente schools service and the unequal treatment that working-class Spanish-speaking students and their parents may receive, several of the school officials included in this study are challenging English-only efforts and are creating more inclusive spaces for Mexican immigrant parents and students. Along with these school officials, many respondents are also advocating for bilingual education, which may have positive implications for race/ethnic relations.

Among the Mexican American school employees interviewed for this study, most of their community-building activities stem from their attempts at creating more inclusive environments for immigrant parents and students. Speaking and validating the Spanish language is key in this process. For Jane

Hanson, an instructional aide at a La Puente school, speaking Spanish to immigrant parents has been important, especially when she observes teachers who ignore parents:

> Some of the teachers don't want to talk to those parents, so I talk to them. For instance, years back I was working with this teacher [and] this parent comes in to open house, and the teacher just turned around and didn't attend to her. I knew why—because she spoke only Spanish. [The teacher] spoke Spanish, but she just walked away. Then I go, "Buenas tardes." I started talking. I said in Spanish, "He's reading much better." The teacher, I could tell, didn't want to talk to her, and she didn't. She never did. I talked to the parent.

While in the previous chapter Jane describes avoiding Spanish-language masses because of her experience with an immigrant woman whom she perceived as "pushy," here she intervenes when she notices that a parent is being avoided by a schoolteacher.

In addition to the support provided by Mexican American instructional aides, some Mexican American school principals are speaking Spanish on the school campus, conducting bilingual parent assemblies, holding parent meetings in Spanish, and encouraging parent involvement. Forty-one-year-old school principal Lourdes Fernandez reflects on the positive effect of interacting with students in Spanish:

> Seeing their faces when you speak to them in Spanish and they understand, that makes your day. When we get [students] that have gone to other schools, they really hurt when they say, "Oh well, they didn't like me over there. The teachers were real mean to me. I didn't know what they were doing. They were teaching in English." So they come over here and know that they are treated with respect.

Lourdes describes how she also tries to include immigrant parents by speaking Spanish:

> Some parents are reluctant to enter into an office setting. We make sure that they feel welcomed. We speak their language. We do whatever it takes to help them out, basically. For recent arrivals from other countries, we get them acclimated with the procedures and systems of the U.S. educational system.

In addition to creating an environment where immigrant parents feel more comfortable in the school's office, Spanish is spoken at School Site Council (SSC) meetings at which elected teachers, parents, and school employees discuss and advise the principal on the school plan, school budget, and school-based programs. Of the language used for the SSC meetings, Lourdes says, "It was interesting. We did our meetings in Spanish. Only one of our teachers spoke English, so we would translate for her, and she's fine with that." Another Mexican American school principal, Roberta Zavala, includes both English- and Spanish-speaking parents in school affairs by conducting bilingual parent assemblies. She does this despite negative reactions by some parents who support speaking only English during assemblies:

> When we do our assemblies in English and then in Spanish, some people just roll their eyes because they hate to go. It takes longer to do. So they [say], "Why should we go through it in Spanish. We should be doing it all in English." If I have to translate, that's no problem. It bothers me, though, when I hear people [saying], "Well, they should be saying it in English." Well, that's true, but let's be a little compassionate.

It is important to note that Roberta favors English-language immersion for Spanish-speaking students. However, despite her view and the fact that some parents oppose her decision to speak Spanish during assemblies, she continues to run bilingual parent assemblies to be more inclusive. By conducting meetings in Spanish or bilingually, these principals are enabling Mexican American and Mexican immigrant participation. As was suggested in the previous chapter and advanced by the contact hypothesis, increasing opportunities for intra-ethnic participation may improve attitudes and interactions. Furthermore, to the extent that school officials and parents are working together to improve the educational experiences of the community's children, Spanish-language and bilingual meetings may also engender a sense of partnership.

Encouraging this partnership is what school principal Denise Villarreal is attempting by stressing respect and "making compromises." During interviews with prospective teachers, Denise emphasizes teacher respect for parents and encourages parental participation in education. She tells them:

> Please don't mistreat them. They employ us, whether you like them or not or agree with them philosophically . . . If you don't like parents, if you don't like baby buggies, if you don't like parents that don't understand that the parent conference hour is from three to three-twenty on Wednesday, not Thursday, don't accept my offer [to work here].

While some teachers believe that Denise concedes to everything parents desire, Denise characterizes her actions as "making compromises." She feels that the school belongs to the community and that parents should be able to freely enter their children's classrooms. To her, parental access to the school is important in creating an environment where Mexican parents are more at ease when leaving their children. Denise describes her philosophy regarding the inclusion of parents in their children's education this way:

When I got here, they didn't want the parents on the property. Mexican mothers take their kids to the door and say, "Ms. Ochoa, this is Alfredo. He is yours for the year. Take care of him for me." That's all they want to do . . . I had to tell a few of my friends here, and some of them left because they can't accept it. I said, "What is the big deal? What is there to hide? Remember, it takes a village to raise a child, and we're the village. If you don't want to participate in the village of La Puente, please go somewhere else. [The parents] got their way of thinking, and I'm telling you, they're coming in with those baby buggies!"

Part of creating an inclusive community in schools is addressing insensitive statements and intra-ethnic conflict. Denise Villarreal describes multiple occasions when she has had to confront teachers' racist comments. She remembers how following a day of swimming with some students, a White teacher said to a Latina student: "God, Gina, you got black outside. What are you going to look like at the end of the summer? We're not even going to see your eyes." Denise confronted the teacher about her racist statement. In addition, she met with the student and said:

Oh Gina, you're so lucky—like me. We hit the sun and we turn tan. Isn't it funny, those Anglos always soaking up the sun trying to get dark? Don't worry about it. They're just jealous because we get suntanned. We're just lucky.

Similarly, several school officials explained how they are attempting to alleviate intra-ethnic conflict by intervening when students make derogatory comments. Denise Villarreal explains how she has addressed anti-immigrant views on the part of some Mexican American students:

I have children who are probably second- and third-generation Hispanic, Latinos, Chicanos, American Mexicans, Mexican Americans, who say, "I'm not going to go play with those Mexicans." I look at them and that hurts me so, and I say, "What did you say? I'm not going to play with those Mexicans?" Or there would be a fight on the playground because they were fighting with the Mexicans. I say, "Let's look at my skin. Let's look at your skin. Let's look at their skin. I've got news for everybody. We're all Mexicans, same way we got grandparents that came from Mexico."

As La Puente teachers, Margarita Villa and David Galvez are also react-ing to Mexican American students' disparaging comments:

MARGARITA: Around here, they'll call them "the wetbacks." I just look at them. I always hated that word. When a kid says that today, I say, "Excuse me, you're talking about my family." I start in on them. I go, "Your parents probably came the same way or your grandparents." I get on that whole issue with them. It quiets them down.

DAVID: When I hear kids say [wetback], I take it as an opportunity to educate them. I try to tell them, "Look, where were your par-ents from? Are you going to go home and call your parents wet-backs today?"

In these examples, school officials challenge anti-immigrant sentiment by emphasizing and affirming the similarities between Mexican Americans and Mexican immigrants. They accomplish this by pointing out skin color and immigration histories. As Mexican American school officials, they are in positions to include themselves in making these connections and in dif-fusing some of the conflict.

As a couple of teachers explain, part of improving intra-ethnic relations in a more sustained manner is fostering a sense of awareness, knowledge, and pride among students whose histories, values, and experiences have often been devalued or rendered invisible in the course curriculum. In con-trast to his own schooling experiences in La Puente when the expectation was that students would accept mainstream values and identities and pre-vailing ideologies, Geraldo Romero is trying to develop a positive working-class and Latina/o identity among students in his classes. He does this by "talking about Latino issues":

I'm also seeing the kids realize that they're Latino . . . I showed them the Chicano film "Taking Back the Schools." I gave an introduction to it. They were all into it . . . We had a great discussion about it. I asked, "How many of you have heard of this before? How many of you have had discussions about Latinos in L.A. before?" The vast majority of them said, "No, never, ever."

Based on their educational experiences, the belief among teachers such as Geraldo is that if students are aware of the history and experiences of Lati-nas/os, they will be more likely to develop a positive sense of self, a critical analysis of society, and a commitment to social justice. As we have seen with respondents who articulate a power-conflict approach to race/ethnicity, such a perspective may also reduce anti-immigrant sentiment and intra-ethnic conflict.

Just as a few respondents describe the social benefits of a course curriculum that enhances students' awareness of Latinas/os and fosters critical thinking, many respondents endorse bilingual education because of the psychological, social, and economic benefits of bilingualism. This support mirrors the 63 percent of Latina/o voters in California who in 1998 opposed Proposition 227, the anti-bilingual education proposition (Davis 2000, 122).

Overall, most respondents' support for bilingual education is rooted in their negative evaluations of the assimilating processes and messages that they received in schools. Drawing on her own experiences, school principal Lourdes Fernandez supports bilingual education and directly challenges assimilationist models by emphasizing the links among language, culture, self-esteem, and academic performance:

> I value the fact that kids have a natural resource of speaking Spanish, and I think right now the climate is really bad towards immigrants and people that speak other languages. I feel that kids should be proud of who they are because they can't separate their culture and their language. Language is part of their culture, and I remember that feeling when I went through school where you didn't want to speak Spanish. You didn't want to say what type of food you were eating at home because maybe nobody else ate it. But I think that's really important now. I know self-confidence has a lot to do with how kids are going to feel about themselves and about school, whether they come or not.

Remembering the shame that she encountered in a school system that favored assimilation, Lourdes stresses how bilingual education can foster a positive sense of identity among Spanish-speaking children.[5]

Reflecting on her own educational experiences, Mary Marquez, a third-generation Mexican American woman, says that because of the growth in the Mexican-origin population, bilingual education should be a requirement in schools:

> I'm all for it. I wish it was a standard class to take. I wish that if a teacher knew Spanish, they would talk to their kids in both Spanish and English. Any little bit that you hear, kids will grasp and stick with it. I think it should be taught because, face it, there are a lot of Mexicans in California now. It's not predominantly English anymore, so I'm for it.

Though there are various forms of bilingual education, Mary endorses a program that would teach the Spanish language to all children. Such forms of bilingual education, referred to as "dual-language immersion" or "two-way bilingual immersion," bring together English-dominant students and English-language learners into one classroom with the goal of developing bilingualism and biliteracy. Such programs are based on an additive approach in which students are improving their home languages as they acquire a second language.[6]

Educational policies and practices such as bilingual education programs that are premised on "linguistic and cultural integrity" have potential for improving academic success and race/ethnic relationships (Soto 1997, 90–91). Scholarship has documented that bilingual children demonstrate superiority in concept formation, mental flexibility, and verbal problem-solving abilities (Lindholm 1995, 274).[7] In terms of improving race/ethnic relationships, Soto's work on a Puerto Rican community in Pennsylvania indicates that the development of home languages and cultures within the educational system is a way of "enhancing intergenerational communication" (90). Besides challenging "coercive power relations" between school district officials and bilingual families, she finds that bilingual education programs may foster healthy self-concepts and positive relationships between Spanish-speaking parents and their children. Likewise, bilingual education programs such as dual language immersion programs may be especially effective in creating a classroom environment where students across race/ethnicity, generation, and language have the opportunity to interact. As opposed to systems of curriculum tracking and "cultural tracking," which divide and rank students by perceived abilities and English language skills, dual language programs affirm the values of multiple languages and the knowledge and language base that, in this case, English- and Spanish-speaking students bring to the classroom.[8] In this way, students gain greater potential to strengthen not only their human capital in the form of language skills but also their social capital as they establish friendships across a wider range of peers (see Valenzuela 1999).

The preceding examples of school officials' strategies are among the many ways that progressive instructional aides, teachers, and principals are (re)structuring classrooms and schools. Through the voices of eight teachers, Darder (2002) also demonstrates the critical role that educators who are committed to "changing the structure of social and economic injustice" are having (149). Employing some of the same strategies as the La Puente school officials profiled here, they likewise affirm and foster biculturalism and seek to establish collaborative relationships with parents.

The scholarship on Latina/o teachers also suggests that they are striving to be caring teachers who create inclusive classroom settings. Through in-depth interviews with six Latina/o teachers, Elizabeth Sugar Martínez

(2000) illustrates some of the teaching philosophies and pedagogical practices of new Latina/o teachers that have been informed by their own experiences as immigrant, Spanish-speaking, and/or working-class students. She finds that encounters with insensitive and ignorant teachers fueled these individuals' desires to become loving teachers and advocates for bilingual education and to effect change in their school systems. As a result of their lived experiences, they may be better able to observe and to challenge exclusionary beliefs and practices.

In the previous chapter, we learned of the structural constraints within the schools that can limit Mexican American–Mexican immigrant relations. To the extent that schools emphasize assimilation, hinder opportunities for teacher-parent communication, and employ teachers who are removed from and unaware of the communities in which they teach, they generally work in ways that "subtract" cultural and social resources from students of Mexican descent and constrain opportunities for the involvement of working-class parents of color (Romo and Falbo 1996; Shannon 1986; Valenzuela 1999). In comparison, the examples of the school officials presented in this section illustrate the possibilities of enhancing intra-ethnic relations and immigrant integration by altering everyday interactions and school policies. By working within their spheres of influence, they are "making compromises" with parents, conceiving of La Puente schools as community sites, and creating a climate within schools to validate the Spanish language. Though they may be constrained within their positions and the structure of their respective school systems, these professionals' activities are raising parent participation within the schools, enhancing the educational experiences of students of Mexican descent, and fostering greater interaction between Mexican Americans and Mexican immigrants.

Conclusion

When placed in the sociohistorical context of Americanization programs, English-only movements, and anti-immigrant sentiments, the attitudes and actions of the Mexican Americans respondents in this chapter illustrate that many are challenging dominant notions of assimilation and the existence of a racial/ethnic hierarchy. While traditional conceptions of resistance have tended to focus on public activities such as elections, strikes, and demonstrations within unions and political parties, this chapter documents the often invisible and unacknowledged forms of resistance and community-building happening in homes, communities, churches, and schools (see Collins 1990; Hardy-Fanta 1993; Pardo 1998).

As communities such as La Puente continue to undergo demographic shifts, established residents and recent immigrants are engaged in processes of adjustment. Immigration is influencing the lives of Mexican Americans, and La Puente residents are engaging in everyday, concrete activities of building community and ethnic solidarity with recent Mexican immigrants.

Just as institutions and ideologies may structure and reproduce negative or conflictual racial/ethnic relations (as described in the previous chapter), they have the potential for enabling community-building. The findings discussed in this chapter illustrate the importance of Latina/o participation in community decision-making positions and processes. As progressive members of the Mexican-origin community gain greater representation in positions of power within churches and schools, they can play even stronger roles in developing more inclusive multicultural spaces. Overall, as increasing numbers of Mexican immigrants continue to settle in predominantly Mexican American communities, Mexican Americans—in particular, those who have adopted a power-conflict perspective—can play more significant roles in easing immigrants' transition and incorporation into their new communities.

Respondents' narratives suggest that individuals who articulate an awareness of sharing history and experiences of exclusion or mistreatment with immigrants are more likely to express attitudes and to interact in ways that fall along the solidarity end of the continuum. This is most evident among the La Puente residents who articulate a power-conflict perspective. Access to empowering education has been key to the perspectives of several of these respondents, illustrating the role that schools can play in raising individual and collective awareness and commitment to social transformation. And although examples in Chapter 5 suggest that some Mexican Americans express support for assimilation and criticize the use of Spanish in public spaces, when confronted with others' derogatory comments, many respondents align themselves with immigrants.

While the Mexican American respondents profiled in this chapter are engaged in community-building activities in their everyday lives, to structurally address the inequality and power differentials that continue to influence racial/ethnic relations, it is important to alter institutional practices and prevailing ideologies. Collaborative and inclusive practices over hierarchical and English-only policies not only increase opportunities for cross-generational and cross-racial/ethnic interaction but also foster an environment conducive for critical thinking.

Even with the implementation of such practices, in the case of working-class communities like La Puente, the unequal political and economic structures undermine individual and community opportunities. For La Puente,

City of Industry garners much of the labor and taxes of La Puente residents, and the school board continues to be controlled by residents in Hacienda Heights. Thus, the resources of La Puente residents remain limited, and their concerns may be unheard or unaddressed.

As described in the next chapter, parents are organizing against some of these inequalities. Moving from an analysis of the individual actions of residents, Chapter 7 examines in depth how two groups of Mexican Americans and Mexican immigrants in La Puente are working collectively to apply pressure to the local school district to meet community demands.

Chapter 7

Constructing Puentes: Mexican American and Mexican Immigrant Mobilization

"¡Sí, se puede! ¡Sí, se puede! ¡Sí, se puede!" Hundreds of marching parents and students shout in unison outside the Hacienda–La Puente Unified School District. Their chants become louder as passing motorists honk and yell words of encouragement. As many as five hundred La Puente-area residents have come together this June 1996 evening to demonstrate their support for bilingual education. Just days earlier, word had spread that a member of the school board had proposed its elimination. To consider the state of bilingual education, a school district study session was scheduled for this evening, and community residents have come out in force.

FIELD NOTES, June 11, 1996

To casual observers, the participants in this demonstration are united. They share a common concern for bilingual education and similar racial/ethnic and class positions as working-class and Spanish-speaking or bilingual Latinas/os from the La Puente area. It is this combination of cultural commonalities and connections based on shared social locations and experiences of institutional inequality within the school district that has brought them together. While they are unified in their pursuit of a common goal—the maintenance of bilingual education—among the demonstrators we find much variation. There are organizers of two distinct parent groups—Puente Parents and Parents for Quality Education—who differ in activist experience, gender, age, and ideology.

By centering this display of Mexican American–Mexican immigrant political mobilization, this chapter focuses on the solidarity end of the conflict-solidarity continuum and brings together some of the key issues raised in the previous chapters. It illustrates the factors and situations that led to Mexican American–Mexican immigrant mobilization against the Hacienda–La Puente Unified School District (HLPUSD). As parents before them have, La Puente residents criticized the district for not adequately serving their community. They organized to demand that they be heard and

Parents and students demonstrate for bilingual education, June 1996

that the district be held accountable. The two primarily Mexican-origin parent groups emerged whose organizers adopted power-conflict perspectives. As we have learned in the previous chapter, this worldview may strengthen the possibilities of cross-generational solidarity and collective action. By analyzing the factors that resulted in the formation of these two groups, this chapter demonstrates the simultaneity of Mexican American–Mexican immigrant unity and diversity. It also points to the influence of institutions on immigrant integration and Mexican American–Mexican immigrant group formation. In this case, we learn how residents are confronting institutions that do not address community demands and that maintain regressive policies and practices. In particular, we see the critical role that long-term Mexican immigrants are playing in organizing La Puente's Mexican-origin community.

Puente Parents and Parents for Quality Education emerged in 1996 as a direct result of efforts by the Hacienda–La Puente Unified School Board to change some of the practices in the district. Puente Parents formed in January to challenge school closures, and Parents for Quality Education organized six months later to prevent the elimination of bilingual education. While these two groups were distinct, at times they coalesced in their struggle for bilingual education. The development of these groups illustrates how parents' concern for the Spanish language intersected with their awareness of the unequal schooling provided to La Puente–area students and resulted in intra-ethnic solidarity and political activism among segments of the

Mexican-origin community. Greater analysis of the intricacies of these two groups reveals the complexity of identities among individuals of Mexican descent and the resulting intra-ethnic diversity within the community. Influenced by their respective social locations and experiences, in their struggles surrounding the school district, organizers from the two groups maintained disparate philosophies and strategies but coalesced at strategic moments. The salient factors influencing the two groups' organizing philosophies and strategies were the life experiences, ideologies, and gender of the groups' organizers.

To explore more closely the intersection of external and cultural factors on group formation and the significance of social location (primarily race/ethnicity and gender) on group dynamics, this chapter centers on the factors and situations that resulted in the formation of Puente Parents and Parents for Quality Education. This is accomplished by locating the activities undertaken by these two groups in the lives and experiences of their organizers. Following a discussion of the structure and the policies of the school district that serves the majority of La Puente students, this chapter introduces the Puente Parents organizers, their philosophies, and their strategies for organizing. It then presents Parents for Quality Education. This chapter ends with a comparison and analysis of these two groups. Emphasis is placed on the institutional processes that resulted in the formation and coalition building of both groups, the factors influencing their forms of activism, and the hurdles that they encountered in their efforts to mobilize the Mexican-origin community.

The Structure of the Hacienda–La Puente Unified School District (HLPUSD) and Issues of Concern for Mexican-origin Residents in La Puente

Participants of Puente Parents and Parents for Quality Education reside in the Hacienda–La Puente Unified School District (HLPUSD), one of the largest districts in the East San Gabriel Valley. In 1996, at the time of the groups' formations, the district's thirty-five campuses had an enrollment in kindergarten through twelfth grade of more than 22,000 students. While most students in the district live in the city of La Puente and in the unincorporated area of Hacienda Heights, some are from Valinda, another unincorporated region of Los Angeles County whose racial/ethnic and class composition more closely resembles that of La Puente than of Hacienda Heights.[1]

Though they share a common school district, the schools as well as the

Table 7.1 *Advanced Placement (AP) Course Offerings at Hacienda–La Puente Unified School District (HLPUSD) High Schools, 2000–2001*

	Total Number of AP Courses (2000–2001)	Total School Enrollment (1999–2000)
La Puente–area high schools		
La Puente High School	4	1,678
Workman High School	7	1,503
Hacienda Heights high schools		
Los Altos High School	17	1,787
Glen A. Wilson High School	12	1,789

(Source: California Department of Education, Educational Demographics Unit)

communities of La Puente and Hacienda Heights are distinguishable. They are physically separated by railroad tracks, the Pomona freeway, and City of Industry's Valley Boulevard, a major industrial thoroughfare. These markers divide the two communities, and in most cases students attend schools in their respective towns. As illustrated in the previous chapter, in the minds of the majority of La Puente respondents, schools in Hacienda Heights and in La Puente are also distinct. The physical plant, school resources, and, as La Puente High School student Mel Sandoval says, "even the food" are better in Hacienda Heights. Mel says students are acutely aware of these differences, leading some to refer to their school as a "ghetto school" in comparison to some of the schools in Hacienda Heights, which teachers and students have described as "country clubs."[2]

An analysis of school district data confirms such perceptions of inequality between schools in La Puente and Hacienda Heights. For example, vast discrepancies exist in the level of courses offered at the high schools in the La Puente area (including Valinda and City of Industry) and in Hacienda Heights. As indicated in Table 7.1, during the 2000–2001 academic year the two La Puente–area high schools, La Puente and Workman, had four and seven advanced placement (AP) courses, compared to seventeen and twelve, respectively, at Hacienda Heights' Los Altos and Glen A. Wilson High Schools.[3] Combined, the two Hacienda Heights high schools offered nearly three times more AP classes than the La Puente–area high schools. In addition to Wilson High School's twelve AP classes, it also boasts an International Baccalaureate (IB) program, offering to select students courses such as

Theory of Knowledge, Twentieth-Century History, and Chinese Literature. As described in Wilson's course catalogue, "The International Baccalaureate (IB) program is an honors college preparatory program offering an academic challenge to bright, motivated students" (Wilson High School 2001, 5). Such differential access to AP and other specialized college-preparatory courses has ramifications for the types of education that students are receiving as well as students' opportunities for gaining access into prestigious colleges and universities.[4]

Racially/ethnically and in terms of class position, the two communities are also distinct. La Puente is a predominantly working-class, Latina/o community, and Hacienda Heights is a primarily middle-class community where in 2000 about 22 percent of the population was White, 38 percent was Latina/o, 38 percent was Asian American, 2 percent was African American, and 1 percent was Native American (U.S. Bureau of the Census 2001).[5] In 1996, at the time of a school board member's proposal to eliminate bilingual education, nearly half of the La Puente students entering kindergarten did not speak English, compared to 25 percent of the students in Hacienda Heights. Of the entire student population in kindergarten through twelfth grade, 15 percent of the students in the district were designated "limited English proficient" (Gouglas 1996b).[6]

While the majority of residents within La Puente and Hacienda Heights have shared a common school district since 1970, the school board members have tended to come from Hacienda Heights, which includes the wealthier and more White and Asian American section of the district.[7] The school district is governed by a locally elected five-person school board; in 1996 four of the five members resided in Hacienda Heights and one in La Puente. The one school board member from La Puente was also the only Latina/o on the board. Thus, residents within La Puente and Hacienda Heights have not been equally represented in decision-making positions. As a result, many in La Puente believe that student and community needs have not been fairly met. Within this context, it may not be surprising that in 1995 and 1996 La Puente–area residents mobilized when school board members considered school consolidation and a proposal to eliminate bilingual education.

In 1995 the school district raised the issue of school consolidation. The district superintendent argued that some schools in the district were being underused because of a 13,000-student decrease since the 1970s (J. Cardenas 1996). As a way of saving money, district administrators considered closing schools and using the savings to hire more teachers, invest in classroom materials, and improve school facilities (ibid.). Thus, in April 1995, at the direction of the school board, the superintendent formed a District Consolidation Committee to study possible consequences of closing schools. This committee was composed of students, parents, teachers, classified staff, and administrators. During the 1995–1996 academic year, committees met and public forums were held at local schools to discuss the ramifications of consolidation.

Conscious that La Puente students have not always been treated fairly, La Puente residents expressed concern that their neighborhood schools would be closed. During a 1996 interview with me, a principal at La Puente High School reported that a number of La Puente parents did not trust the district. Remembering the closing of four schools in the 1980s, some parents remained angry and skeptical (J. Cardenas 1996). Still other parents were concerned that La Puente students would be bused to Hacienda Heights to prevent the closing of schools in that area. La Puente parents were fearful that their children would suffer worse consequences of the school closures than the children in Hacienda Heights would, and this issue served as an impetus for community organizing.

A second issue raised by the school district that triggered the mobilization of the Mexican-origin community was a proposal to eliminate bilingual education. A member of the school board raised this issue near the completion of the 1995–1996 school year. A June 7, 1996, press release by a District Bilingual Advisory Committee member reported that a school board member had proposed abolishing bilingual education for kindergarten and first grade, eliminating Spanish reading for all grades, ceasing teacher training for bilingual credentials, and establishing an English-only policy for the school district. A study session was held a few days later by members of the school board to review this proposal. No changes were made to the district's Bilingual Education Master Plan at that time. However, because an English-only instructional policy was proposed in a district where a large proportion of students enter school speaking a language other than English, parents organized in response to the proposal.

The Mobilization Efforts of Puente Parents and Parents for Quality Education

As a result of the actions and issues raised by the HLPUSD, Puente Parents and Parents for Quality Education formed. Although Puente Parents was led mostly by Mexican immigrant men and a Mexican American woman, both groups were composed largely of women of Mexican descent, and both groups employed power-conflict perspectives in their struggles to improve the educational opportunities for La Puente–area students and to maintain bilingual education. However, they differed in their analyses of the school district and in their strategies for organizing community residents and effecting change.

Stemming from their extensive history of activism and knowledge of the school district, Puente Parents organizers developed a critical view of the HLPUSD and creatively sought ways to organize outside of the schools. Puente Parents adopted an approach that was explicitly anti-racist. Its organizers challenged multiple forms of racism and sought to unite Spanish and bilingual speakers. The long-term goals of some of the organizers include the development of politically engaged and active residents and the creation of community-based institutions.

As with Puente Parents, the organizers of Parents for Quality Education also adopted an approach that was opposed to the racial/ethnic hierarchy that favors English over Spanish. However, they endorsed working with school officials for educational reform. They emphasized the individual benefits of bilingualism within the existing social structure and advocated that racial/ethnic groups, such as the Mexican-origin community, maintain their languages, traditions, practices, and values. Moreover, the group's organizers, a Mexican immigrant woman and a Mexican American woman, employed a gender-conscious approach that involved devising strategies to integrate women and families in their fight for bilingual education.

Overall, both groups' organizers advanced philosophies and engaged in strategies that were intimately connected to their distinct experiences and gendered positions, revealing the internal diversity within the Mexican-origin community. However, at strategic moments, such as during the school board study session described at the beginning of this chapter, Puente Parents and Parents for Quality Education presented a united front that opposed the elimination of bilingual education. Demonstrating the benefits of both groups' approaches, their activities were effective in applying pressure to the school board and in increasing public consciousness. Also, by advocating for bilingual education and keeping the Spanish language in the schools, they confronted the assimilationist imperative and racial/ethnic hierarchy.

Puente Parents

The Organizers

The threat of school closures in January 1996 was the impetus that brought together Puente Parents. However, the four key organizers—Francisco Delgado, Roberto Delgado, Ilene Gómez, and Joaquin Macias—are longtime residents in the city who have a history of activism and participation in the school district. At the time of the group's formation, the organizers had lived in La Puente for an average of thirty-one years, moving to the city as youths in the 1950s and 1960s. The three men are Mexican immigrants who came to the United States when they were between the ages of twelve and fifteen, and Ilene Gómez is a second-generation Mexican American woman. Three graduated from La Puente High School, and all four have children who have attended schools in the district.

The activism of the organizers has been long and varied, including participation in school- and city-based groups as well as electoral and grass-roots politics. Three were involved in various ways in the Chicano movement in the 1970s. Three have been active in the schools and have been critiquing the actions of the school district for decades; as early as the 1980s, some collaborated to demand that the school district ensure equal access to core curriculum for students in the bilingual education program. Several were also involved in the struggle in 1995 to guarantee that Workman High School, one of two La Puente–area high schools, remain open.

While their entree into political activism was linked to experiences and an awareness of prejudice, discrimination, and inequality, some initially became involved in the school system because of concern for their own children. However, as they became more aware of school and district practices, their struggle embraced Spanish-speaking, Latina/o, and La Puente youth. The history and knowledge that Puente Parents organizers have acquired throughout the years resulted in their growing dissatisfaction with the school district and their decision to organize.

The brothers Francisco and Roberto Delgado in many ways have been leading these struggles within the school system. They migrated with their parents from Mexico and eventually settled in La Puente in the 1960s. Forty-three-year-old Francisco Delgado, who was twelve when his family migrated, attended La Puente High School, where he remembers prejudiced and discriminatory teachers. Francisco says this awareness of the ways schools and other institutions denigrate Mexicans and the Spanish language has enabled him to better understand the experiences of Mexican Americans and to make cross-generational connections between Mexican Americans and Mexican immigrants:

A lot of [Mexican Americans] grew up with shame because they spoke Spanish. The people tended to make fun of them, and they grew up with shame of who they are. They didn't grow up with a very strong knowledge of their background, so they tend to discriminate against immigrants.

As a student at La Puente High School during the Chicano movement, Francisco became increasingly active in politics. He was among a group of students who started El Movimiento Estudiantil Chicano de Aztlán (MEChA) at La Puente High School, and he worked with local Mexican-origin communities and organizations in struggles to stop police brutality and to improve education and access to better housing.

Since the 1980s Francisco has been watching and challenging the practices he has observed in the HLPUSD:

> I have taken time out of my personal life to visit some of the schools and some of the classrooms to see what materials are in the classrooms, to see the curriculum that the teachers are presenting. What are the things that the teachers need? What school budgets do they have? How do they manage the school budget? What kind of school committees do they have? How are the parents participating? How is the principal to the parents? How are the students affected? What kind of campus do they have? I'm sorry to say, but they are pigsties.

Francisco monitors La Puente schools and addresses the school board at its bimonthly meetings; he is also a member of several school-based parent groups.

Francisco's involvement with the schools has led him to believe that the school district does not sufficiently meet the needs of Latina/o students or of La Puente residents:

> The school board very strongly discriminates against Hispanics. The schools here in the district are out of compliance, and they have been for many years. When the schools in Hacienda Heights are well equipped, our schools here in La Puente are lacking a lot of equipment and instructional materials. That's one of the things that has irritated me. Others are the overpopulation of the schools and in the past the way they managed the district, in which notes were being sent home in English only without the consideration of those parents who have not been able to acquire English with fluency. They're unable to get the news like the rest of us.

Because the majority of the HLPUSD board members come from Hacienda Heights and only a few have been Latina/o, Francisco feels that the interests of the La Puente community are not being served. He attributes the discrepancies between the two communities to the people who are in positions of power:

> The majority of the representatives in the school board have been people who live in Hacienda Heights, who raised their kids in Hacienda

Heights, whose children are going to Hacienda Heights, and who have forgotten that our children also generate revenues for the district, and that our children also deserve equal education and equal access to core classes.

Francisco's activism in La Puente transcends working on behalf of his own children. Rather, he has been trying to achieve a La Puente presence on the school board to more fairly represent all students and parents in the school district. One way he has attempted to shift the unequal balance of Hacienda Heights representation on the board has been through assisting Latina/o immigrants with their citizenship applications and registering voters. In this way, more Latinas/os and La Puente-area residents will be able to participate in school board elections. Francisco has been influential in helping immigrants become U.S. citizens by offering citizenship classes, consultation, and voter information sessions.

Roberto Delgado, Francisco's older brother and Puente Parents co-organizer, was fifteen when he moved to the United States. Now, at the age of forty-six, he connects his struggle on behalf of Mexican-origin students to his experiences growing up in a neighboring working-class community where he was ridiculed by school officials and prevented from speaking Spanish at school. Roberto reflects on the stigmatizing of Mexicans in the San Gabriel Valley schools he attended in the 1960s: "When I went to school, to speak Spanish was wrong, to eat beans was wrong. To eat tortillas was wrong." Anti-Mexican experiences such as these have led Roberto to empathize with both Mexican Americans and Mexican immigrants, facilitating his ability to make cross-generational connections in the Mexican-origin community and motivating him to bring about change in the schools:

> I think the Mexican Americans here in La Puente are good people. There are some people that have been brainwashed since the beginning that to speak Spanish is wrong, to let people know that you eat tacos is wrong, to let them know that you eat beans [is wrong] . . . Some, they even say now, "I'm sorry. I wish that I could speak Spanish, but I don't." I don't blame them for not knowing the language because they were taught, and I can look back to the years when I was in high school, that to speak Spanish is wrong . . .

> My experience with [Mexican immigrants] is very positive. I have high regards for that kind of people because I was an immigrant at one time. I walked in their shoes.

Francisco has a long history of working for the betterment of the Mexican-origin community. Like his brother, he has participated in several school-based parent groups, including the Parent-Teacher Association

(PTA) at one elementary school. In this capacity, he helped to raise money by selling food and organizing carnivals and Cinco de Mayo celebrations.

Over time, however, Roberto grew increasingly dissatisfied with school committees, school officials, and the structure of schools. In the case of the PTA, much of his disillusionment came with the realization that the organization was more concerned with maintaining the status quo than with working with La Puente parents and the community to bring about positive changes in the school:

> I haven't been in the PTA for the last three years. When [another principal came to the school], I said, "Forget it. You don't want community involvement. Forget it. I don't want to involve myself with you. You don't want me around, and I don't want you around me." A lot of parents feel the same way. PTA has practically disappeared at [that school].

Also like his brother, Roberto criticizes the discrepancies that he has observed between schools in Hacienda Heights and those in La Puente:

> In Hacienda Heights, the school population is low, the classroom sizes are low. There are air-conditioned classrooms. We don't have anything that is [completely] air-conditioned. Like [one elementary school] for instance, there's only one classroom that's got air-conditioning other than the principal's office. How can you expect a child to learn when outside it's a hundred and five and inside the classroom is a hundred degrees?

Roberto remembers the quality of La Puente schools at the time he became active in the 1980s:

> When we started to get involved in the schools, nine years ago, the grounds were dirty. Trash and weeds were everywhere. Nothing that would stimulate the students to go back to school the following day. The food was bad. A lot of kids got sick, and it was just one thing after another.

Roberto believes Spanish-speaking students have been mistreated in the school district:

> They treat our children, the Hispanic kids, like they were a bunch of cows like you do when you load a cow in a truck. They are not cows. They are humans. They don't have a handicap . . . It is not a crime not to know a language. It's not a crime. Don't condemn them, but the district did not want to help them.

Roberto's observations of the school district, especially the lack of resources provided for Spanish-speaking students, led him, along with several other individuals, to file a number of charges of racial discrimination with the State Department of Education and the State Office of Civil Rights (OCR) against the HLPUSD in 1992.[8]

Francisco and Roberto Delgado's activism emerged from their social positions and experiences. As Spanish-speaking Mexican parents, they were concerned about the quality of education that their children and other Latinas/os were receiving in La Puente. It was their experiences with school officials and working within the school system that caused them to seek alternative, less integrationist methods for change. Their power-conflict perspectives and positions as long-term immigrants with life experiences of adjusting to a new society and an awareness of the assimilation processes encountered by Mexican Americans have strengthened their abilities to better understand the experiences of both Mexican Americans and Mexican immigrants. For the Delgados, this vantage point has enabled them to see the similarities Mexicans share across generations and to potentially unite Mexican Americans and Mexican immigrants.

The Delgados' fellow Puente Parents organizer Ilene Gómez likewise has formed her perspectives on the HLPUSD based on her experiences and observations. As a pre-teen in the 1950s Ilene moved with her parents from Texas to La Puente. After graduating from La Puente High School, she eventually earned a master's degree in bilingual education and administration that she applied in more than twenty years of teaching in the HLPUSD. Ilene characterizes her best times teaching as those when she taught English as a Second Language and citizenship classes because, she says, "I told the truth, and I spoke in Spanish when I needed to. I told them that they were empowered, if only they knew, and they had to know how empowered they were."

In her capacity as a teacher and resource specialist in the district, Ilene observed the inferior education that Spanish-speaking students were receiving. She realized that there were not enough bilingual teachers to meet the needs of students. Students designated "limited English proficient" did not have sufficient educational materials, despite the amount of state money that they should have been receiving. In some cases, Ilene found students in bilingual education programs with books in English that should have been in Spanish. At times she observed comments and actions by administrators who were against bilingual education and who advocated learning English because "this is America."

With four other district teachers, Ilene worked toward remedying these discrepancies by challenging the school district, "running all over trying to fix the world," and becoming "a constant thorn." Organizing against such inequalities, Ilene and a group of teachers began to get parents involved in this struggle:

> We helped them to understand how to get involved, how to take part, this is wrong for your kids. I saw some kids languishing. I saw death and destruction, and I would cry . . . I saw kids holding on for their dear life.

Like Francisco and Roberto Delgado, Ilene reached a breaking point where she could no longer work under the system set up by the school district. For her, it was in the mid-1980s at a district meeting with superintendents and district personnel discussing bilingual education. At one point during the meeting, one of the administrators turned to Ilene and said that maybe with the enactment of the 1986 Immigration Reform and Control Act, the English-language learners "will all go back, and we won't need your program." At that moment, Ilene had enough. She reflects on her growing frustration and her decision to resign from her position:

> Years of frustration, years of having allowed this and to continue thinking, "Well, we'll fix it. Well, we'll put a little here, and we won't tell them. We'll spend this little bit of money. We'll take some from Chapter 1." I [finally] said, "No, I'm helping you perpetuate a system that's disgusting, and it's immoral, and you realize it."

After twenty years, Ilene Gómez left her job as a teacher in the HLPUSD. A group of La Puente parents, determined to change the school district, urged Ilene to run for the school board. With their assistance and the help of others, she was elected. Ilene's participation on the school board was just one more way that she and community residents thought that they could improve students' educational opportunities and address parents' concerns. While these were their intentions, it did not take them long to realize the difficulties that lay ahead of them. Elected as the first Latina on the board, Ilene recalls her first real glimpse of the dynamics at the district level:

> I knew the inside. I had been in there as a student, teacher, and an administrator. So I knew, but at the same time, I didn't. I hadn't been in the inside, the real, deep inside . . . Then I got inside. That was a horror what I saw.

In her new capacity, Ilene continued challenging the practices and policies of the board as well as other board members' perceptions of her as a Latina:

I was the first Latina ever on the school board. They thought I was going to come in with a rose and play the guitar, and I did. I did. I said, "Hey, I'm going to play the guitar for you, and I'm going to sing 'Rancho Grande.' If you don't like it, too bad." So I met all of their expectations, except for a couple of them. One is, I'm intelligent, and I'm educated, and I've been in the department long enough that I could deal with many, many issues that came before the board.

While she was aware of some of the district officials' stereotypical views of Latinas/os, Ilene did not concede to such misperceptions. She used her expertise to raise questions and to try to effect change. Nevertheless, Ilene often found herself outvoted on the school board. Overall while she was on the school board, Ilene believes, "I really demonstrated that I was an educated Chicana, and I went one for one with them on the school board, and man, I made their lives miserable, and man, they made my life miserable." Though she ran for a second term, she was not reelected.

The other Puente Parents co-organizer, Joaquin Macias, is a longtime resident in La Puente and a labor and community organizer, though fairly new to organizing in his own city. Born in Mexico, Joaquin was fourteen when his family moved to the United States in the 1960s. Three years later, his mother purchased a home in La Puente, where Joaquin spent his last semester of high school. As a student, Joaquin encountered Mexican Americans who ridiculed immigrants. However, he realized that it is the societal pressures to acculturate that influence some Mexican Americans' attitudes and behaviors. As with the Delgado brothers, this awareness has provided Joaquin with a greater understanding of the factors and processes influencing cross-generational relations:

We were attacked by U.S.-born kids. Later on, I came to understand why. There's some self-hate involved in that. This guy's trained, conditioned that way, and the more they put down those feelings that remind them in some way of themselves, the better they feel. Once you understand that, then it opens up a way to bear it. I don't really see any fundamental differences between Chicanos and Mexican immigrants . . . Once in awhile, we find some of those people who hate themselves very much. They really buy a lot of the myths of this country, and they hate anybody who speaks Spanish or who is Mexican. They make it a point of letting you know that they are not Mexican, even though they are a Martinez or a Gonzalez.

Following high school, Joaquin attended college, where he became active in MEChA and enrolled in Chicana/o studies courses. As is the case with several respondents described in the previous chapter, Joaquin traces his political activism to such educational experiences.

Prior to his involvement in Puente Parents, Joaquin was not politically active in La Puente. He nonetheless was known by some of the residents because of the organizing that he had done in Los Angeles and other communities. In particular, he was known for the crucial role he had in organizing the largest anti–Proposition 187 demonstration in Los Angeles in 1994, in which hundreds of thousands of people, including La Puente residents, marched through downtown Los Angeles. He was also known for his work in the early 1990s of organizing undocumented Mexican immigrant workers. Having seen him on television and in the newspaper, La Puente parents had tried to recruit Joaquin on previous occasions to assist them with their struggles, but he was involved with other organizing campaigns. This time, when parents called him regarding the issue of school consolidation, he was able to participate. He describes his conversations with parents about working for change and his organizing philosophy:

> This time, once again with this consolidation, people started calling me, and then I started throwing it again, "Look, I'll be willing to participate in something if we do it right, if we use our brains not just our hearts because this is not about heart." People were more receptive to that, and so that's how I ended up in this.

Working to create change in the HLPUSD is just one of the many ways that Puente Parents organizers have fought for social justice. As evidenced by their multiple activities both inside and outside of the city, Puente Parents organizers have made life commitments to such struggles. While the threat of school consolidation was the catalyst that brought them together, most had become increasingly frustrated with the school district. Thus, influenced by their long histories in La Puente and their interactions with the school district, Puente Parents organizers sought less conventional avenues to organize residents. They adopted a power-conflict perspective and an autonomous approach to bringing about change. This involved challenging larger systems of inequality, highlighting historical and contemporary patterns of discrimination, and working for change outside of the established mechanisms.

"We want to do it independently as a parents' group":
Organizing Philosophies

A key goal of Puente Parents is to effect significant changes by fighting for a school district that meets the needs of the Mexican-origin, Latina/o community. Its July 1996 mission statement lists as the group's first underlying premise that "education is truly the key to the future of our children, our community, and ourselves as Latinos/Mexicanos." Recognizing La Puente parents' lack of power within the school district, the group is trying to rally parents to become active participants in the decision-making processes in the schools and at the district level. Besides increasing parents' influence within the school district, the group wants to hold school board members and administrators more accountable (Gouglas 1996c). Joaquin Macias describes the group's strategy to work toward these goals: "Rather than work through those committees, we want to do it independently as a parents' group."

Puente Parents organizers believe that to achieve their goals requires changing the institution, not just the individuals within it. Thus, in addition to focusing on equity and having a voice in the school district, a strong emphasis is placed on working toward the creation of a politically educated and organized community that can better influence institutional changes. Joaquin describes the group's long-term goals:

> In the long run, I think [organizing independently] is much more worth the investment because you can have a community-based structure. Forget consolidation—you can go after all the other problems that exist in the district and be able to deal and negotiate and confront them or whatever, whomever one on one as opposed to from the bottom up.

As Joaquin reveals, while education is one of the group's key concerns, a long-term aspiration is to organize the community to develop a sense of ownership of the institutions that are ostensibly designed to meet its needs. Developing a "community-based structure" is seen as integral to acquiring the decision-making power that would allow for schools, a school board, a city council, and so forth that are truly community-run. This would place parents in positions of power rather than on the defensive, where they are forced to go through bureaucratic means or "from the bottom up" in an attempt to address their concerns.

Puente Parents leaders have been motivated to organize independently because of the limitations that they perceive in the traditional modes designed for parent participation. Puente Parents organizers maintain that the PTAs, school site councils, and bilingual advisory committees are controlled and shaped by the school board and the school principals. Since committees are constructed and overseen by school officials, they believe that school-based groups tend to concentrate on those issues that are deemed important to teachers or administrators—not necessarily the ones of concern to students and parents. As such, these committees have not been effective means for the Mexican-origin and La Puente community to discuss relevant issues and concerns. Joaquin Macias elaborates:

> Communicate, yes, we will do that, but in terms of working with them to solve problems, that hasn't worked. I think that's exactly what has been wrong because the institution is the institution. It has a tendency to want to resist change and perpetuate itself in the interest of those who have interests within it. A lot of parents have worked with the bilingual committee, with the Cinco de Mayo Committee, with the PTA, but all of these committees have been designated by the institution and are subjected to the agenda, the timing, everything of the institution.

Confirming Joaquin's view of the origins and purposes of school-based groups, in a 1996 interview a school principal described the role of committees such as the school site council and the bilingual advisory committee:

> There are bylaws which say what they have to do. [The school site council] is a legal body, and their legal function is to approve the plans for those school-based coordinated programs but also to approve the budgets and how they are spent . . . [The bilingual advisory committee] advises the principal of the school on the quality of the bilingual education in the school.

As legally constituted bodies, these organizations have designated issues to discuss and must post agendas, announce meeting times, and meet stipulations regarding the participation of the school principal and teachers. It is this format and focus that Puente Parents organizers believe constrains parent participation. Joaquin explains that the way school-based groups are structured is

> like saying, "You can tell me anything you want about my house inside, but come inside and tell me in front of me." It doesn't work . . . the committees have no power, and so [parents] cannot forcefully get their messages across to the people that make the decisions, whether it be the principals, superintendents, or the school board.

Puente Parents organizers say parental exclusion and the stifling of parents' active participation in school affairs emerged during the district's discussions of school consolidation. Members of Puente Parents were incensed because though the district appeared to desire parental input on consolidation, this was not parents' reality. Puente Parents member George Lopez describes how the principal at his daughters' school actually excluded parent participation:

> The principal decided who they're going to have. She decided that she didn't need any parents' ideas because she never asked anyone. She never passed out any flyers, and she decided it would be her and one of her teachers representing [us]. Well, I beg to differ. First of all, she has no children in that school. The teacher that she chose is a very young teacher who is very loyal to her because she gave her a job, and she's going to go in whatever direction [the principal] wants her to go.

George explains the principal's response when he offered to be a parent representative:

> I told her that I was willing to be a representative, that I had parents who were willing to allow me to represent them, and I was willing to do that. I was turned down. She said it was too late. Okay, so it's all politics. It's all a game.

Joaquin Macias agreed with George Lopez that the district was not interested in hearing their comments. Joaquin strongly opposed consolidation, believing that the decision to close schools had already been made:

> My personal objections to consolidation are not that in itself, but it's the way in which it has been put forth to people and trying to fool people into thinking that look, we haven't decided yet, it's up to you, tell us what you think, when in fact I know they have decided to consolidate.

Just as the traditional construction of school-based organizations may constrain democratic participation, some school officials might not wish to create spaces for parental involvement. This was precisely the sentiment expressed by one Mexican American school principal. When asked his perspective on parent participation, he replied rather abruptly:

> I don't know what parent participation means. Parent participation is not always a good thing. For example, when I was the principal at [another] school, we had to check with the different parent groups before we could get anything done. I don't want to have a bitch session.[9]

Despite these constraints to parental involvement, La Puente parents have attempted to work within the established parameters arranged by the school district. Through these means they have expressed their concerns about the quality of education to teachers, principals, and district officials. However, parents report not being taken seriously. Joaquin Macias says parents have been ignored in their efforts to raise their concerns with school officials:

> In the past, what I've seen the parents do is they get together because their frustration reaches such a level, and they go and complain. They make very eloquent arguments at the school board meetings, to principals, to teachers, and to administrators. They speak very eloquently with a sense that they know what they're saying. They can do it politely, and they've done it politely, and it's ignored. They've done it in an angry way, and it's not only ignored but it's ridiculed. That [technique] hasn't worked, so we're trying to do things differently in response to the parents. We try to channel them in a different way. We'll see if it works.

One member of Puente Parents and mother of four adds, "We've been going to the board with five or ten people, and we're ignored. In a group, united, we will be heard" (Gouglas 1996c). By meeting independently, organizing and educating community residents, contacting the media, and raising awareness of larger patterns, in the words of Joaquin, Puente Parents were "trying to do things differently."

Having tried to work within the traditional system and believing it has failed, Puente Parents organizers advocate working outside of the current system. Roberto Delgado argues against playing by the same rules:

> [We] believe that we've been neglected by the district, and it's about time people wake up and say, hey, it's time for us to make our rules. Forget about the board. The board better listen to us or else we'll get them out.

Puente Parents' critiques of the school district's attempts to stifle parent participation were confirmed during the group's organizing attempts, when they were eventually locked out of schools and intimidated. The school district's resistance to parent organizing was evident in Puente Parents' struggle to find a meeting space. While initially they gathered at different La Puente schools, after several meetings their access to these facilities was restricted. Puente Parents member George Lopez explains how the school district excluded parents:

> Well, what happened was that they were allowing us to utilize the schools. At the schools, we were having our meetings. And then they said we couldn't continue to do that, if we did not involve the princi-

pal or some aspects of the actual school there. So we said, "No, all we want is to utilize the facility. We don't want to tie ourselves to anyone else. We're our own entity, and we're just concerned parents." They said, "No, you can't do that."

In response to parents' concerns of such exclusion, a La Puente school principal allowed Puente Parents to meet at the school where she worked. However, to abide by the district's regulations the group had to meet during school hours, and the principal introduced the meetings before handing the floor to Puente Parents. While these restrictions limited the participation of individuals who worked during school hours, convening at the school ensured that the group had a place to gather. Also, since they met in the morning, parents who dropped their children off at school could theoretically stay for the meeting. Eventually, however, the use of this facility came under attack as well. Some believe that the school district began to apply pressure to the school principal so that she would prohibit the parents from meeting. Joaquin describes the district's tactics to stifle participation:

They've locked us out of the school for meetings, for everything. Imagine that—their own parents are locked out. They don't let them in. To me because somebody from the district called the principal, "Don't let them in." We go, "Well, if you lock us out again, we'll do what we did last week. We'll meet outside again, and you know what, I'm going to have some of the media here so they can see what you do." So, miraculously the place opened up with the threat of the media.

Shortly after this meeting, the principal informed Puente Parents that she was receiving pressure from the school district, so she asked the parents to meet elsewhere. Finding it difficult to acquire a public space, Puente Parents were compelled to hold meetings at members' homes. In some ways, denying them the use of school facilities may have worked to ostracize the group and to marginalize their concerns, limiting the amount of credibility they could achieve from other community residents.

According to organizers, intimidation was another attempt used by district officials to squelch parent activism. Francisco describes the use of intimidation as a tool to limit the assistance of potentially supportive administrators, such as the principal who opened the school to parent meetings:

Right now, we have a principal, and the district harasses her so much. She even gets reprimanded when the parents speak out at the school board meetings. She says, "Well, how can I control the parents? I have no way of controlling the parents." She gets reprimanded, and I guess right now [that school] is one of the schools with the most active bilingual advisory committee on this side of the district because of the way that the principal is working with the parents.

Retribution is another form of intimidation that some parents believe school personnel have used in an attempt to silence dissent. A couple of individuals describe how their children have been treated unfairly by teachers and principals because of their activism. For example, Roberto Delgado recounts several instances where his children "received retribution" for his outspokenness. In one incident, his daughter's citizenship grade for behavior suffered consequences:

> At the beginning of the semester, she received an A for citizenship. I have never had any problems with citizenship with my kids. She got an A for her first grading period. She got an A on the second grading period, and then at the end of the semester, she received an F. It didn't make any sense . . . I went to the school. I asked for a meeting with the teacher, and nobody could come up with why this was . . . things that were supposed to have one or two demerits, she was getting ten, fifteen demerits. So in two weeks she went from an A to an F.

As a result of their encounters with the school district, some Puente Parents members maintain that their children have suffered not only from an unequal education institutionally but unfair treatment because of their own struggles with the school district.

Puente Parents attributed the district's reactions to their use of school facilities and their intimidation tactics to a fear that parents might "overthrow" district decisions. George Lopez explains:

> There's some apprehension on their part about what [Puente Parents] is all about. They don't understand it. It's fear of the unknown. Some of them I'm sure are speculating that we're just out to make waves for them and maybe also to overthrow some of their decisions. That's not it. We want to talk about what's best for our kids. And not just my children, but when I say our kids, I mean the kids of La Puente.

Joaquin Macias says the group's attempt to work outside of the school's committees was met with anger:

> That's got the school board pissed off and the teachers and principals very angry because it's "How dare we?" number one. Secondly, we must be wanting to cause conflict or else we would work with them.

Puente Parents' concerns about the limited avenues available for parent participation mirror the patterns that others have documented in schools throughout the United States (see Shannon 1996; Shannon and Latimer 1996). Working-class parents and Latinas/os may encounter a double bind. While school officials may complain that Latina/o parents are not sufficiently involved with their children's educations, they may only desire parental involvement when it serves the status quo of the school. Thus, teachers and administrators may expect parents to attend back-to-school nights and parent-teacher conferences or to organize events for Cinco de Mayo celebrations, activities that may not question or challenge the policies or practices of the classroom or of the school. When Latina/o parents move beyond passive roles in school affairs to roles as critical advocates for their children, they typically encounter what Puente Parents organizers describe — being ignored or perceived as demanding. As education scholar Shannon (1996) has written, "Teachers . . . generally want parents to assume the role of audience" in their relationship to schools (72), but when "low status" parents such as Mexican-origin parents challenge the dominant practices of schools and teachers, they have been dismissed or labeled "irrational" (83).

To the extent that school district personnel attempt to stifle parent activism or dictate the parameters of their activism, groups such as Puente Parents who try to organize outside of the mainstream encounter difficulties. Such reactions and actions by school personnel are barriers to organizing parents, in that they may impede the process of gaining credibility among the community and may limit a group's access to necessary resources.

Organizing Strategies: Making Cross-Racial and Historical Connections

Despite these constraints, Puente Parents organizers mobilized Latina/o parents by conducting meetings in Spanish and by making structural, cross-racial, and historical connections.[10] In particular, they connected school board actions and policies to larger systems of inequality, made linkages between the exclusion and mistreatment encountered by Latinos and African Americans, and related historical and contemporary patterns of discrimination. These techniques brought Spanish-speaking Latinas/os together by highlighting cultural commonalities as well as shared racial/ethnic and class positions. By providing a larger framework for understanding the experiences of Latinas/os, the organizers were also setting the stage for their long-term goal of developing a politically active community.

Puente Parents organizers connected school board policies and their detrimental implications for Latinas/os to other contemporary events. Underlying such connections was an analysis of the systemic and historical character of racism. For example, the subject of one Puente Parents meetings was the 1996 police chase and beating of Mexican immigrants Alicia Sotero Vasquez and Enrique Funes Flores, which ended in the nearby San Gabriel Valley city of El Monte. While throughout California there were divergent perspectives on this event, the thirty members of Puente Parents present during that April meeting interpreted the police officers' actions as atrocious, and many believed that they easily could have been the ones on the receiving end of the police officers' blows.[11] Confirming this general sentiment, Joaquin Macias, the main organizer at the meeting, argued that it was because the victims were Mexican and Latino that the police accosted them.

Besides focusing on the significance of the victims' race/ethnicity, discussions at the meeting equated this videotaped police beating with the videotaped police beating of African-American motorist Rodney King in Los Angeles in 1992. By making such cross-racial comparisons, Joaquin Macias explained how, like African Americans, Latinos have been the targets of racism and xenophobia. He also dispelled the common sentiment that such events are "isolated incidents." By connecting the two police beatings, he indicated that they are part of a larger pattern and history of police brutality against African Americans and Latinas/os. Group discussions of such events in the context of a history of systematic inequality allowed Puente Parents members to see some of the actions and policies of the HLPUSD in a more macroscopic way. Collective dialogues on these issues also highlighted the common struggles faced by Latinas/os (across country of origin) and African Americans.

During a June 1996 meeting at which Puente Parents planned their response to the district's proposal to eliminate bilingual education, the organizers once again made cross-racial connections as they discussed the persistence of racism. Implying that the movement to end bilingual education was a racist attempt to squelch the use of Spanish, Joaquin Macias gave the example of the more than thirty African American churches that had been recently burned to substantiate his belief that racism was increasing. Joaquin's example drew on the collective memory of African Americans facing prejudice and discrimination in the United States. By explicitly comparing the burning of African American churches with the attack on bilingual education, Joaquin's argument suggested that racism, while perhaps experienced differently by African Americans and Latinas/os, is nonetheless prevalent and destructive to both groups' lives and cultures. Since African Americans have faced exclusion from dominant arenas and from decision-making positions, Black churches have historically been significant social, cultural, and political spaces that have provided a source of group cohesion among African Americans (Morris 1984). For the Mexican-origin community, despite the long history of Spanish-language repression, the Spanish language and the "symbolic commitment" to its maintenance have been important for fostering a sense of unity (Lopez and Espiritu 1990) and, at times, political activism (Padilla 1985). Thus, both the burning of African American churches and the attack on bilingual education may be seen as forms of cultural genocide and attempts to stifle a sense of collective identity and political struggle. By making such comparisons, Joaquin's example also speaks to the possibilities of African American–Latina/o coalitions around similar histories and experiences.

Organizers also highlighted the history of racism and exclusion that Latinas/os have experienced in the school district and in the United States overall. During meetings, Joaquin Macias spoke of past and present school board members who opposed bilingual education. He gave multiple examples of the pejorative ways that some board members have viewed the La Puente community, including one board member who consistently referred to La Puente residents derogatorily as "you people down there."

Puente Parents organizer Roberto Delgado connected the movement to eliminate bilingual education with his own experiences growing up in a neighboring working-class community where he was ridiculed by school officials and prevented from speaking Spanish at school. He remembers that

> for the teacher to call me a wetback every day, it was tiring. I used to ask to see the counselor. She would tell me, "I don't have no interpreter here, so I cannot see you." She used to turn me down. When I got out of high school, they told me, "They just put you on the list of graduating students because they felt sorry for you."

The sharing of this history at Puente Parents meetings helped to provide a framework in which members could connect the contemporary struggle for bilingual education to a larger history in which Mexicans, the Spanish language, and cultural practices have been denigrated in the school system and in society. For Mexican immigrants who may be unaware of the assimilating pressures and exclusionary practices that Mexican Americans have encountered in the United States, these historical connections may also be helpful for improving intra-ethnic relations and immigrants' understanding of the experiences of Mexican Americans.

Puente Parents organizers also equated the movement to eliminate bilingual education to contemporary forms of nativism and anti-Latino sentiment. At a June press meeting, they linked this movement to anti-immigrant sentiment of which California's Proposition 187 was just one part. Joaquin

Macias argued that "from a political perspective, anything Latino is fair game" (Eftychiou and Gouglas 1996). He described the school board's decision to hold a study session on bilingual education as a "racially motivated effort to suppress Mexican or Latino culture" (ibid.). Organizer Ilene Gómez also placed the school board member's proposal to eliminate bilingual education into the larger English-only movement.

Puente Parents members attended school-based events to vocalize their discontent with some district policies. For example, at public forums considering the ramifications of school consolidation, Puente Parents presented an organized and unified voice in opposition to school closures. Likewise, in a display of Latina/o unity and power, on June 11, 1996, the day of the bilingual education study session, Puente Parents demonstrated in support of bilingual education. They chanted, distributed flyers, and carried placards with their group's perspectives and mission in Spanish and English. As apparent in the photographs on pages 177 and 201, the demonstrators' placards reflected the themes that emerged in the group's meetings:

Shame on You [School Board Member]! No Tienes Vergüenza!
[Superintendent]: Bilingual Education is Not Your Toy!
Stop Corruption at HLPUSD
HLPUSD=A Perfect Dictatorship!
No English-Only
Stop Educational Racism
Bilingual Education Is Good
Muchos Idiomas → Muchas Puertas Abiertas
[Superintendent], Parents Do Matter!
Puente Parents—Limpiamos la Mesa Educativa
[Superintendent], Las Escuelas Son Nuestras, No Tuyas!

Determined to convey these messages to the school board, the demonstrators were not silenced once the study session began. Their placards were visible throughout the crowded room, and from the chamber's window one could see parents outside the building waving their banners. During the session, parents were also quick to correct board members' English pronunciations of schools with Spanish-language names, such as La Subida. This occurred several times during the meeting when parents called out in unison the correct Spanish pronunciation of various schools. The image of the mainly non-Latina/o school district personnel discussing bilingual education and being corrected by the largely Latina/o audience revealed the gap between those who would be determining the fate of bilingual education and those who would be most affected. The power differentials were evident, but

Placards at June 1996 rally denounce English-only proponents and proposal

the message being sent by the Latina/o parents that night was clear: "While you might be opposed to bilingual education, the Spanish language is all around us, and we are here to maintain it." When one of the school board members who supported abolishing bilingual education expressed concern that the children present at the meeting would probably be going to bed at a late hour, parents scoffed loudly. To the parents, this interest in their children's bedtime but not for their bilingual education was a farce that they would not let pass without comment.

Overall, Puente Parents organizers presented an alternative approach to the long-standing emphasis on assimilation and the dominant perception that speaking Spanish is a detriment. They used the Spanish language as a mechanism to organize members of the La Puente community, and they made cross-racial and historical connections. Their group's organizing approach and philosophy indicated that they would not be silenced, even when confronted with various institutional constraints.

Continuing the Struggle

Shortly after the demonstration at the district's study session on bilingual education, district administrators assured parents, teachers, and community residents that bilingual education in the district would continue. Nevertheless, parents remained wary of such claims, and Puente Parents, intent on organizing the community beyond the issue of bilingual education, moved forward with their long-term goal, as Joaquin Macias explains:

> If we are successful in raising the political awareness level of people in La Puente, eventually more than just Latinos but everyone, I think we can make a statement to other cities, to Los Angeles, to ourselves that things can be solved. It doesn't have to be this lovey-dovey, multicultural, diversity, Cinco de Mayos at every school, learning to know about each other's food, like that's a problem.

Emphasizing the importance of political action, Puente Parents organizers aspired to work beyond the confines of the school.

Building on their momentum from the struggle to maintain bilingual education and with the hope of achieving their long-term goals, Puente Parents collaborated with two other parent groups in neighboring school districts to organize a daylong conference on education in 1996. Like Puente Parents, those two groups described being ignored by district personnel when they expressed their concerns about bilingual education, school facilities, and limited funding (H. Gonzalez 1996). The groups came together as the San Gabriel Valley Organizing Council to hold the conference to educate parents about their rights and to increase parent participation. Thus, this conference was seen as an important step toward organizing Latinas/os to gain political clout in schools and communities. More than one hundred people participated in the conference, including MEChA students and faculty from nearby colleges. Held in Spanish and led by professors, community leaders, and parents, the conference workshops focused on bilingual education, special education, preschool education, and immigration.

Throughout their meetings and events in 1996, Puente Parents organizers emphasized acquiring political power through registering citizens, encouraging voting, and gaining representation on school boards and city councils. To this end, Joaquin Macias ran for a seat on the La Puente City Council in March 1997. Community members assisted with his campaign by registering voters, distributing absentee ballots, and walking precincts. Although Joaquin was defeated by twenty-one votes, the extensive community support he received was a positive indication for future elections.

A continuing goal of Puente Parents organizers is to endorse and elect candidates to the Hacienda–La Puente Unified School Board. Joaquin Macias says they hope to transcend contemporary discussions of diversity and multiculturalism that tend to focus on cultural appreciation and "getting along" without interrogating systems of inequality. Instead, they envision fighting for power and justice. While the long-term goal of organizing "more than just Latinos but everyone" has not quite been met, Puente Parents organizers effectively brought together Spanish-speaking Latinas/os, and they continue to work individually and collectively against various forms of injustice.[12]

Parents for Quality Education

The Organizers

Parents for Quality Education formed in June 1996. Upon hearing of the proposal to evaluate bilingual education in the school district, this group of Spanish-speaking Latina/o parents met to discuss strategies to prevent the board from altering the program. During their first meeting, they created a committee to inform community members, the media, and local politicians of the proposed changes. Initially, the group was developed solely to alert community members of the district's proposal to eliminate bilingual education; however, they received such overwhelming support that they became a permanent group.

Unlike the Puente Parents organizers, the two organizers who started Parents for Quality Education, Raquel Heinrich and Irene Renteria-Salazar, were relatively new to the community, having moved to the La Puente area in the 1980s. Their knowledge of the local schools and the HLPUSD came from the three to five years that their children had been enrolled in an area elementary school.

In comparison to Puente Parents, Parents for Quality Education embraced a method that advocated working with school officials to improve education. In particular, the organizers were concerned with maintaining bilingual education, which they characterized as an important tool for students' individual, economic, social, and psychological advancement. As Raquel Heinrich and Irene Renteria-Salazar sought to organize the community, they were especially attuned to women's gender-role responsibilities as "reproductive laborers,"[13] so they explicitly devised strategies to ensure the participation of women and families in their group's activities. Thus, as with Puente Parents, their organizing philosophies and strategies were intimately linked to their experiences with the school and their own social positions. As such, they were instrumental in gaining support for bilingual education and in redefining gender role expectations.

Migrating from a small town in Mexico in the 1970s at the age of eighteen, Raquel came to Los Angeles with the "wish to just better myself in every area I could think of." In the mid-1990s, she enrolled in labor studies courses, which have informed her activism. These courses focused on immigrant rights, labor studies, women's history, third world women's organizing, the history of U.S. racial/ethnic groups, and the development of the labor movement.

Prior to organizing parents in the La Puente area, Raquel Heinrich had spent years representing workers. After completing four years of college and receiving a degree in culinary arts, Raquel began working with the Hotel and Restaurant Employees Union. From there, she went on to work as a field representative in Los Angeles for Justice for Janitors, affiliated with the Service Employees International Union. In this capacity, she has represented workers by enforcing contracts, filing charges, investigating civil suits and labor charges, and participating in negotiations. She has also trained members of the union on how to become leaders.

When Raquel's daughter began elementary school in the 1990s, Raquel became more familiar with her neighborhood schools. Being bilingual, Raquel felt strongly about enrolling her own children in the bilingual education program. She believed that such enrollment would help to ensure that her children were proud of their racial/ethnic background as well as expand their life and career opportunities:

> The importance of [bilingual education] has a lot to do with making sure the child will have a career that has no limits. Having a child be fluently bilingual will not only open the doors in this country, but anywhere else . . . Every child should be able to have two languages, and what better language than Spanish, which is one of the most spoken around the world . . . It helped me, and it opened many doors, and now more than ever I am the most proud to be bilingual. So I can have that pride and know that my children, when they become bilingual, they are going to feel proud of themselves.

When her daughter started the bilingual education program in kindergarten, Raquel was encouraged by school personnel to get involved in the advisory committee at both her school and at the district. Following this advice, she eventually became co-chair of the district bilingual advisory committee and gained the trust and respect of parents and school officials. Raquel characterizes her encounters with school and district personnel while on these committees as positive:

> My experience with the board has been very good. They open the doors to any suggestions that I make. They listen. I work with parents, and I utilize my knowledge on how to negotiate with them. When I call the superintendent or any principal, they are available. I have a lot of support from teachers and parents from other schools.

Raquel recounts examples of the supportive responses she received from the school board when she approached them with concerns about the bilingual education program. Representing the district, she attended local and statewide conferences and was introduced to the many resources available to teach bilingual education. Thus, when she visited bilingual education classrooms in the HLPUSD that were lacking resources, she met with district personnel to devise ways to make the resources available. It was exchanges such as these that confirmed Raquel's belief about the importance of parent participation. It was this history of organizing and her experiences with school-based personnel and organizations that Raquel brought to the development of Parents for Quality Education.

The co-organizer of Parents for Quality Education, Irene Renteria-Salazar, moved to the La Puente area when she married. She had spent the first twenty-five years of her life living in Los Angeles with her Mexican immigrant parents. Since her husband already owned a home in the area, she agreed to the move. The demands of raising two young daughters and maintaining a full-time management position restricted Irene's ability to become familiar with her new community. She professed that until recently she "didn't know very much of what was going on" in the area.

Irene was also relatively new to organized political activism. However, she adopted her parents' belief that one should "not forget where you come from . . . that it doesn't matter what language you speak, as long as you are able to stand up for what you are." Irene has been standing up for who she is by maintaining a strong race/ethnic and class identity on a daily basis, though it has not always been easy for her in the face of peer pressure to assimilate.

Being bilingual and with family in Mexico, Irene also strongly believes in raising children to be bilingual. As someone who began school speaking Spanish, Irene explains the benefits of bilingual education:

> I think that bilingual education boosts the morale of the child, the confidence level. It also makes them be more of an extrovert . . . It opens doors to jobs, to help other people that are not English-speaking . . . I think it is wonderful that we are allowing the opportunity to teach our children in bilingual instruction. They learn and master their language, and eventually the English will be picked up.

It was through her children's enrollment in the bilingual education program in the early 1990s that Irene became more aware of her neighborhood school and the district through working with teachers and contacting the school principal. Over time, Irene's working relationship with the bilingual resource teacher even developed into a friendship.

Irene also positively characterizes her interaction with the school principal, who "always receives my phone calls." This has also been true for the school board members:

I think that all board members are very open. You call them, and they will come to the phone. They want to hear from all of the community. They have taken my phone calls.

Though Irene's work schedule prevents her from contributing as fully as she wishes in the bilingual program, she has participated on the District Bilingual Advisory Committee (D-BAC). While she is not fully entrenched in its meetings and activities and is new to organizing, Irene's occasional involvement with this committee facilitated her ability to join forces with Raquel Heinrich to form Parents for Quality Education as they fought to preserve bilingual education.

"How can we help on something that is going to benefit the community and the children?": Organizing Philosophies

Key among Parents for Quality Education's philosophies was working collectively with school and district officials to ensure that all children in the district obtain a quality education. This emphasis on collaboration stemmed from the organizers' prior experiences with teachers and district officials and was based on their premise that parents and school personnel are equally concerned with the betterment of all students' education. Raquel explains the group's underlying ideology:

In this community, we are always going to have children. We are always going to have schools, and we are always going to have teachers and parents. None of these entities can function without the other. So we have to develop an organization that is going to maintain and sustain the quality education for our child, regardless of which community we are.

Importance was placed on collaboration on multiple levels. According to the group's mission statement, one level involved developing "a partnership" with teachers by parents participating in classrooms and school events. Another level entailed providing advice and assistance to school and district officials as well as attending school board meetings. Raquel elaborates on these group goals:

The goal is to develop an organization that will be able to be there to work hand and hand with the district, with the administration, with the teachers, with the principals, and with the board that is going to say,

"Okay, which way is the right way to approach education? What programs are good? How can we help on something that is going to benefit the community and the children?"

Collaboration with school officials involves working within the system. Organizers believe that it is important to maintain representatives on the Bilingual Advisory Committees and to sustain open lines of communication with school board members, as Raquel explains:

If we don't have a say at the school level and we don't have a say through our D-BAC, we don't have any input at the board, and this is why it is very important for us to keep that.

To illustrate the importance of working with school officials, Raquel and Irene say it was because of their involvement with the District Bilingual Advisory Committee that they became aware of the school board proposal to eliminate bilingual education.

With their emphasis on working together, the organizers characterize their group as inclusive. They argue that it is not only La Puente students and parents who are affected by the decisions of the school district but also families in the unincorporated areas. Raquel points out that the name Parents for Quality Education in itself demonstrates the group's inclusivity:

"Parents for Quality Education" doesn't include only La Puente. It doesn't exclude Valinda or Hacienda Heights. It includes everybody, including businesses or communities around our district.

She says the group's intent parallels the rationale behind its name:

We have to develop an organization that is going to maintain and sustain the quality education for our child, regardless of which community we are. We're not isolating anybody. We don't want to say this is only for English-speaking or only for La Puente parents, or only for Valinda parents because the unified school district covers four cities.[14]

As a group that formed in direct response to the proposal to eliminate bilingual education, Parents for Quality Education accentuated the benefits of being Spanish-English bilingual. Irene includes psychological advantages among these,

because you do not feel left out. I think it is very important for the child to be able to fit in an environment that is comfortable to him, that he is learning at the same speed that his peers are learning.

She adds that bilingual instruction brings economic rewards as well:

> It is an advantage because I know when I was working in sales, there was an extra group of people that I could actually communicate with. You are compensated for it.

Raquel mentions the ability to provide assistance to Spanish-speaking people:

> When you are in a meeting or a hospital and someone needs help because they do not understand the language and you are able to do it for that person, you cannot measure that gratitude that that person has because you have helped them.

Like Puente Parents organizers, Raquel and Irene link the movement to end bilingual education to the larger English-only movement. Raquel sees the issues La Puente–area residents are encountering as a reflection of what is happening throughout California:

> [The Hacienda–La Puente Board member] who is very heavily involved with trying to eliminate the bilingual education program just accomplished that in Westminster [California]. What they did in Westminster is the same thing they wanted to do it in our district—under the table without anyone knowing.

Coming together in support of bilingual education, Parents for Quality Education made education the group's central organizing focus. Raquel contrasts her group's local and single-issue focus to Puente Parents' broader emphasis: "It's not about housing. It's not about the city council. It's not about anything other than education . . . The primary goal is education." The group's mission statement is illustrative:

> Parents for Quality Education is committed to creating a vigilant group for quality education for the Hacienda–La Puente Unified School District community, where there is a strong need for parents to participate in the daily activities, not only at school and throughout our communities, but also at home.

Organizing Strategies

With an emphasis on collaboration and inclusiveness, Parents for Quality Education organizers sought various ways to involve members of the community in their activities. They attempted to make participating more viable and appealing for women and families, and they integrated elected officials, religious organizations, and business owners by approaching them with opportunities to provide assistance.

Raquel and Irene describe their strategic thinking in planning group meetings and events to best accommodate the competing demands that they as well as most of the group members have as working women with families. Raquel emphasizes the importance of considering such multiple commitments:

> I know more or less how to do it, and I can probably get it done, but I know that doing it alone is not possible not just because I have two kids but because I see the other parents who are working. We are going to have to mold it around their schedules. We are going to have to mold it around the ones that do have a lot of time, but without burning them out, either.

Aware of people's time constraints and many responsibilities, the group tended to organize meetings at Raquel's home, a convenient place known by many families in her community because of the intimate relationships Raquel has developed with her neighbors. Families were invited to meetings, and in many cases, food and drink were provided. Raquel explains, "So I don't burn out myself or anybody else, we have to go around our family needs. I like to include the family."

As well as designing group meetings that were family-friendly, other activities were also characterized as "family events." For example, following their meeting at a local Catholic church that more than seventy-five people attended, Parents for Quality Education established various committees. One involved gathering signatures on a petition in support of bilingual education and inviting people to the protest and vigil that they were organizing for the evening of the school board study session. As part of this committee, a family volunteered to disseminate information before the morning masses at a neighborhood Catholic church. Raquel remembers how the family arrived outside the church Sunday morning at 7:30 and worked together to inform the community of the school board's study session and the activities of Parents for Quality Education:

> They showed up, not only husband and wife. They were carrying a baby, and they had a stroller with a two-year-old, and their ten-year-old was passing out flyers with them. So they took turns signing people up, passing the flyers out, inviting them to the meetings, and signing the petition. So I was very proud to see that it was a family event.

As with Puente Parents, the majority of participants in Parents for Quality Education were women. Of the fifteen people who consistently attended meetings, just one was a man. The higher level of women's involvement in both parent groups supports the existing literature that illustrates the connection, especially for women of color, of motherhood and a concern for one's children to community involvement (Collins 1990; Pardo 1991; Hardy-Fanta 1993; Naples 1998). It also demonstrates how women of color are usually responsible for the reproductive labor that may include activities within their communities, their local schools, and their neighborhood churches (Collins 1990; Glenn 1992; Baca Zinn 1994; Dill 1994; Goode and Schneider 1994; Naples 1998; Pardo 1998). Many women involved with both parent groups were motivated by a concern for their children and a hope for their futures (see Gilkes 1994). Parents for Quality Education member Norma Mendoza articulates this motivation in the group's first newsletter:

I, as a mother, am very happy to [give] a little bit of my time to defend the rights of my children. I want their future to be better than mine . . . Bilingual education is very important for me because I want my children to be able to defend themselves, so that they don't go through what most of us go through because we are not able to defend ourselves. They have [humiliated] me, but I will do everything I can to make sure that my children are not humiliated. Let's unite so that our children are better off than us.

Norma's political activism emerged from her experiences of discrimination and her position as a mother defending her children's rights.

Similarly, Irene discusses the significance of gender in the community activism of Latina members of Parents for Quality Education by reflecting on her own experiences and the interdependence between the role of Latinas as reproductive laborers and their participation in school affairs:

In the Hispanic community or the Hispanic family . . . women are the ones that take care of the education of the children, so I think that's the reason why we have more women involved in it, even though we had a lot of men out there marching, but they're not willing to give their time to come to meetings . . . Once you tell them exactly what's going to be done, they'll be there in the front, but they won't be always at the planning end. "No, that's women stuff." It's almost like . . . in the house . . . my dad used to be the same way. He never would go to any meetings, but if you told him he would have to be there at a certain time to do something, then he'd be there, but Mom always took care of all the stuff that has to do with education.

Irene and Raquel attribute women's and men's activism in Parents for Quality Education to their respective gender roles. They equated the division of labor within their organization to the division of labor in the household. Attributing the mostly female involvement in the daily running of the group's activities to women's gender role responsibilities, Irene expects men to be supportive of their activities and to appear when requested at specific events. As evidenced by her quote, Irene is acutely aware that while men may not be "willing to give their time" for meetings, "they'll be there in the front" at such public events as demonstrations.

Raquel also highlights the significance of men's support in the group's activities and the infrequent but nonetheless important participation in key events—in this case, their involvement in the June 11, 1996, demonstration before the bilingual education study session. Her husband videotaped the vigil before the bilingual education study session, and she watched the video for the first time at the group's meeting on Fathers Day:

It was the first time that I saw the magnitude on the part of the men on the picket line. And that was what I was very proud of. So regardless of who takes part in the event planning, as long as the men are there to support what we are doing, I am happy with it.

The extensive participation of men that Raquel observed in the video may be a visual reflection of Irene's point that men tend to "be there in the front," while the women are actually the ones planning and organizing activities. At this demonstration it may have been the men who were physically near the front of the protesters, thereby appearing in larger numbers on the video. Regardless of what might account for the large numbers of men on the picket line, Raquel, like Irene, is pleased with their support. Defining men's responsibilities as being "supporters" in the struggle for bilingual education challenges dominant conceptions of political activism, in which men are usually conceived as the organizers and women are typically cast in auxiliary roles (Robnett 1997).

Given their philosophy of working collaboratively and within the established parameters provided for parent participation, it is not surprising that during their movement to preserve bilingual education, Parents for Quality Education sought ways to work with members of the school district. In June 1996, appearing on a radio show devoted specifically to the issue of bilingual education, Raquel shared with the listeners how their group continued to endorse working with the school board:

Just this morning I spoke with [a school board member] and told her that we were ready to work with them in resolving or solving the existing problems in the district. I told her that we were open to suggestions that they, together with us, wish to make because we know problems exist in the district, but they are not irreparable.[15]

Parents for Quality Education frequented community sites as they tried to enlist more participants and increase public awareness of bilingual education, the school board proposal, and their own group. Catholic churches were described as instrumental in providing a gathering place for the largest meeting of Parents for Quality Education, and religious officials helped by making public announcements about their scheduled events. Raquel recalls the efforts to get the word out about the study session and the group's planned activities surrounding it:

> It took two weeks to organize. We went to the churches. I told Father at Saint Martha. They were very open. They were announcing every hour on the hour at their services that there was going to be a meeting.

And organizers credit local businesses with donating food and drinks for some of the group's events.

Parents for Quality Education also gained the backing of local Latina/o elected officials. Through press releases, letters, phone calls, and invitations to parent meetings, Raquel and Irene kept local politicians abreast of their struggle to maintain bilingual education. While several politicians wrote letters to the school board indicating their support for bilingual education, others attended meetings or sent representatives to Parents for Quality Education meetings.

While Raquel and Irene tell of the generally favorable receptions that they received from those whom they approached, Irene recalls some parents they encountered while leafleting at local schools who received their messages much less kindly:

> When I was handing out flyers at school, a Hispanic woman approached me, and I said, "Oh, here. I would like to give you a flyer on supporting bilingual education. We are having a meeting on this, and the community is invited." She looks at me, and she says, "I don't believe in bilingual education. I am all English only. It's a lot easier. We are here now, might as well learn the language." She crumbled the paper and threw it away.

Raquel had a similar experience. However, after sharing her views on the benefits of being bilingual, she persuaded a fellow parent to sign a petition in favor of bilingual education.

When I was collecting signatures, I went inside the classroom, and I asked a parent aide who was assisting preschoolers whether she would sign the petition. She said, "No, I don't believe in bilingual education." She spoke perfect English . . . I asked her, "Where is your husband from?" She said he was from Mexico. I said, "Your child will not be bilingual?" She said, "Of course not." I said, "Well, guess what? You are closing to your kid an extra door. That is what you are doing. All of his friends, look around you, all of the kids are Latino. So is your kid, whether you like it or not—he is Latino. You are closing a door on him because what you are doing is putting him in a position that if he wants to go to Mexico, Central America, anywhere in the world . . . By the year 2000, Spanish is going to be the language of the world, and you are closing the door on him. So if you want to do that to your kid . . ." She said, "Okay, where do I sign?"

Raquel's argument to a potential supporter of bilingual education parallels the linkages that she and Irene make between motherhood, a concern for one's children, and community participation. In this case, Raquel seems to equate not teaching one's children Spanish and not supporting bilingual education to poor mothering. By stating that the woman is "closing a door" on her child because she does not speak Spanish, Raquel calls into question how a mother could knowingly limit her child's opportunities. The implication is that since Raquel is advocating for the needs of Latina/o children and the community by fighting to maintain bilingual education, she is a "good mother" (see Naples 1998, 113–114). Raquel's conceptualization of "good mothering" directly challenges dominant perceptions that speaking Spanish to one's children makes one an "unfit parent."[16]

In response to the proposal to eliminate bilingual education and the planned school board study session, Parents for Quality Education organized a vigil and a signature campaign and demonstrated with Puente Parents in support of bilingual education. For technical and organizational support, they contacted the media, elected officials, and members of various organizations. Like the vigil, the collection of more than five hundred signatures was intended to influence the school board's commitment to bilingual education by demonstrating the large number of bilingual education supporters. Parents for Quality Education presented to the board members the list of signatures along with a plea to maintain bilingual education and an offer to provide assistance with school policies.

Shortly after the June vigil and demonstration, Parents for Quality Education began establishing opportunities for parent leadership training programs in the area of education. Drawing on her connections with various organizations serving the Mexican-origin community, Raquel made arrangements with the Mexican American Legal Defense Fund (MALDEF) to provide scholarships for a group of parents to receive such training. Irene describes the group's long-term goals:

> I think that eventually our group will grow because we are willing to offer training. That is one of the things that we are looking into—developing a lot of individuals into leaders and really to just solely concentrate on educational law.

During our interview, Raquel said their goal of developing community leaders stems from the belief that "a parent well informed is a parent prepared to assist his or her children with their education."[17]

Conclusion

As described in the previous chapters, many respondents, including those not involved with these two parent groups, express dissatisfaction with the HLPUSD. They disapprove of some school officials' stereotyped views, the use of dated school materials, poor school facilities, and the overall unequal education that they believe La Puente residents are receiving in comparison to students in Hacienda Heights. What becomes salient is that the hierarchical structure of the educational system has resulted in La Puente residents having little power within the school district. Most of the board members neither live in the La Puente area nor share the experiences of the primarily working-class Latina/o community. The ramifications of such community, racial/ethnic, and class gaps between those who determine school policies and those who bear the policies' impacts was made explicit in the parents' struggles to prevent school closures and to maintain bilingual education.

Too many parents find that rather than attempting to build schools and a district that are community-friendly, school officials may stifle, ignore, or ridicule the opinions, voices, and actions of parents who advocate on behalf of their children. Not only may parents be subjected to surveillance, exclusion, and repercussions when they attempt to use school facilities to organize, as was the case with Puente Parents, but some principals and teachers may be subjected to such practices as well.

The philosophies and actions of Puente Parents and Parents for Quality Education must be seen in this larger context of overall frustration with the education provided to La Puente–area students. As a result of the practices and proposals by the HLPUSD, Puente Parents and Parents for Quality Education mobilized to fight for what they believe to be in the best interests of the children in the school district. These two groups are examples of how Mexican Americans and Mexican immigrants are aligning against institutional policies that are seen as detrimental to the Mexican-origin community. Since the school district is perceived, especially by Puente Parents, as an institution hindering the advancement of both Mexican Americans and Mexican immigrants, it became a focal point around which intra-ethnic and Latina/o solidarity emerged.

The formation of Puente Parents and Parents for Quality Education demonstrates how in particular circumstances and under certain social conditions, racial/ethnic consciousness and resilience of ethnic culture can be used as instruments of solidarity and mobilization (see Padilla 1985). In this case, we see how a similar social position on the racial/ethnic and class hierarchies—especially as it relates to inequality within the school district, as well as a concern for the Spanish language resulted in political activism among the Mexican-origin community. The power-conflict perspectives of the two groups' organizers have been influenced by their positions, experiences, and observations as bilingual Mexicans in La Puente. Their organizing philosophies and strategies, though distinct, included analyses of the ramifications of the racial/ethnic hierarchy on the maintenance of bilingual education and on the lives of those in the Mexican-origin community. Among the organizers, it was Mexican Americans and long-term Mexican immigrants who played a critical role in the mobilization effort. Given their immigration experiences and knowledge of U.S. institutions, long-term Mexican immigrants in particular may be strategically positioned to build cross-generational connections that lead to political mobilization.[18]

An examination of the dynamics within each of the parent groups allows for a greater understanding of the diversity within the Mexican-origin community and the intricate ways that experiences, gendered positions, and ideologies influence organizing philosophies and strategies. Frustrated during years of observing institutional inequality in the district and by thwarted attempts at approaching school officials to effect change, Puente Parents organizers adopted a critical perspective of the HLPUSD and an autonomous approach to organizing. Making cross-racial connections, they employed a historical and macrostructural analysis of inequality. Believing that education is just one of many institutions that reflect and reproduce racial/ethnic and class disparities, Puente Parents organizers were interested in building a politically informed and active Spanish-speaking community whose members could effect change in multiple arenas. To them, this involved transcending contemporary multicultural movements that focus more on cultural celebration than on a redistribution of power.

In comparison, the organizers of Parents for Quality Education were relatively new to the school district. Employing terminology such as developing "a partnership," "working hand and hand," and supporting an "open-door policy," they drew on their exchanges with school officials to advocate working together. Stemming from their own positions as working mothers who are balancing multiple gender-role responsibilities, Raquel Heinrich and Irene Renteria-Salazar consciously developed strategies to include women and families in their group's activities.

As research on political activism demonstrates, women may be more inclined to combine everyday relationships with political activism (Hardy-Fanta 1993, 29). As a result of their familial obligations as reproductive laborers, women often do the "social work of neighboring" (Goode and Schneider 1994, 148) by going door to door to sell food, nurturing and watching neighborhood children, and enlisting assistance for neighborhood projects or concerns (see also Lamphere 1992; Conquergood 1992; Hagan and Rodriguez 1992). It is these gendered responsibilities that may also explain how in comparison to their male counterparts, women leaders of Mexican descent have been described as more likely to stress working collaboratively and engaging people with common interests (Hardy-Fanta 1993; Méndez-Negrete 1999). Thus, Parents for Quality Education's explicit emphasis on collectivity and including families may stem from the organizers' social positions as women. Likewise, the relationships that Raquel Heinrich has developed with her neighbors may have facilitated women's active participation. Just as long-term Mexican immigrants have the potential to build alliances across generations, these patterns parallel what others have suggested, that women may be drawing on their gendered networks to also build community and to influence change (Hondagneu-Sotelo 1994; Pardo 1998).

Despite the differences between the two groups' organizing philosophies and strategies, there were occasions when these differences were seen as secondary to their common struggles. As we saw with the June 1996 demonstration and vigil, concerned parents, students, and members of both groups came out together in a display of intra-ethnic alliance against eliminating bilingual education. Mexican Americans, Mexican immigrants, and other Latinas/os united in the face of adversity and in the pursuit of a common goal. When Puente Parents organizer Joaquin Macias ran for the La Puente City Council, he contacted and received the endorsement from Parents for Quality Education organizer Raquel Heinrich. Thus, while differences existed, in a larger context both groups were seeking positive change for Latinas/os.

Individually and together, both groups were effective in applying pressure to the school board, causing the board to rule against the proposal and to continue with the district's bilingual education program—at least until the passage in 1998 of California Proposition 227, which resulted in severely restricting bilingual education in public schools statewide. In pressuring the school board for change, the groups contested the hierarchy that favors the English language over the Spanish language. Concerned about educating children and adults, they advocated for the betterment and advancement of Latinas/os, and they raised political awareness and participation among La Puente–area residents. Using their respective social locations to organize community members, the leaders and participants in both groups directly challenged myths about Mexican-origin parents as apolitical, uninterested, or apathetic regarding their children's education. The participation of large numbers of women in both groups and as the key organizers in Parents for Quality Education also dispelled stereotypes about Latina passivity and submissiveness. By doing so, they chipped away at the gender hierarchy that may limit or confine women's political activism.

Just as the examples of Puente Parents and Parents for Quality Education illustrate the continued potential of Mexican American–Mexican immigrant mobilization, the organizers' perspectives and the groups' activities reveal the potential for fostering Latina/o pan-ethnic solidarity and cross-racial/ethnic solidarity and mobilization. For Puente Parents, whose primary concern is organizing the Spanish-speaking community, some of the organizers emphasize the historical, economic, and political connections Mexicans share with other Latinas/os and with African Americans. Such historical and contemporary linkages may be setting the stage for realizing the group's goal of developing political awareness and political participation in the community. Likewise, acknowledging the range of communities included in the school district, Parents for Quality Education articulated an inclusive agenda that would "maintain and sustain the quality education for our children, regardless of which community we are."

The cases of Puente Parents and Parents for Quality confirm the significance of shared cultural factors and experiences of exclusion or mistreatment on Mexican American–Mexican immigrant unity and political activism. They also shed light on the contemporary ways that members of the diverse Mexican-origin community are organizing. Within such examples of racial/ethnic, class, and geographic solidarity, diversity remains. The analysis of Puente Parents and Parents for Quality Education reveals this diversity. In addition to demonstrating the importance of both cultural and structural factors in collective action, the formation and activities of these two parent groups illustrate how the social location of community organizers influences their philosophies and their approaches to change. As individuals and as members of their respective groups, the organizers profiled in this chapter continue to struggle for quality education and against school policies and practice that are perceived as detrimental to the Mexican-origin community and to La Puente residents.

Chapter 8

Revisiting and Envisioning the Processes of *Becoming Neighbors*

The telephone rings late Monday evening on July 22, 2002. The familiar voice on the other end of the receiver updates me on the intricacies occurring in La Puente schools—a knife was found on a playground, elementary schoolchildren are being expelled, parents are organizing, there is dissatisfaction with a principal. Amidst the update on these dynamics in the local schools, the conversation shifts to the hiring of a new city manager in La Puente. I am told that the City Council may hire a former member of the Hacienda–La Puente Unified School District—a twenty-year veteran of the board who was involved in discussions to close schools and to eliminate bilingual education. This individual is widely known in local political circles, and he is a controversial figure among some community activists.

The following evening, the bimonthly La Puente City Council Meeting has begun. Mexican American and Mexican immigrant activists are at the meeting to demonstrate their opposition to the hiring of the former board member. Among them are several students who are relatively new to politics. Their youth and their matching white T-shirts make them hard to miss among the older residents who typically attend City Council meetings. They are MEChA students from a La Puente high school. Having just revived this organization at their school, they are present at the meeting proudly displaying their self-designed MEChA T-shirts.

As the meeting progresses, a community organizer addresses the council. He criticizes the former school board member and now contender for the city manager position because of what the organizer describes as a history of nepotism and mishandling of funds—using money from the school district's general fund for a stadium at Glen A. Wilson High School in Hacienda Heights. He warns the City Council that members of the community, including the students from MEChA, are watching them.

Not all in attendance support this assessment. Another longtime resident and business owner presents his perspective to the council. He explains that though he may not agree with some of the previous speaker's comments, he supports his right to "freedom of speech." However, he is troubled by his observation that the speaker did not place his hand over his heart during the Pledge of Allegiance, leading him to believe that the speaker may want the benefits of freedom but that he is not willing to honor such traditions and the work of American veterans. His comments are greeted with applause and yells of support by some of the older attendees.

The La Puente City Council afterward hired an interim city manager rather than the former member of the school board. The issues and events surrounding this debate encapsulate the patterns of conflict and struggle emerging from the unequal distribution of power that has characterized communities such as La Puente. In this case, we observe the differing interests that surround the hiring of a city manager. Though there are some among La Puente's community, including elected officials and business owners, who endorse his hiring, as we have seen in the past other members are challenging institutional policies and individual beliefs and actions they feel are detrimental to the interests of Latinas/os and the working class. Such community residents continue to watch, question, resist, and organize. Yet at times they may be tolerated by the political establishment or ignored, dismissed, and seen as troublemakers with their own personal agendas.

For members of the Mexican-origin community whose Americanness has too often been questioned, they may find that by challenging the status quo, their citizenship and allegiance are doubted. As we saw at La Puente's City Council meeting, questioning the allegiance of those who speak out may especially be the case in the contemporary conservative political climate in which one's level of patriotism is increasingly measured by public displays of the American flag, the reciting of the Pledge of Allegiance, and unwavering support for the actions of the U.S. government. With the 2001 passage of the USA PATRIOT (Uniting and Strengthening America by Providing Appropriate Tools Required to Intercept and Obstruct Terrorism) Act, such questions of Americanness and allegiance may be even more closely scrutinized.

In spite of this climate and what may appear to be continual setbacks, groups of Mexican Americans and Mexican immigrants who see their shared interests continue to unite and to mobilize. What is apparent in La Puente in the year 2002 is that there is a new generation of political activists, MEChA high school students, who on the evening of the City Council meeting have come together with longtime community organizers. At least one

Members of MEChA attend La Puente City Council meeting, summer 2002

of these MEChA students is the son of a La Puente activist, suggesting that we may see additional examples of intra-ethnic and cross-generational (by country of origin and by age) solidarity and mobilization in the future. As others have also indicated, the political activism of parents may positively influence their children's political consciousness, community involvement, and commitment to social justice (Naples 1998).

Much has happened in California over the eight years since I began this project. A state proposition designed to prevent undocumented immigrants from receiving social services was passed. Affirmative action and bilingual education were eliminated, and a new so-called "racial privacy" initiative is set to be voted on in California in October 2003. Supporting the perspective of being "color-blind" (read: power-evasive), the aim of this initiative is to prohibit state agencies from collecting racial and ethnic data. At the same time that these propositions and policy changes are arising, California's population is becoming increasingly Latina/o, with nearly 33 percent of Californians identifying as such in 2000, compared to 25 percent in 1990 (U.S. Bureau of the Census 2001, 1991).

Two generations of La Puente activists, summer 2002

In this sociopolitical context, the histories, experiences, and narratives that emerge in this study provide us with an understanding of the processes under which Mexican Americans and Mexican immigrants are becoming neighbors. Furthermore, when we look more broadly at four overarching conclusions, we see that they may be applied to the dynamics in other communities and to race/ethnic relationships in general:

First, contemporary race/ethnic relations and examples of conflict have been shaped by historical factors and processes. These include a history of U.S. conquest and colonization, the establishment of a racial/ethnic hierarchy, patterns of labor exploitation, and institutional racism and discrimination. In Mexican-origin communities such as La Puente, this history includes de jure and de facto segregation in schools, neighborhoods, and other community spaces.

This historical structuring of inequality has resulted in a general underrepresentation of the Mexican-origin community in positions of power. Moreover, even when some enter into such positions, the fundamental structure of society and its institutions have not been transformed. Thus, the community remains largely excluded from decision-making processes, and individuals in relative positions of power who are intent on effecting change may find that they too are constrained by the established structures.

The inequality and racial/ethnic relations are being maintained and reproduced in such contemporary policies, practices, and ideologies as the structure of school districts, as in the Hacienda–La Puente Unified School District, curriculum tracking, the assimilationist imperative, and the treatment of and attitudes toward Mexican Americans and Mexican immigrants.

Second, just as historical and contemporary factors have influenced the opportunities, experiences, and intra-ethnic relationships among the Mexican-origin community, they also have fostered narrow, binary, and static conceptualizations of Americanness and Mexicanness. The narrow constructions of a cultural, national, and racial/ethnic identity in the United States as Anglo and White have resulted in stereotypes of Mexicans as immigrants whose citizenship is questioned. In addition, Mexican immigrants may use Spanish-language skills, country of birth, and skin color to determine whether Mexican Americans are authentically "Mexican." Within these narrow constructs, Mexican Americans are claiming and justifying their own racial/ethnic identities.

Third, when policies and practices are seen to adversely affect both Mexican Americans and Mexican immigrants, there are examples of everyday forms of resistance, community building, and political organizing. As neighbors, community leaders, teachers, and principals, some Mexican Americans are assisting immigrants in their incorporation by challenging derogatory statements, providing aid, forming political alliances, and using their relative positions of power within the school system to create an inclusive environment. These examples depict the important role that the Mexican-origin community has in the adaptation process of Mexican immigrants.

Finally, this work is as much about how Mexican Americans are negotiating identity, language, and interactions with immigrants as it is about the role of structural factors and ideological processes on race/ethnic relations. Thus, there are two positions from which we can reflect on what this research suggests about the processes and dynamics that might enhance intra-ethnic relations and race/ethnic relationships in general. The first involves analyzing respondents' individual attitudes and perceptions. The second entails a more macro analysis of the institutional factors that if changed may more effectively foster a sense of community.

From Conflict to Solidarity: How Individuals Are Negotiating the Processes of Becoming Neighbors

Respondents expressed a range of racial/ethnic identities and perceptions. Throughout this work, a conflict-solidarity continuum—from intra-ethnic conflict to a shared connection to racial/ethnic mobilization—was used to capture both the fluidity and diversity among the respondents' perspectives. Rather than a fixed and discrete typology to categorize respondents, the dynamic character of a continuum suggests the possibilities of change. Also, as we have seen, those individuals who have adopted a power-conflict perspective, often including long-term immigrants and women, may be well positioned to make intra-ethnic connections and to engage in community-building activities.

The Conflict-Solidarity Continuum

Illustrating the situational and fluid nature of racial/ethnic identity and perspectives, some Mexican Americans express conflictual attitudes toward immigrants who they believe are not assimilating. However, these same respondents may challenge disparagement directed toward Mexicans and toward use of the Spanish language. For example, Rosario Jones' simultaneous support for immigrant acculturation, desire to acquire Spanish, and endorsement of Spanish-language church masses demonstrates this complexity. Rosario describes shopping outside of La Puente to avoid immigrants, but she attends Spanish-language mass and listens to Mexican music to improve her Spanish-language skills and to acquire a better understanding of her Mexican background. She engages in such practices despite the negative perceptions that her White husband, her in-laws, her pastor, and other outsiders have of Mexicans. Likewise, while in the comfort of her family room, Shirley Garcia may advocate for immigrant acculturation; she nonetheless speaks out against similar pronouncements by Whites.

This book's use of a conflict-solidarity continuum also allows us to observe how perspectives may be historically, regionally, and temporally specific. While Pete Saldana grew up identifying as White in 1940s New Mexico, today in La Puente he adamantly declares that he is "not White." Similarly, as a pre-teenager, David Galvez ridiculed immigrants and disassociated from La Puente, the Spanish language, Mexican music, and Mexican food. After attending college during the student activism of the 1990s and enrolling in Chicana/o studies courses, he is now a La Puente teacher and self-described "advocate" for immigrants.

Just as the continuum captures the oftentimes fluid attitudes of Mexican

Americans, it also allows for the range of perspectives within the Mexican-origin community. Thus, while some may express intra-ethnic conflict, along the solidarity-end of the continuum we find the formation of Mexican American–Mexican immigrant political alliances. In particular, when certain institutional forces such as the threats of school consolidation and of the elimination of bilingual education were imposed on the Latina/o community, Mexican Americans and immigrants mobilized in Puente Parents and Parents for Quality Education.

Adopting a Power-Conflict Perspective

Because of this fluidity and variation of perspectives, the possibility exists that people can change. As we heard from several individuals, this possibility is heightened with the adoption of a power-conflict perspective that may emerge from various experiences and observations, including patterns of discrimination, access to an empowering education, or involvement in political struggles. Such change is exemplified in Rita Lopez Tellez' narrative of a period when she distanced herself from Mexican immigrants to avoid being associated with the negative stereotypes that she had accepted of them. However, as a result of the anti-immigrant sentiment surrounding Proposition 187, she became increasingly aware of the struggles Mexican Americans and Mexican immigrants share. This awareness solidified her adoption of a power-conflict perspective that fostered for her a macrostructural analysis of inequality. She now sees herself connected to immigrants and links the struggles faced by immigrants with those encountered by women, gays, and lesbians. Thus, the conflict-solidarity continuum captures the changes in perceptions of self and society that may occur over an individual's lifetime.

Narratives such as Rita Lopez Tellez recounts indicate how the acceptance of various ideologies might also influence people's perceptions of immigrants. While we have seen how the prevailing ideology of assimilation may foster intra-ethnic tension, Rita's experiences indicate how a power-conflict worldview can enhance cross-generational connections as well as political consciousness and a commitment to social justice.

Knowledge of the historical and macrostructural factors and ideologies influencing the Mexican-origin community may improve cross-racial/ethnic relations as well as intra-ethnic relationships. As sociologist C. Wright Mills (1959) has argued, greater awareness of historical continuities and differences and the relationships between social issues and personal lives better enables us to recognize problems, to create solutions, and to bring about change. By highlighting the historical and macrostructural factors influencing Latinas/os and African Americans, the organizers of Puente Parents illustrate how such awareness can strengthen cross-racial/ethnic understanding and connections and may set the stage for future acts of mobilization.

Long-term Immigrants and Women Making Connections

Though more work in this area is needed, this study suggests the critical role that long-term immigrants and women in particular may have in intra-ethnic solidarity. While the experiences and voices of Mexican Americans have been the focus of this book, interesting patterns emerged among some of the Mexican immigrant respondents regarding community building. As evidenced by Puente Parents and Parents for Quality Education, four of the six organizers of these two groups are long-term Mexican immigrants. Their narratives suggest that they were effectively able to draw on their experiences and Spanish-English bilingual skills to bring together Mexican Americans and Mexican immigrants in their struggle to maintain bilingual education. Thus, as Roberto Delgado describes it, having "walked in their shoes" may strategically position long-term Mexican immigrants in positions to foster cross-generational connections. Having gone through the processes of settlement and adjustment in a new country and with experiences in U.S. institutions, they may be able to create, maintain, or strengthen the bridges by which Mexican Americans and Mexican immigrants are becoming neighbors.

Likewise, this study reveals how men and women are perceiving and constructing intra-ethnic relations in their homes, schools, churches, supermarkets, and communities. Since it is often women who are actively engaged in these arenas, they have much to say about the changes that they are observing and how they are negotiating such shifts. As I was talking informally to a retired La Puente resident about the city, he told me rather abruptly, "You should talk to my wife. All of those years while I was working outside of La Puente, my wife was taking the kids and grandkids to school. She was participating in the church and doing the shopping." While women in La Puente may also work elsewhere and La Puente men also work within the city, it is generally women who are responsible for the reproductive labor that may bring them into community sites and into greater contact with their neighbors. The analysis of the philosophies and activities of Puente Parents and Parents for Quality Education provides additional insight into how women are using their gendered responsibilities and networks to mobilize the community in different ways than some of the male organizers.

Restructuring Institutions and Communities

As this work illustrates, exclusionary practices and ideologies negatively impact attitudes, interactions, and experiences. Therefore, work needs to be done on contesting and eliminating such practices and beliefs. While this may be more difficult to do at the state level, strategies may be employed in La Puente and in other communities to foster cooperation and community building. Since the school system was an issue of concern raised by many respondents, most of the following recommendations focus on this institution. However, the overall emphasis on a redistribution of power and a remaking of institutions that are characterized not by hierarchical divisions but by inclusion and collaboration may be applied to other arenas as well.

As community organizers argue, within the Hacienda–La Puente Unified School District, steps must be taken to achieve a more representative and equitable school board. As of yet, La Puente residents and the community's interests are not sufficiently represented by school board members and district officials. Four of the five school board members continue to reside in Hacienda Heights. Thus, the situation remains that many who are affected by school policies are excluded from the processes that determine and result in the implementation of school practices. Though La Puente residents have organized against such disparities, the need for institutional changes persists. Such alterations might involve allowing all community residents to vote regardless of citizenship status and establishing proportional representation on the school board.

In addition, to offset the class, racial/ethnic, generational, and community imbalance at the school-district level and what some describe as the top-down approach employed by school, city, and church officials, greater attempts need to be made to collaborate with community residents. Developing more opportunities for community participation and input would involve conducting bilingual community meetings in accessible places. Such meetings should be scheduled regularly and not simply implemented when officials wish to gain the support of residents for already determined actions or policies (as parents perceived to be the case with school consolidation and bilingual education). Also, since access to space has been a major concern for community organizers, school and city buildings need to be redefined and constructed as community institutions and spaces that are open to residents. Although we see some individuals committed to this process, they often are working within spheres that are dictated and controlled by district policies or administrative influences. For example, school principal Denise Villarreal is working with teachers to re-envision the classroom space as an area open to students and parents, but members of Puente Parents who initially convened meetings in a school cafeteria experienced the repercussions of a school district that was "threatened" by parents organizing outside of the traditional parameters. Thus, one of the hurdles that Puente Parents consistently had to contend with was finding a space where they could meet to address community concerns while still maintaining their autonomy.

At the institutional level, increasing the number of Spanish-speaking, Mexican American, and Mexican immigrant institutional representatives and restructuring social arenas may lead to increased feelings of cooperation and inclusivity among all community residents. The aggressive movement in some areas to hire bilingual personnel to meet the needs of the growing Latina/o and Asian American populations is one step that may be taken. Such actions may prevent the repetition of exchanges like the one documented in Chapter 3 in which a postal worker belittled and ignored a Spanish-speaking customer.

The experiences and perspectives of a significant number of La Puente school administrators and teachers do not reflect those of the residents of the largely Latina/o and working-class community. As education scholars have documented, racial/ethnic backgrounds of teachers and their cultural knowledge may influence the educational experiences of students (see Sleeter 1993; Shannon 1996; Galguera 1998; Valenzuela 1999). Since teachers tend to enter the classroom with their own presuppositions of race/ethnicity based on their experiences, White teachers may be more inclined to articulate a "color-blind" or power-evasive approach to race (Sleeter 1993). While such an approach may be a reaction to earlier essentialist views that inaccurately linked racial differences and group position to biology (Frankenberg 1993), trying not to see or claiming not to see what exists in a racially stratified and race-conscious society can make one unaware of the significance of race/ethnicity in shaping life chances (Sleeter 1993). By failing to consider the larger societal factors that affect peoples' lives differently depending on their social locations, this power-evasive approach may lead some teachers to blame groups of color for their positions in society and to reinforce the prevailing notions of rugged individualism and meritocracy (Frankenberg 1993; Sleeter 1993; McIntosh 1995).

As well as being unaware of the structural constraints students may encounter, teachers may also be unfamiliar with the cultural practices of the students, families, and communities with which they are working. Within the classroom, this may result in teachers who emphasize speaking English and assimilating, as we heard from the La Puente–area fourth-grader whose teacher yelled, "In this class, you will speak English. This is America. If you want to speak Spanish, go back to where you come from." Focusing on Mexican-origin high school students, Valenzuela (1999) argues that "as long as those in charge [of schools] are neither themselves bilingual nor educated on the needs of either Spanish-dominant or culturally marginal, Mexican American youth, schooling will continue to subtract resources from them" (256). To the extent that school policies and teachers' practices advocate assimilation, denigrate the practices and knowledge of communities of color, and perpetuate the power-evasive ideology, the educational and life experiences of individuals of Mexican descent will be negatively affected. The narratives of respondents across age groups show us how school policies and practices of assimilation constrain Mexican American–Mexican immigrant relations among youth as well as adults.

While merely placing members of the Mexican-origin community into relative positions of power may not necessarily change how various institutions are run, it can have a positive impact. Studies indicate that Latina/o students prefer Latina/o teachers and favor teachers whose language choice parallels their own (Galguera 1999). As evidenced by the descriptions of the Mexican American teachers and principals portrayed in this book, their shared working-class origins and race/ethnicity can enable them to make critical connections with parents and students. They are also facilitating the incorporation of immigrants through speaking Spanish or creating a comfortable classroom or school environment for students and parents. Actions such as these can be an important step toward challenging assimilationist practices that can be divisive and have often denigrated Mexicanness and speaking Spanish.

In particular, we find that school officials who are knowledgeable of the experiences of the Mexican-origin community are integrating historical and contemporary analyses of Latinas/os into their course curriculum and classroom discussions. Instruction in Chicana/o studies has provided these school officials with the skills to challenge shortcomings in their own primary and secondary educations that focused on assimilation, lacked an emphasis on developing critical thinking skills, and neglected discussions of identity, power, class, and political activism. As revealed by those who have completed Chicana/o studies courses, to the extent that teachers provide students with critical thinking skills, access to multiple forms of knowledge, and course curriculum that is grounded in discussions of diversity and power, there exists the potential for producing politically conscious students who will have the knowledge to make cross-racial/ethnic connections on the basis of historical and structural commonalities.

As is apparent throughout this work, access to quality multiracial/ethnic education is critical for developing a positive sense of self and of others. For one salient example, with Spanish as the second most common language in the United States and the one most used in the Western Hemisphere, rather than advocating English only, all would benefit if the United States embraced teaching Spanish and additional languages in schools (J. Gonzalez 2000, 272). Most respondents remember educational experiences that stressed learning English and acquiring Anglo and middle-class values, traditions, and expectations. Through their voices, we are made aware of the impacts that language repression and other assimilating experiences have had on previous generations' sense of self and their perspectives of Mexican immigrants. A school environment and society that are not premised on assimilation—and that instead respect the cultural integrity of diverse groups encourage bilingualism and multilingualism, teach multiple and intersecting histories, and deconstruct power and inequality—enable cross-generational and cross-racial/ethnic connections.

Unfortunately, with the growing pressure on improving standardized test scores and the emphasis on teaching through phonics rather than on whole-language development, schools, teachers, and students are becoming increasingly stifled. As teachers are encouraged to "teach to the test," more classroom time is spent in activities in preparation for tests and in skills that stress rote memorization—thereby limiting classroom opportunities for discussion and activities that may foster greater critical thinking, active engagement, and political awareness.

Finally, individuals and institutions must acknowledge the diversity of identities, attitudes, and experiences within the Mexican-origin community. This includes considering the relative forms of privilege and subordination which individuals within the Mexican-origin community may experience because of their differing social locations (such as generation, gender, and class position) in the United States. Connected with this recommendation is the need to place individual attitudes and experiences within a historical and macrostructural context. Thus, a space needs to be created where Mexican Americans and Mexican immigrants can discuss their similarities and differences and their underlying causes. Discussions should also include other Latina/o groups, the growing Asian American communities, Whites, and African Americans. Community activists as well as institutional representatives can provide the arena to discuss such issues through community meetings and school forums.

Overall, the processes of becoming neighbors are multifaceted, complex, situational, and being negotiated. While individuals are actively engaged in activities that are facilitating this process, as those who articulate a power-conflict perspective argue, becoming neighbors involves more than cultural appreciation and "getting along." It requires deconstructing dominant ideologies, restructuring community arenas, and redistributing power to allow for coming together in a manner not constrained or structured by hierarchical relationships.

To the extent that people are involved individually and collectively in challenging exclusionary practices and ideologies, there remains the potential for not only becoming neighbors but also for becoming politically engaged. Organizer Joaquin Macias powerfully articulates the possibilities: "There's going to be political awareness, political participation, and political competition." It is this politicizing process and potential for change that provide some with hope for the future.

Appendix

The Politics of Research

It is November 1997—La Puente's annual 5K run. The mainly Latina/o runners have just completed the hardest mile of the race. We are greeted by community residents who have risen early this Sunday morning. Standing in front of their homes, they cheer us on—"Come on. Good job. Keep going. ¡Vamos! ¡Vamos! ¡Andale! ¡Andale!" From the group of runners, we hear someone yell, "Speak in English. This is America." Suddenly I hear myself respond, "This is La Puente. We speak in Spanish and in English." My heart beats faster, and I run ahead.

FIELD NOTES, November 1997

Feminists, scholars of color, and progressives have extensively critiqued the assumptions underlying traditional social science methodological approaches that assert that scholars should maintain distance and a "value-free" stance from their research topics and the people being studied (hooks 1989; Collins 1990; Frankenberg 1993). Such critics have argued that research questions, research design, data collection, analysis, and conclusions are influenced by a researcher's social location and his or her views of the world as a raced, classed, and gendered individual. Thus, all research, whether explicitly stated or not, is based on political perspectives and political decisions (Nyden et al. 1999). There is no "disinterested position to be adopted in scholarship" (Frankenberg 1993, 30). Also, maintaining distance may reinforce power differentials and objectify individuals and communities (hooks 1989; Collins 1990). As with other forms of research, certain politics are involved in conducting a qualitative study of a working-class community of color (Baca Zinn 1979; Zavella 1987; Blea 1995). As a self-identified Latina, a bi-ethnic Nicaraguan and Italian-American woman, born in La Puente and raised in a lower-middle-class household doing research in a predominantly working-class, Mexican-origin community, it has been important to reflect both on the research process and my own position.

As a feminist and Chicana/o studies scholar concerned with achieving social justice, I was not a neutral researcher. I agreed with many of the issues raised by parents regarding the quality of schools and the unequal power dynamics of a Hacienda Heights–controlled school board that does not sufficiently represent the entire school district. When the decision to eliminate bilingual education arose, I, like many vocal residents, raised my concerns. I assisted in some of these struggles by speaking at a school board meeting in support of La Puente parents and teachers and by supporting progressive candidates with their campaigns for City Council and the school board.

As I reflect on the relationships between my identity and experiences and the research process, my position as a simultaneous insider and outsider among the Mexican-origin community in La Puente appears most salient. Though I spent the early years of my life in La Puente and am currently living in the city, I was raised primarily in Hacienda Heights, often referred to by La Puente residents as "the other side" (of the tracks). When people hear that I attended Glen A. Wilson High School, they often reply with a simple "Oh" and a roll of their eyes—indicating to me that they too are aware of the inequality in resources between La Puente–area and Hacienda Heights schools. Thus, class and racial differences between the two communities combined with my current educational background clearly mark my class privileges.

Despite differences in community, educational, and racial/ethnic background, a few individuals shared with me how other factors of my identity and experience were helpful in the research process. Knowing that I am Latina, that I live in La Puente, that I was interested in doing a study on the city, and that my mother has taught middle school students in La Puente for nearly thirty years seemed to facilitate the research process. Also, the fact that many of the people whom I interviewed were recommended by other respondents was helpful. Thus, before the actual interviews, individuals were already familiar with my work, and they expressed an interest in participating.

Since I was interviewing people on group attitudes and interactions, I attempted to present as open-minded an image as possible by attentively listening to people, encouraging them to ask me questions, and honestly revealing aspects of myself. At most times during the interview, this was easy. However, in situations where individuals revealed experiences of discrimination or their own prejudiced views, it was difficult not to be affected. I could not have remained expressionless or emotionless when people shared personal experiences of discrimination or abuse. I could understand much of the pain, frustration, and anger they shared with me, and on a professional level to have remained aloof likewise would have been unconscionable—it would not have been conducive to relationship-building or supportive of my feminist principles. When some made prejudiced statements or expressed rather exclusionary attitudes, I tried to keep their perspectives in context, to understand the whole person, and to keep in mind their experiences and the ways ideological processes and structural factors have influenced our beliefs. It is my hope that people's attitudes are contextualized in this way throughout the book.

As with those who shared their life experiences with me, my experiences and perspective also have been influenced by my upbringing, by discrimination, and by pressure to assimilate. In particular, my relationship with the Spanish language is complex and in some ways parallels the experiences of some of the people I interviewed. While my mother was a Spanish major in college and is a fluent Spanish-speaker, my father, whose first language was Spanish, strongly supported the common sentiment of the time that English was the first language that my brother and I should learn. His beliefs were influenced by the dominant emphasis on assimilation and by his attempts to shield us from the color and language discrimination that he encountered. Thus, Spanish was only spoken in our home when our parents wanted to conceal something. However, during weekly visits with my paternal grandparents, I sat quietly listening as my family reminisced about and discussed events occurring in Nicaragua, sharing stories, and enjoying one another's company all in Spanish. Interacting with my Spanish-speaking grandmother, I became very adept at understanding her Spanish and responding in English. While I have employed various mechanisms to acquire the language, as those presented in this book testify about their own lives, it has been a difficult process at multiple levels.

People seemed to respond to me and my work in a range of ways. For example, a couple of school officials emphasized how they were glad to see a Latina working on a Ph.D. These same individuals described how they revealed material to me that they had not shared with others. Despite the candidness of some, a few were more reluctant to disclose information. This tended to be the case with some individuals who held public offices whose public position may have made them more leery.

While the amount of personal contact I had with the La Puente residents and institutional representatives tended to be limited to the interviews, my contact with community organizers has been more frequent. It generally involved the interview, multiple meetings (both in their homes and mine), informal interactions at city and school events, and phone conversations. Nevertheless, establishing rapport with a few of the community organizers involved a somewhat different process. Initially, I was not sure if I was being "tested" to determine the extent to which I was committed to the issues and concerns that organizers were addressing or if I was being educated on critical community issues. For example, following a meeting by a group of community organizers, I was asked to accompany a parent to a hearing at the HLPUSD regarding the possible suspension of her elementary school-age son. As one of the longtime community leaders was already attending the hearing as a Spanish-English translator, I was unsure of my role. Before the actual morning of the hearing, I believed that the community organizers were interested in learning my willingness to ally with them in cases against the school district. However, as I observed the interaction of school district administrators, the parent, and the organizer, I began to realize that I was not being "tested" but educated. Some La Puente residents have spent years and even decades struggling with institutional representatives in the school district trying to ensure that children in La Puente receive quality educations, that Latina/o parents are respected, and that community concerns are addressed. It was clear that community organizers wanted me, a relative newcomer to the city's politics, to see firsthand the attitudes and behaviors of some of the district personnel and the issues that residents were attempting to overcome. Following this hearing, as my research progressed and I have spent more time in La Puente, I have been moving from an observer at meetings with community leaders to a participant, a community member, and someone who is becoming more involved in community affairs.

Notes

Chapter 1

1. While almost all said they did not mind if their names were used, to ensure their privacy and the privacy of their family members, respondents' names have been changed. The name changes were either provided by the participants or selected to approximate the racial/ethnic ancestry of individuals' actual names. Quotations here and throughout this work are typically used to indicate that these are the sentences, phrases, and words used by the participants in this study.

2. Out of awareness of the politics of racial and ethnic labels, this work uses the terms most often employed by the people I interviewed. "Mexican American" is used when referring to Mexicans born in the United States, and "Mexican immigrants," "Mexicanas," and "Mexicanos" are used when referring to people born in Mexico who are currently living in the United States. "Mexican," "Mexican-origin," and "Mexican descent" are used to refer to both Mexican Americans and Mexican immigrants. Though used less frequently by the individuals included in this work, "Latina/o" refers to anyone of Latin American descent.

3. Throughout this book, I use the term "race/ethnicity" to best capture the experiences of the Mexican-origin population in the United States. I use race/ethnicity not to conflate race and ethnicity but instead to acknowledge that they are two interrelated systems that have worked together in ways that shape the life chances and experiences of the Mexican-origin community. While Mexican Americans are usually discussed as an ethnic group that shares cultural characteristics, in the United States they have been racialized and socially constructed as distinct from European Americans both racially and ethnically.

4. With a realization that all racial/ethnic labels are political, camouflage diversity, and vary geographically, historically, and situationally, I use the terms and definitions typically used in public and academic discourse. Therefore, throughout this work, I use the terms "Asian American," "African American" or "Black," and "White" or "Anglo" (these last two terms are used when referring to non-Latina/o whites of European descent). As a group, Whites in the United States historically and contemporarily have

been located on top of the socially constructed racial hierarchy and have been granted the privileges that accrue to their light skin. However, within this category is much variation. In the United States, preferential treatment often has been given to individuals, traditions, languages, values, and so forth from Northern Europe as opposed to those who trace their ancestry from Southern and Eastern Europe. Thus, in recognition of this cultural hierarchy that has existed among Whites and cultures within Europe, I use the term "Anglo" occasionally in this study and particularly when discussing the values, traditions, and expectations that are deemed superior in the United States. I also use "Anglo" when presenting historical information on the White population before the large migration of Southern and Eastern Europeans who were initially not thought of as White (Brodkin 2000).

5. Proposition 227 mandates that all children in California public schools be taught in English. Parents or legal guardians may apply for (but are not guaranteed) a waiver for their child to participate in bilingual education.

6. In a review of *At the Crossroads: Mexico and U.S. Immigration Policy,* edited by Bean, de la Garza, Roberts, and Weintraub (1997), Vila (1998) argues that there is a striking omission of a discussion of intra-ethnic attitudes of anti-Mexican sentiment. He argues that this absence is significant, given current indications of support from Latinas/os for limiting undocumented immigration and to eliminate social services to undocumented residents in California.

7. Throughout this work, I use the term "intra-ethnic relations" to refer broadly to the relationships within the heterogeneous Mexican-origin population. I occasionally use the terms "cross-generational relations" and "inter-generational relations" to highlight the relationships that exist across generations in the United States, particularly between Mexican Americans and Mexican immigrants.

8. A couple of respondents from the neighboring largely Mexican-origin, working-class community and unincorporated area of Valinda also are included in this study. Racially/ethnically and in terms of class position, many areas of Valinda and La Puente are not distinct, and some Valinda residents share resources and material conditions with La Puente residents. Given the school district boundaries, for example, some Valinda residents attend schools with La Puente residents in the Hacienda–La Puente Unified School District.

9. Unlike quantitative research that emphasizes surveying large random samples of the population, this is not the intent of qualitative research. The aim of qualitative research is to provide detailed, in-depth, and nuanced understandings of the issues being explored, to get at members' meanings (Seidman 1991). Due to the emphasis on detail and depth in the data collection process, qualitative research relies on far fewer cases and on more variables (Hakim 1987, 27; Creswell 1998, 15–16). Saturation is an important criterion that is used by qualitative researchers to know when to stop collecting interviews. When no new information emerges from interviews and the interviewer begins to hear the same themes and issues, this is the point of saturation, and the period when the data collection process is usually ended (Seidman 1991, 45).

10. While I completed the English interviews, a second interviewer conducted the interviews in Spanish. Given the focus of this research, I felt that Spanish-speaking indi-

viduals would be more likely to discuss their attitudes and experiences with individuals who are equally fluent in the language. As it turned out, I interviewed all of the respondents who are Mexican American and are long-term immigrants (individuals who have spent the majority of their lives in the United States).

11. As is typical in qualitative research, this study draws extensively from respondents' interviews (see Creswell 1998). The use of respondents' quotes throughout this book serves three main purposes: to illustrate key patterns, to allow readers to come to their own conclusions, and to center the voices of the individuals included in this work.

12. My familial ties and knowledge of the area were helpful in designing this study. As a longtime resident born and raised in the area, I moved back to La Puente in the 1990s while beginning this research. This is the same city where my own family had settled. My maternal grandparents, aunts, and mother moved from New York to La Puente in 1960, and my father, uncle, aunt, and paternal grandparents left Nicaragua and came to the city in 1956. When my parents were able to purchase a home in the 1970s, we moved to the neighboring unincorporated area of Hacienda Heights. We maintained close contact with La Puente through our weekly visits with family members and my mother's work at a La Puente middle school. During college I remained connected to my hometown through my weekend stays. While completing graduate school, I moved back to La Puente and have been living in the city since 1995.

As a result of personal ties and my own connection with the community, I established relationships with several individuals including teachers and residents. From these initial interviews I relied on techniques commonly used by qualitative researchers—snowball sampling and referrals—to obtain as diverse a nonrandom sample of participants as possible. I began by soliciting names of potential respondents from several residents who differed by age, occupation, educational background, and race/ethnicity. In this way I was introduced to several different networks, increasing the possibility that I would meet a range of La Puente residents. Following each interview, I asked people to recommend individuals I might contact. In addition, through my participant observations at various community meetings, I met and interviewed several La Puente residents involved in city and school affairs.

13. The two other school districts in the La Puente area that are not studied in this work are the Basset Unified School District and the Rowland Unified School District. While some La Puente students attend schools in these two districts, they primarily serve students in the unincorporated areas of Basset and in the city of Rowland Heights.

14. Latina/o youth leave high school without a diploma twice as often as White students do (Romo and Falbo 1996, 1). As a whole, 61 percent of Latinas/os finish high school; two out of every five Latina/o students do not (Della Piana 1999, 11).

15. Throughout the book, the terms "structural factors" and "structural constraints" are used to refer broadly to economic conditions, institutional inequality, and discrimination. "Cultural factors" refers here primarily to language, but it also encompasses religion, values, norms, traditions, and symbols. As will be discussed in greater detail in Chapter 2, the term "ideological processes" is used as an umbrella term to refer to the systems of beliefs that have maintained, shaped, and/or reproduced racial/ethnic relations. Of particular consideration for the Mexican-origin community are the prevail-

ing ideologies of assimilation and Anglo superiority or white supremacy. These dominant ideologies have had a significant role in influencing Mexican American–Mexican immigrant relationships. Occasionally, the term "external factors and processes" will be used in reference to both structural factors and ideological processes.

Chapter 2

1. In particular, I draw from the work of Frankenberg (1993) and her use of Omi and Winant's (1986 first edition) stages in the scholarship and discourse on race/ethnicity. Frankenberg equates the assimilationist paradigm to what she refers to as "color evasiveness" and "power evasiveness." One aspect of a power-conflict approach that she highlights is "race cognizance." She uses these approaches to understand how White women conceptualize and think through race (Frankenberg 1993, 14–16).

2. The phrase "becoming American" is used here to refer to the adoption of the English language and dominant middle-class and Anglo American values and traditions. Quotations are used to illustrate that this is a phrase articulated by a few of the people I interviewed and to indicate that the idea of "becoming American" is a social construct based on narrow conceptualizations of what it means to be "American."

3. By connecting respondents' worldviews to these differing perspectives, my intent is not to simply present a dichotomized image that respondents articulated one or the other perspective. Rather, it is to illustrate how such popular paradigms are influencing race/ethnic relations. As will be apparent in Chapters 5 and 6, there are examples of individuals who express multiple beliefs and attitudes that demonstrate both perspectives.

4. As Omi and Winant (1994) have described, prior to the 1930s the ethnicity-based paradigm (from which the assimilationist approach would emerge) was an "insurgent approach" that directly challenged biological determinist approaches that equated race with biology and assumed that non-Anglos were biologically inferior (Omi and Winant 1994, 14–16).

5. Because of the problematic equation of the term "color-blindness" with a physical disability, I prefer to use Frankenberg's concept of "power-evasiveness," which more accurately captures this dominant ideology.

6. While this increase may be attributed to the growth in the Latina/o population, Whites nonetheless continue to attend highly segregated schools in areas where the percentage of Latina/o students has increased (Orfield and Yun 1999, 31). More than 60 percent of White students still attend schools that have 90 to 100 percent White enrollment (Rojas and Gordon 1999, 10).

7. Milton Gordon (1961) describes "Americanization" as "a consciously articulated movement to strip the immigrant of his [her] native culture and attachments and make him [her] into an American along Anglo-Saxon lines—all this to be accomplished with great rapidity" (266).

8. One exception was the Confederación de Uniones Obreras Mexicanas (CUOM), which was established in 1938. It rejected notions of assimilation, endorsed the rights of immigrants, and emphasized enthnocultural and class solidarity among the Mexican-origin community (Gutiérrez 1995; Ruiz 1998; G. Gonzalez 1999).

9. Orozco (1992) documents that the Mexican American middle class was not equivalent to the European American middle class. Most of the former were first-generation middle class from working-class families.

10. Historian David Gutiérrez (1995) notes that during the Depression years, common sentiment among LULAC leaders was that Anglos' negative views toward Mexican immigrants, not the persistence of racism and structural inequality, was the cause of Mexican American discrimination. Thus, they believed it important to distinguish between Mexican American citizens and Mexican immigrants, to work toward the interests of Mexican American citizens, and to raise public awareness that Mexican Americans are Americans. Historian Cynthia Orozco (1992) argues that while LULAC was acting within a particular time period and from a middle-class and masculinist perspective, its anti-racist activism was nonetheless beneficial for the entire Mexican-origin community. Furthermore, she illustrates that the social distance between Mexican Americans and Mexican immigrants was not as stark as some of the ideas and philosophies that appeared in LULAC's documents. For example, responding to community needs, women involved in LULAC engaged in grassroots activities to assist immigrant and U.S.-born Mexicans (see also Ruiz 1998).

11. According to Menchaca, there are also distinctions among Chicanas/os and immigrants, and ethnic labels differentiate among "old families," "new Chicanas/os," "old immigrants," and "new immigrants" (Menchaca 1989, 220).

Chapter 3

1. Fifty-nine percent and 71 percent of voters in La Puente opposed Propositions 187 and 209, respectively (Los Angeles County 1994, 1996).

2. Rowland was born in Maryland in 1791 and Workman in Westmoreland, England, in 1802. They met in Taos, New Mexico, where they became business partners (Sandoval 1994).

3. In contrast to the daughters of working-class Mexican and Native American families, European Americans tended to deem the daughters of the elite Californio families as worthy of marriage. Marriages to such wealthy women strengthened the economic and political opportunities of Anglo families (Almaguer 1994).

4. After receiving the requisite approval of priests, Rowland took the Workman-Rowland land grant application to the governor of Alta California, Juan Bautista Alvardo in Monterey, who had the power to distribute land grants. While the governor initially wavered on the distribution, Rowland explained that he was carrying one thousand dollars in gold that he was prepared to pay to the governor for back taxes and for assessments of the land. When the governor heard this, John Rowland and William Workman's application for a Rancho La Puente was accepted, and they were granted the 48,790.55 acres of land (McIntosh 1960, 1; La Puente Valley Historical Society 1976, 9–10).

5. Since limited scholarship exists on Rancho La Puente outside of the material on the Rowland and Workman families, it is difficult to determine the occupations of the Mexican-origin population who lived and worked in the area. However, as was the case in Santa Barbara during the rancho period, Mexican mestizos usually con-

stituted the small skilled working class of foremen, vaqueros, craftsmen, and black-smiths (Camarillo 1979, 12).

6. At this time, Rancho La Puente became known simply as Puente. In 1956 the city was incorporated as La Puente (informal interview with a member of La Puente Valley Historical Society, June 6, 2002).

7. Until its closing in 1947, La Puente had the largest walnut-packing plant in the world (La Puente Valley Historical Society n.d.).

8. To assist during the walnut season, day laborers, including children, also were re-cruited from more established communities such as East Los Angeles (Fields and Guerrero 1978).

9. From the little material mentioned on the Japanese in Puente during this period, it ap-pears that they played an important role in the agricultural trucking industry and in farming strawberries and grapes (Andriesse 1987; Sandoval 1994; personal interview with Cecelia Lower Wictor, January 11, 2001). Some Spanish-speaking individuals of Spanish and Basque descent were also encouraged or required to attend Central Ave-nue (Sandoval 1994; Wictor interview 2001).

10. As Lucas (n.d.) describes, "Of the 66 graduates, 36 have been boys and 30 girls; of those entering high school, 26 were boys and 19 girls; of the high school graduates . . . 10 have been boys and 9 girls" (7).

11. In 1957 a fire damaged the church, and it was demolished (*History of La Puente Valley California* 1960, 12).

12. A half-million Mexican Americans served in the armed forces during World War II (Takaki 1993, 393). In Los Angeles, Mexican Americans comprised one-tenth of the population but accounted for one-fifth of the casualties in the war (McWilliams 1990; Takaki 1993, 393).

13. Focusing on this time period, studies have found that as Mexican Americans moved geographically closer to Whites, they tended to select more Europeanized racial/ethnic labels (Vigil 1980).

14. As of the 1990 Census, 50 percent of the houses in La Puente had been built between 1950 and 1959. Seventy-seven percent of the houses were built between 1950 and 1969, making 1959 the median year when houses were built in the city.

15. For varying reasons, not all in Puente endorsed incorporation. For example, as San-doval (1994) notes, Jim Stafford, a wealthy rancher and real estate investor, opposed incorporation of Puente because of his "reliance on Mexican labor" (75). For a dis-cussion of the role of Stafford in the formation of the City of Industry and the Bank of Industry and his eventual arrest and imprisonment for "18 criminal charges, including fraud, obstruction of justice and conspiracy" see Valle and Torres (2000).

16. Such legislation included the 1964 Civil Rights Act, the 1965 Voting Rights Act, and the 1968 Federal Housing Act (Acuña 1998, 19).

17. Though critical of most of the school officials he came in contact with as a high school student, Francisco Delgado was quick to credit one school counselor for her attempts to offset the stereotypes and barriers Spanish-speaking students confronted.

18. This quote and the one preceding it were recorded in my field notes from an August 15, 1995, Planning Commission meeting regarding an ordinance amending the city code on domestic animals. The two comments were made by Latina/o La Puente residents.

19. Field notes, Planning Commission meeting on reviewing an application to subdivide one lot to build five condominium dwelling units, July 5, 1995. This comment was made by a White La Puente resident.

20. Information gathered from a November 14, 1995, Community Advisory Committee meeting organized by the County of Los Angeles Sheriff's Department on "illegal vendors."

21. Field notes, City Council meeting, July 24, 2001.

22. Lola Storing, the only non-Latina/o council member, was opposed to the bilingual newsletter, saying during the July 24, 2001, City Council meeting that it was biased against "the Oriental people that cannot read Spanish."

23. Field notes, City Council meetings, July 10 and 24, 2001.

24. Field notes, City Council meeting, June 27, 1995.

25. Informal interview with Mexican American La Puente–area resident, January 30, 2001.

26. Field notes, January 2001.

27. Ibid.

Chapter 4

1. As discussed in Chapter 2, in 1848 the Treaty of Guadalupe Hidalgo granted U.S. citizenship to Mexicans who decided to stay in the region. Though Mexicans were extended citizenship and legally defined as White, intra-group variation by color and class resulted in vastly different experiences. Thus, members of the working class were viewed and treated in ways similar to other racialized groups. Likewise, by the turn of the century, as Anglo speculators and developers took over the lands of wealthy Californios, many of these individuals also became a politically and economically powerless group (Camarillo 1979; Almaguer 1994).

2. The equation of Mexicanness with speaking Spanish may be more common among mestizo (Spanish and Indian) Latinas/os as opposed to indigenous Latina/o immigrants whose first language may not be Spanish.

3. Some scholars argue that due to the lack of visibility, Latinas/os are being "symbolically annihilated" by network news (C. Rodríguez 1997, 15).

4. This is a recurring pattern between unequals when those in power have fewer restrictions in terms of asking personal questions to those who are in positions under them (Goffman 1956; Rollins 1985).

5. A few of the self-identified Chicana/o respondents explained how more assimilated Mexican Americans as well as Whites may also react negatively to people who identify as Chicana/o.

6. Buriel (1987) and Tienda and Ortiz (1986) have also found this use of multiple terms

among Mexican Americans, and Hurtado and Arce (1987) and Gómez (1992) find that this variation often is linked to generation or to social situation.

7. Because difference from the socially constructed White norm is what is often marked, such patterns may be more apparent among those individuals who are Mexican and White. Among the respondents who identified as multiracial/ethnic, none indicated that he or she was Asian or Black.

8. David Galvez' and Geraldo Romero's criticisms of the educational system for the Mexican-origin community are reminiscent of the key issues raised by youth during the early years of the Chicano student movement. In the 1960s and 1970s, students argued for opening educational opportunities and establishing educational programs on Chicana/o history and experiences.

9. In opposition to the chancellor's decision not to create a department and to reduce funds to the Chicana/o campus library, David Galvez, as part of a newly created organization, Concerned Students of Color, participated in a rally that resulted in the take-over of the UCLA faculty center. David, along with ninety-eight other students, was arrested. The arrest of these students helped to strengthen campus and community support for the creation of a Chicano studies department. After students staged a two-week hunger strike and multiple demonstrations and gained support from local unions, grassroots activists, and elected officials, UCLA administrators agreed to the formation of the César Chávez Center for Interdisciplinary Instruction in Chicana and Chicano Studies (Acuña 1996).

Chapter 5

1. Focusing on the construction industry in Florida, Grenier et al. (1992) found that distance between groups of workers in Miami resulted from the division of labor and from spatial separation, both of them connected to a racial/ethnic hierarchy. In their study, African American and Haitian tradespeople are viewed as having the lowest prestige in the construction industry. In contrast, those trades requiring state licenses, such as electricians and plumbers, have the highest prestige, and a majority who hold those licenses are European American. Carpenters, who are primarily Latino, are in the middle of this hierarchy (850).

2. In her edited volume, Lamphere (1992) also observes how power within institutions often varies by immigrant status such that established residents typically "have de facto power over immigrants" (4).

3. In the La Puente–area schools of the Hacienda–La Puente Unified School District, 60 percent of all teachers were White and 24 percent were Latina/o during the 2000–2001 school year. This compared with the 88 percent of students who were Latina/o and 4 percent who were White (California Department of Education 2001a, 2001b).

4. My meeting with Erica Handel occurred before the passage of Proposition 227, which empowered the school district to severely limit bilingual education. Thus, the program she describes at her school is no longer in effect.

5. In 1997 and 1998, the movement to eliminate bilingual education in California reached a climax. Businessman Ron Unz proposed the elimination of bilingual education

through the California state initiative "English Language Education for Children in Public Schools," a campaign which he funded. The passage presented here appeared in one of Unz' letters soliciting support to include his initiative as a proposition on a statewide ballot.

6. When asked to discuss her interactions with and perceptions of immigrants, Rosario Jones handed me a newspaper clipping of a letter to the editor that she and her sister had submitted to a local newspaper.

7. Focusing on internalized racism, race and ethnicity scholars have discussed the concept of internalization for people of color (Harris and Ordoña 1990; Yamato 1991). Harris and Ordoña (1990) argue that as a result of a history of institutionalized racism, people of color have been instilled with the same racist and white supremacist values and attitudes that have oppressed them (314).

8. In "Assimilation in American Life" (1961), Gordon discusses three ideologies of ethnic assimilation. These include: Anglo-conformity, the melting pot thesis, and cultural pluralism. I use the ideology of Anglo-conformity to explain the attitudes and behaviors exemplified by some respondents.

9. This term was coined by Rodolfo Alvarez (1971) and also has been used by Mario García (1989).

10. As described by other respondents and based on personal observations, the Spanish-language masses tend to draw the most people. Due to the high attendance rate, the Catholic churches in La Puente and the surrounding communities have added additional Spanish masses.

11. Field notes taken from phone interview June 18, 2002, by Daniela Pineda with one of the original parishioners of the church. This parishioner met with other church volunteers to compile this list of priests. Since the last names of priests were used, the number of Latina/o priests is an estimate. It may include Spanish priests.

12. Other racial/ethnic groups likewise have disassociated themselves so as to avoid any racial/ethnic lumping that may result from being perceived as part of a particular group (Hayano 1981; Espiritu 1992; Waters 1999). For example, fearing that they would be mistaken for Chinese immigrants during Chinese exclusion in the late nineteenth century, Japanese immigrants distanced themselves by wearing American work clothes and eating American food (Ichioka 1988; Espiritu 1992). During World War II and the incarceration of many Japanese in the United States, people of Chinese, Korean, and Filipino ancestry, especially along the U.S. West Coast, wore buttons, made identification cards, and dressed in their regional clothing in an attempt to avoid being the targets of anti-Japanese activities (Takaki 1989; Espiritu 1992). More recently, West Indians have highlighted their ethnic status and cultural values to distance themselves from African Americans (Waters 1999).

13. This conception of immigrants as absolutely destitute is part of an image of "huddled masses" and a larger mythology that depicts immigration as a process that is fueled by poverty. This conception may not consider the historical and macrostructural processes of a history of U.S. recruitment, economic restructuring, and globalization that shapes and influences immigration. Moreover, contemporary studies find that because

of the cost of migration, it is usually not the most destitute who migrate (Portes and Rumbaut 1990). Instead, the socioeconomic backgrounds of Mexican immigrants are comparable to or surpass the country's average (Portes and Rumbaut 1990).

14. Through an analysis of exit-poll data in California in 1988, Schmid (1992) found that Latinas/os born before World War II were more likely to support language restrictions than were younger Latinas/os.

Chapter 6

1. For Roberta, learning Spanish through the "foreign language" model in high school and college was "a cinch," so she may believe that learning another language will be easy for others as well. Rather than beginning in elementary school by teaching students another language or strengthening the home languages with which students may enter school, this model typically begins in high school and often assumes that students have little or no prior experience with the language.

2. Though such patterns are not always the case, they highlight the inequality of a U.S. educational policy that may differentially encourage the acquisition and maintenance of Spanish. Such differential encouragement may vary by class position, by race/ethnicity, and by which language is being acquired. This may result in a situation of wealthy children encountering educational institutions and receiving societal messages that encourage them to learn another language and to study abroad, while the Spanish that working-class immigrants and second-generation Latinas/os may speak when they enter school is downgraded, perceived as a hindrance to their advancement, and replaced with English until they enter high school, where they can take it as a "foreign language" (Valenzuela 1999; Cummins 2000). Highlighting some of these inequalities, Tse (2001) notes that "the number of programs to help students develop their native language [in elementary school] is minuscule compared with the number allowing foreign-language participation" in middle and high school (56).

3. Although there is extensive literature on the significance of networks in facilitating immigration or as "catalysts for migration," as Menjívar (2000, 234) suggests, not all immigrants may have the resources to continue providing assistance to one another once they have settled in the United States.

4. Field notes taken June 18, 2002, from a phone interview by Daniela Pineda with one of the original parishioners of the church, and from the web page for the Archdiocese of Los Angeles (http://www.sgpr.org/).

5. Rates of academic performance for Latina/o students have been found to be higher in well-implemented bilingual educational programs than in English-only programs or in those that emphasize quickly moving students into English-only programs (Cummins 2000, 229). Likewise, studies on racial/ethnic identity also reveal positive correlations among racial/ethnic identification, academic success, and psychological adjustment for Latina/o students (Vasquez 1997, 457–458).

6. They do this through the use of one of two models—90/10 and 50/50, indicating the percentage of time spent on the two languages, in this case Spanish and English. As with other well-implemented bilingual education programs, dual-language immersion

programs have proven to be more effective scholastically than English-only programs or programs whose focus is not on creating bilingual or biliterate students (Cummins 2000).

7. Lindholm (1995) finds that "by third grade in the bilingual/immersion program, after only one academic year of reading instruction in English, bilingual students scored higher, but not significantly higher, than English-dominant students in language achievement, though equivalent in reading achievement. In addition, bilinguals outperformed the English-dominant and Spanish-dominant students in English math achievement and in Spanish reading achievement" (284).

8. For a discussion of "cultural tracking" and the differential course placement of English language learners see Valenzuela (1999, 31) and Mendoza-Denton (1999).

Chapter 7

1. Of the nearly 22,000 Valinda residents, 75 percent are Latina/o, 12 percent are White, 11 percent are Asian and Pacific Islander, 3 percent are African American, and 2 percent are Native American (U.S. Bureau of the Census 2001).

2. Formal and informal interviews with Wilson High School officials and Mexican American La Puente–area residents, 2001.

3. Advanced placement courses are described as "college-level classes," and students may earn college credits for these classes if they successfully pass specially designed examinations (Wilson High School 2001, 5).

4. While there are differences between schools in the La Puente area and in Hacienda Heights, students within each of the schools also have varied experiences. For example, observations at Wilson High School and interviews with school officials and students during the 2000–2001 school year suggest that while Latina/o students constitute about 38 percent of the student body, they make up 5 percent of the students enrolled in AP courses (Gilda Ochoa and Dianna Moreno, field notes). As scholars have observed elsewhere, in addition to being severely underrepresented in honors and AP classes, Latina/o students are extremely overrepresented in non–college preparatory classes (see Oakes 1985).

5. See Chapter 3 for a detailed description of La Puente's racial/ethnic composition.

6. In 1996 roughly 24 percent of "limited English proficient" students enrolled in public schools in California, and for 78 percent of them, Spanish was their primary language (Gouglas 1996a).

7. On March 11, 1969, the Hudson Elementary and La Puente Union High School Districts described in Chapter 3 were dissolved when residents voted for unification (Cochrane 1969, 1). Unification entailed combining the educational programs for kindergarten through twelfth grade under one board of directors. The school district that has served the majority of La Puente residents since 1970 is the Hacienda–La Puente Unified School District.

8. The OCR found that the school district was in violation of two of the complaints filed by the parents. First, the OCR found that due to a lack of translation services at the

school board meetings, Spanish-speaking parents were prevented from fully participating in public meetings. This violation was seen as a "denial of equal educational opportunity" to the students of Spanish-speaking parents. Second, the OCR found that a significant number of limited English proficient (LEP) students were not being adequately served, partly because of a "profound shortage" of instructional personnel trained to teach LEP students. The school district was also lacking "sufficient quantities of texts and other instructional materials designed for LEP students." Finally, the district was not "implementing a consistently applied system for the redesignation of students from LEP to fully English proficient (FEP)" (U.S. Department of Education 1993).

9. Informal interview, May 2001.

10. The decision to conduct meetings in Spanish was a complex one. On the one hand, as we saw in the previous chapter, creating spaces where the Spanish language flourishes may be seen as a form of resistance, an act that challenges assimilationist expectations and English-only movements. However, since not all La Puente residents speak Spanish, a couple of parents who attended the group's first few meetings expressed concern about conducting the meeting solely in Spanish. Puente Parents organizers explain that conducting meetings in Spanish was important for mobilizing a population that has been disenfranchised, especially in light of public antagonism toward immigrants and toward the use of Spanish. Such meetings were also effective in uniting Spanish-speaking residents as well as fostering a sense of belonging and ownership in the city, key goals of Puente Parents organizers.

11. This event received much notoriety because it was videotaped and aired multiple times on prime-time television in both English and Spanish.

12. In the November 2001 Hacienda–La Puente Unified School Board elections, members of Puente Parents ran their own candidate. While their candidate was endorsed by several area teachers, professors, elected officials, businesses, community organizers, and residents, the three incumbents on the school board were reelected.

13. "Reproductive labor" includes but is not limited to buying and preparing food and clothing, providing emotional support, care, nurturance, and socialization for family members, maintaining and transmitting culture, and maintaining family and community connections (Dill 1994, 167; Baca Zinn 1994, 308; Glenn 1992).

14. HLPUSD encompasses La Puente, Hacienda Heights, Valinda, and Rowland Heights.

15. In June 1996 organizers from Parents for Quality Education and Puente Parents were interviewed on KPFK's *En Foco Latino* program.

16. This perception was made explicit when on August 28, 1995, a state district judge threatened a Texas woman with losing custody of her five-year-old daughter if the mother did not speak to the child in English (J. Gonzalez 2000, 206).

17. During fall 2001 Raquel Heinrich was working with a group of La Puente–area parents to improve the high school drama department. The department lacked resources, and the school's theater—having been used for several years for school detention—needed repair. In November more than a dozen parents met with the school's drama teacher at Raquel's home. As in previous meetings, Raquel provided food (beans,

chips, salsa, and chapurrado, a drink). Though Irene Renteria-Salazar's children still attended middle school and she had a new job that required long hours, she attended the meeting to demonstrate her support (field notes, November 8, 2001).

18. Valenzuela (1999) also suggests that long-term immigrants, particularly those who migrated to the United States as children, may be able to build alliances with Mexican Americans and with Mexican immigrants. Focusing on youth, she attributes these possibilities to fluency in two languages and to experiences in U.S. schools (201).

References

Acuña, Rodolfo F. 1988. *Occupied America: A History of Chicanos*. New York: Harper and Row.

———. 1996. *Anything but Mexican: Chicanos in Contemporary Los Angeles*. London: Verso.

———. 1998. *Sometimes There Is No Other Side: Chicanos and the Myth of Equality*. Notre Dame, Ind., and London: University of Notre Dame Press.

Ainslie, Ricardo C. 1998. "Cultural Mourning, Immigration, and Engagement: Vignettes from the Mexican Experience." In *Crossings: Mexican Immigration in Interdisciplinary Perspectives*, ed. Marcelo M. Suárez-Orozco, 285–305. Cambridge, Mass.: Harvard University Press.

Alba, Richard. 1990. *Ethnicity in America: The Transformation of White America*. New Haven, Conn.: Yale University Press.

Almaguer, Tomás. 1994. *Racial Fault Lines: The Historical Origins of White Supremacy in California*. Berkeley: University of California Press.

Alvarez, Michael R., and Tara L. Butterfield. 2000. "The Resurgence of Nativism in California? The Case of Proposition 187 and Illegal Immigration." *Social Science Quarterly* 81 (1): 167–179.

Alvarez, Rodolfo. 1971. "The Unique Psycho-Historical Experience of the Mexican American People." *Social Science Quarterly* 52: 15–29.

———. 1973. "The Psycho-Historical and Socioeconomic Development of the Chicano Community in the United States." *Social Science Quarterly* 53: 920–942.

Amott, Teresa L., and Julie A. Matthaei. 1991. *Race, Gender, and Work: A Multicultural Economic History of Women in the United States*. Boston: South End Press.

Andriesse, Ann B. 1987. "An Oral History Interview with Anne Faure." The Workman and Temple Family Homestead Museum Oral History Project. City of Industry, Calif.

Anzaldúa, Gloria. 1987. *Borderland, La Frontera: The New Mestiza*. San Francisco: Aunt Lute Books.

———. 1998. "To(o) Queer the Writer—Loca, escritora y chicana." In *Living Chicana Theory*, ed. Carla Trujillo, 263–276. Berkeley, Calif.: Third Woman Press.

Baca Zinn, Maxine. 1979. "Field Research in Minority Communities." *Social Problems*, 27 (2): 209–219.

———. 1994. "Feminist Rethinking from Racial-Ethnic Families." In *Women of Color in U.S. Society,* ed. Maxine Baca Zinn and Bonnie Thornton Dill, 303-314. Philadelphia: Temple University Press.

Balderrama, Francisco E., and Raymond Rodríquez. 1995. *Decade of Betrayal: Mexican Repatriation in the 1930s.* Albuquerque: University of New Mexico Press.

Barrera, Mario. 1979. *Race and Class in the Southwest.* Notre Dame, Ind.: Notre Dame University Press.

Barrera, Martha. 1991. "Café con Leche." In *Chicana Lesbians: The Girls Our Mother Warned Us About,* ed. Carla Trujillo, 80-83. Berkeley, Calif.: Third Women Press.

Bean, Frank D., Rodolfo O. de la Garza, Bryan R. Roberts, and Sidney Weintraub. 1997. *At the Crossroads: Mexico and U.S. Immigration Policy.* Lanham, Md.: Rowman and Littlefield.

Binder, Norman E., Jerry L. Polinard, and Robert D. Wrinkle. 1997. "Mexican American and Anglo Attitudes toward Immigration Reform: A View from the Border." *Social Science Quarterly* 78: 324-337.

Blauner, Robert. 1972. *Racial Oppression in America.* New York: Harper.

———. 1999. "Talking Past Each Other: Black and White Languages of Race." In *Race and Ethnic Conflict: Contending Views on Prejudice, Discrimination, and Ethnoviolence,* ed. Fred L. Pincus and Howard J. Ehrlich, 30-40. Boulder, Colo.: Westview Press.

Blea, Irene Isabel. 1995. *Researching Chicano Communities: Social-Historical, Physical, Psychological, and Spiritual Space.* Westport, Conn.: Praeger Publishers.

Bonacich, Edna. 1972. "A Theory of Ethnic Antagonism." *American Sociological Review* 37: 547-559.

Bond, Marian. 1994. "Sheep Gave Way to Home on the Range." *Los Angeles Times,* Jan. 9.

Bourgois, Philippe. 1996. *In Search of Respect: Selling Crack in El Barrio.* Cambridge: Cambridge University Press.

Bowles, S., and Gintis, H. 1976. *Schooling in Capitalist America: Educational Reform and the Contradictions of Economic Life.* New York: Basic Books.

Brodkin, Karen. 2000. *How Jews Became White Folks and What That Says About Race in America.* New Brunswick, N.J.: Rutgers University Press.

Browning, Harry L., and Rodolfo O. de la Garza. 1986. *Mexican Immigrants and Mexican Americans: An Evolving Relation.* Austin: University of Texas Press.

Burawoy, Michael, Allie Burton, Ann Arnett Ferguson, Kathryn J. Fox, Joshua Gamson, Nadine Gartrell, Leslie Hurst, Charles Kurzman, Leslie Salzinger, Josepha Schiffman, and Shiori Ui. 1991. *Ethnography Unbound: Power and Resistance in the Modern Metropolis.* Berkeley: University of California Press.

Buriel, Raymond. 1987. "Ethnic Labeling and Identity among Mexican Americans." In *Children's Ethnic Socialization,* ed. Jean S. Phinney and Mary Jane Rotherman, 134-152. Beverly Hills, Calif.: Sage.

Cadena, Gilbert R., and Lara Medina. 1996. "Liberation Theology and Social Change: Chicanas and Chicanos in the Catholic Church." In *Chicanas and Chicanos in Contemporary Society,* ed. Roberto M. De Anda, 99-111. Boston: Allyn and Bacon.

Calavita, Kitty. 1992. *Inside the State: The Bracero Program, Immigration, and the I.N.S.* New York: Routledge.

California Department of Education. 1998. "Racial or Ethnic Distribution of Staff and Students in California Public Schools, 1996–1997." Educational Demographics Group. Sacramento.

———. 2001a. "Number of Teachers in California Public Schools by District, School, Gender, and Ethnic Group, 2000–01." Educational Demographics Group. Sacramento.

———. 2001b. "Student Enrollment in California Public Schools by Ethnic Group, 2000–01." Educational Demographics Group. Sacramento.

Camarillo, Albert. 1979. *Chicanos in a Changing Society: From Mexican Pueblos to American Barrios in Santa Barbara and Southern California, 1848–1930.* Cambridge, Mass.: Harvard University Press.

———. 1984. "Chicanos in the American City." In *Chicano Studies: A Multidisciplinary Approach,* ed. Eugene E. Garcia, Francisco A. Lomeli, and Isidro D. Ortiz, 23–39. New York: Teachers College Press.

Cardenas, Gilbert. 1986. "The Impact of Immigration in the Ethnic Enterprise." In *Chicano-Mexicano Relations,* ed. Tatcho Mindiola Jr. and Max Martinez, 60–71. Mexican American Studies Monograph No. 4, Mexican American Studies Program. Houston: University of Houston, University Park.

Cardenas, Gilbert, Rodolfo O. de la Garza, and Niles Hansen. 1986. "Mexican Immigrants and the Chicano Ethnic Enterprise: Reconceptualizing an Old Problem." In *Mexican Immigrants and Mexican Americans: An Evolving Relation,* ed. Harry L. Browning and Rodolfo O. de la Garza, 157–174. Austin: University of Texas Press.

Cardenas, Jose. 1996. "The Numbers Crunch: Declining Enrollment Forces District to Consider Closing Some Schools." *Los Angeles Times,* Feb. 7.

Cardoso, Lawrence A. 1980. *Mexican Emigration to the United States, 1897–1931.* Tucson: University of Arizona Press.

Castillo, Ana. 1994. *Massacre of Dreamers: Essays on Xicanisma.* New York: Penguin Group.

Castro, Diego. 1998. "Hot Blood and Easy Virtue." In *Images of Color, Images of Crime,* ed. Coramae Richey Mann and Marjorie S. Zatz, 134–143. Los Angeles: Roxbury.

Charmaz, Kathy. 1983. "The Grounded Theory Method: An Explication and Interpretation." In *Contemporary Field Research: A Collection of Readings,* ed. Robert M. Emerson, 109–126. Prospect Heights, Ill.: Waveland Press.

Chavez, Leo R. 1998. *Shadowed Lives: Undocumented Immigrants in American Society.* Fort Worth, Tex.: Harcourt Brace Jovanovich College Publishers.

Chavez, Linda. 1991. *Out of the Barrio: Toward A New Politics of Hispanic Assimilation.* New York: Basic Books.

Citrin, Jack, Beth Reingold, and Donald P. Green. 1990. "American Identity and the Politics of Ethnic Change." *Journal of Politics* 52: 1124–1154.

Cochrane, William. 1969. "Unification Approved." *Hudson Headlines* (spring): 1.

Cockcroft, James D. 1986. *Outlaws in the Promised Land: Mexican Immigrant Workers and America's Future.* New York: Grove Press.

Collins, Patricia Hill. 1990. *Black Feminist Thought: Knowledge, Consciousness and the Politics of Empowerment.* Boston: Unwin Hyman.

Conquergood, Dwight. 1992. "Life in Big Red: Struggles and Accommodations in a Chicago Polyethnic Tenement." In *Structuring Diversity: Ethnographic Perspectives in the New Immigration,* ed. Louise Lamphere, 95–144. Chicago: University of Chicago Press.

Crawford, James. 1992. *Language Loyalties: A Source Book on the Official English Controversy.* Chicago: University of Chicago Press.

———. 2000. *At War with Diversity: U.S. Language Policy in an Age of Anxiety.* Clevedon, England: Multilingual Matters.

Creswell, John W. 1998. *Qualitative Inquiry and Research Design: Choosing Among Five Traditions.* Thousand Oaks: Sage.

Cummins, Jim. 1996. *Negotiating Identities: Education for Empowerment in a Diverse Society.* Los Angeles: California Association for Bilingual Education.

———. 2000. *Language, Power and Pedagogy: Bilingual Children in the Crossfire.* Clevedon, England: Multilingual Matters.

Darder, Antonia. 2002. *Reinventing Paulo Freire: A Pedagogy of Love.* Boulder, Colo.: Westview Press.

Darder, Antonia, Rodolfo D. Torres, and Henry Gutiérrez. 1997. *Latinos and Education: A Critical Reader.* New York: Routledge.

Davis, Mike. 1998. *Ecology of Fear: Los Angeles and the Imagination of Disaster.* New York: Metropolitan Books.

———. 2000. *Magical Urbanism: Latinos Reinvent the U.S. Big City.* London: Verso.

de la Garza, Rodolfo O., Louis DeSipio, F. Chris Garcia, John Garcia, and Angelo Falcon. 1992. *Latino Voices: Mexican, Puerto Rican & Cuban Perspectivas on American Politics.* Boulder, Colo.: Westview Press.

de la Garza, Rodolfo O., Jerry L. Polinard, Robert D. Wrinkle, and Tomás Longoria Jr. 1991. "Understanding Intra-Ethnic Attitude Variations: Mexican Origin Population Views of Immigration." *Social Science Quarterly* 72 (2): 379–387.

Della Piana, Libero. 1999. "Reading, Writing, Race and Resegregation." *Color Lines* (spring): 9–14.

deMarrais, Kathleen Bennett, and Margaret D. LeCompte. 1999. *The Way Schools Work: A Sociological Analysis of Education.* New York, Addison Wesley Longman.

Dill, Bonnie Thornton. 1994. "Fictive Kin, Paper Sons, and Compadrazgo: Women of Color and the Struggle for Family Survival." In *Women of Color in U.S. Society,* ed. Maxine Baca Zinn and Bonnie Thornton Dill, 149–169. Philadelphia: Temple University Press.

Donato, Katherine M. 1993. "Current Trends and Patterns of Female Migration: Evidence from Mexico." *International Migration Review* 17 (4): 748–771.

Durand, Jorge, and Douglas S. Massey. 1992. "Mexican Migration to the United States: A Critical Review." *Latin American Research Review* 27 (2): 3–42.

Eftychiou, Chris and Michael Gouglas. 1996. "Parents Protest Language Proposal: District Administrators Review Instruction in Bilingual Education." *San Gabriel Valley* (Calif.) *Tribune,* June 12.

Escobar, Edward J. 1999. *Race, Police, and the Making of a Political Identity: Mexican Americans and the Los Angeles Police Department, 1900–1945.* Berkeley: University of California Press.

Espenshade, Thomas J., and Charles A. Calhoun. 1993. "An Analysis of Public Opinion toward Undocumented Immigration." *Population Research and Policy Review* 13: 189-224.

Espiritu, Yen. 1992. *Asian American Panethnicity: Bridging Institutions and Identities.* Philadelphia: Temple University Press.

Estrada, Leobardo F. 1993. "Family Influences on Demographic Trends in Hispanic Ethnic Identification and Labeling." In *Ethnic Identity: Formation and Transmission Among Hispanics and Other Minorities,* ed. Martha E. Bernal and George P. Knight, 163-179. Albany: State University of New York Press.

Estrada, Leobardo F., F. Chris Garcia, Reynaldo Flores Macias, and Lionel Maldonado. 1981. "Chicanos in the United States: A History of Exploitation and Resistance." *Daedalus* 110: 103-132.

Ferrante, Joan, and Prince Brown Jr. 1999. "Classifying People by Race." In *Race and Ethnic Conflict: Contending Views on Prejudice, Discrimination, and Ethnoviolence,* ed. Fred L. Pincus and Howard J. Ehrlich, 14-23. Boulder, Colo.: Westview Press.

Fields, Jacquie, and Yvonne Guerrero. 1978. "Migrant Walnut Workers." In *A History of the Walnut Industry in the La Puente Valley,* 40-46. Community History Project, La Puente High School. La Puente, Calif.

Frankenberg, Ruth. 1993. *White Women, Race Matters: The Social Construction of Whiteness.* Minneapolis: University of Minnesota Press.

Freire, Paulo. 1970. *Pedagogy of the Oppressed.* Trans. Myra Bergman Ramos. New York: Seabury Press.

Galguera, Tomás. 1998. "Students' Attitudes toward Teachers' Ethnicity, Bilinguality, and Gender." *Hispanic Journal of Behavioral Sciences* 20 (4): 411-428.

Gamio, Manuel. 1971. *Mexican Immigration to the United States: A Study of Human Migration and Adjustment.* New York: Dover Publications.

Gándara, Patricia. 1995. *Over the Ivy Walls: The Educational Mobility of Low-Income Chicanos.* New York: State University of New York Press.

Gans, Herbert. 1979. "Symbolic Ethnicity: The Future of Ethnic Groups and Cultures in American." *Ethnic and Racial Studies* 1: 1-19.

García, Alma. 1989. "The Development of Chicana Feminist Discourse, 1970-1980." *Gender and Society* 3 (2): 217-238.

García, John A. 1981. " 'Yo Soy Mexicano': Self-Identity and Sociodemographic Correlates." *Social Science Quarterly* 62 (1): 88-98.

García, Mario T. 1985. "Americans All: The Mexican American Generation and the Politics of Wartime Los Angeles, 1941-45." In *The Mexican American Experience: An Interdisciplinary Anthology,* ed. Rodolfo O. de la Garza, Frank D. Bean, Charles M. Bonjean, Ricardo Romo, and Rodolfo Alvarez, 201-212. Austin: University of Texas Press.

———. 1989. *Mexican Americans: Leadership, Ideology, and Identity 1930-1960.* New Haven: Yale University Press.

———. 1994. *Memories of Chicano History: The Life and Narrative of Bert Corona.* Berkeley: University of California Press.

Gilkes, Cherly Townsend. 1994. " 'If It Wasn't for the Women . . .': African American Women, Community Work, and Social Change." In *Women of Color in U.S. So-*

ciety, ed. Maxine Baca Zinn and Bonnie Thornton Dill, 229-246. Philadelphia: Temple University Press.

Gimenez, Martha E. 1997. "Latino/Hispanic—Who Needs a Name?" In *Latinos and Education: A Critical Reader,* ed. Antonia Darder, Rodolfo D. Torres, and Henry Gutiérrez, 225-238. New York: Routledge.

Giroux, Henry. 1983. "Theories of Reproduction and Resistance in the New Sociology of Education." *Harvard Educational Review* 53: 257-293.

Glazer, Nathan, and Patrick Moynihan. 1975. *Ethnicity: Theory and Experience.* Cambridge, Mass.: Harvard University Press.

Glenn, Evelyn Nakano. 1992. "From Servitude to Service Work: Historical Continuities in the Racial Division of Paid Reproductive Labor." *Signs: Journal of Women in Culture and Society* 18: 1-43.

Goffman, Erving. 1956. "The Nature of Deference and Demeanor." *American Anthropologist* 58: 473-502.

Goldberg, David Theo. 1995. "Made in the USA: Racial Mixing 'n' Matching." In *American Mixed Race: The Culture of Microdiversity,* ed. Naomi Zack, 237-255. Lanham, Md.: Rowman and Littlefield.

Gómez, Laura. 1992. "The Birth of the Hispanic Generation." *Latin American Perspectives* 19 (75): 45-58.

Gómez-Quiñones, Juan. 1990. *Chicano Politics: Reality and Promise, 1940-1990.* Albuquerque: University of New Mexico Press.

Gonzales, María Dolores. 1999. "Crossing Social and Cultural Borders: The Road to Language Hybridity." In *Speaking Chicana: Voice, Power, and Identity,* ed. D. Letticia Galindo and María Dolores Gonzales, 13-38. Tucson: University of Arizona Press.

Gonzalez, Gilbert G. 1990. *Chicano Education in the Era of Segregation.* Philadelphia: Balch Institute Press.

———. 1999. *Mexican Consuls and Labor Organizing: Imperial Politics in the American Southwest.* Austin: University of Texas Press.

Gonzalez, Hector. 1996. "Latino Parents Unite for Better Schools." *San Gabriel Valley (Calif.) Tribune,* Aug. 22.

Gonzalez, Juan. 2000. *Harvest of Empire: A History of Latinos in America.* New York: Viking Press.

González, Rosalinda M. 1983. "Chicanas and Mexican Immigrant Families 1920-1940: Women's Subordination and Family Exploitation." In *Decades of Discontent: The Women's Movement 1920-1940,* ed. Lois Scharf and Joan M. Jensen, 59-84. Westport, Conn.: Greenwood Press.

Goode, Judith, and Jo Anne Schneider. 1994. *Reshaping Ethnic and Racial Relations in Philadelphia: Immigrants in a Divided City.* Philadelphia: Temple University Press.

Goode, Judith, Jo Anne Schneider, and Suzanne Blanc. 1992. "Transcending Boundaries and Closing Ranks: How Schools Shape Interrelations." In *Structuring Diversity: Ethnographic Perspectives in the New Immigration,* ed. Louise Lamphere, 173-213. Chicago: University of Chicago Press.

Gordon, Milton. 1961. "Assimilation in American Life: Theory and Reality." *Daedalus* 90 (10): 263-285.

———. 1964. *Assimilation in American Life: The Role of Race, Religion, and National Origin.* New York: Oxford University Press.

Gouglas, Michael. 1996a. "Multilingual Education on the Table." *San Gabriel Valley (Calif.) Tribune,* June 11.

———. 1996b. "Parents Seek Unity: Bilingual Programs Focus of Meetings." *San Gabriel Valley (Calif.) Tribune,* June 24.

———. 1996c. "Bilingual Programs at Focus of Parent Protests, District Review." *Hacienda Heights (Calif.) Highlander,* July 4.

Grebler, Leo, Joan Moore, and Ralph Guzman. 1970. *The Mexican American People: The Nation's Second Largest Minority.* New York: Free Press.

Grenier, Guillermo J., Alex Stepick, Debbie Draznin, Aline LaBorwit, Steve Morris, and Bernadette Coppee. 1992. "On Machines and Bureaucracy: Controlling Ethnic Interaction in Miami's Apparel Industry and Construction Industries." In *Structuring Diversity: Ethnographic Perspectives on the New Immigration,* ed. Louise Lamphere, 65–93. Chicago and London: University of Chicago Press.

Griswold del Castillo, Richard. 1990. *The Treaty of Guadalupe Hidalgo: A Legacy of Conquest.* Norman and London: University of Oklahoma Press.

Guerin-Gonzales, Camille. 1994. *Mexican Workers and American Dreams: Immigration, Repatriation, and California Farm Labor, 1900–1939.* New Brunswick, N.J.: Rutgers University Press.

Gurin, Patricia, Aida Hurtado, and Timothy Peng. 1994. "Group Contacts and Ethnicity in the Social Identities of Mexicans and Chicanos." *Society for Personality and Social Psychology* 20 (5): 521–532.

Gutiérrez, David G. 1995. *Walls and Mirrors: Mexican Americans, Mexican Immigrants, and the Politics of Ethnicity.* Berkeley: University of California Press.

———. 1998. "Ethnic Mexicans and the Transformation of 'American' Social Space: Reflections on Recent History." In *Crossings: Mexican Immigration in Interdisciplinary Perspectives,* ed. Marcelo M. Suárez-Orozco, 309–335. Cambridge, Mass.: Harvard University Press.

Hacienda–La Puente Unified School District. 1996. "Bilingual Education." Photocopy. June 11.

Hagan, Jacqueline Maria, and Nestor P. Rodriguez. 1992. "Evolving Intergroup Relations in Houston." In *Structuring Diversity: Ethnographic Perspectives on the New Immigration,* ed. Louise Lamphere, 145–171. Chicago and London: University of Chicago Press.

Hakim, Catherine. 1987. *Research Design: Strategies and Choices in the Design of Social Research.* London: Allen and Unwin Publishers.

Hardy-Fanta, Carol. 1993. *Latina Politics, Latino Politics: Gender, Culture, and Political Participation.* Philadelphia: Temple University Press.

Harris, Virginia R., and Trinity A. Ordoña. 1990. "Developing Unity among Women of Color: Crossing the Barriers of Internalized Racism and Cross-Racial Hostility." In *Making Face, Making Soul/Haciendo Caras: Creative and Critical Perspectives by Women of Color,* ed. Gloria Anzaldúa, 304–316. San Francisco: Aunt Lute Books.

Harrison, Lawrence E. 1999. "How Cultural Values Shape Economic Success." In *Race and Ethnic Conflict,* ed. Fred L. Pincus and Howard J. Ehrlich, 97–109. Boulder, Colo.: Westview Press.

Hayano, David M. 1981. "Ethnic Identification and Disidentification: Japanese-American Views of Chinese-Americans." *Ethnic Studies* 3 (2): 157–171.

Heller, Celia S. 1966. *Mexican American Youth: Forgotten Youth at the Crossroads.* New York: Random House.

Hillburg, Bill. 2001. "New Census Report Details Southland's Diversity." *San Gabriel Valley* (Calif.) *Tribune,* Nov. 20.

History of La Puente Valley California. 1960. Reprints from 50th anniversary edition 1910–1960, *La Puente Valley (Calif.) Journal* and supplementary article, Oct. 6.

Hondagneu-Sotelo, Pierrette. 1994. *Gendered Transitions: Mexican Experiences of Immigration.* Berkeley: University of California Press.

Hood, M. V. III, and Irwin L. Morris. 1997. "Amigo o Enemigo?: Context, Attitudes, and Anglo Public Opinion towards Immigration." *Social Science Quarterly* 78 (2): 309–323.

hooks, bell. 1994. *Teaching to Transgress: Education as the Practice of Freedom.* New York: Routledge.

Horton, John. 1995. *The Politics of Diversity: Immigration, Resistance, and Change in Monterey Park, California.* Philadelphia: Temple University Press.

Hoskin, Marilyn, and William Mishler. 1983. "Public Opinion toward New Migrants: A Comparative." *International Migration* 21: 440–462.

Hudson Elementary School District. School Board Minutes, 1925–1951. Hacienda–La Puente Unified School District. City of Industry, Calif.

Hurtado, Aída. 1995. "Variations, Combinations, and Evolutions: Latino Families in the United States." In *Understanding Latino Families: Scholarship, Policy, and Practice,* ed. Ruth E. Zambrana, 40–61. Thousand Oaks, Calif.: Sage.

Hurtado, Aída, and Carlos H. Arce. 1987. "Mexicans, Chicanos, Mexican Americans, or Pochos . . . Qué somos? The Impact of Language and Nativity on Ethnic Labeling." *Aztlán* 17 (1): 103–130.

Hurtado, Aída, Patricia Gurin, and Timothy Peng. 1994. "Social Identities: A Framework for Studying the Adaptations of Immigrants and Ethnics: The Adaptation of Mexicans in the United States." *Social Problems* 41: 129–151.

Ichioka, Yuji. 1988. *The Issei: The World of the First Generation Japanese Americans, 1885–1924.* New York: Free Press.

Johnson, James H., and Melvin L. Oliver. 1989. "Inter-ethnic Minority Conflict in Urban America." *Urban Geography* 10 (5): 449–463.

Johnson, James H. Jr., Melvin L. Oliver, Walter C. Farrell, and Cloyzelle Jones. 1992. "The Los Angeles Rebellion: A Retrospective View." *Economic Development Quarterly* 6 (4): 356–372.

Kasarda, John. 1989. "Urban Industrial Transitions and the Underclass." *The Annals of the American Academy of Political and Social Science* 501: 26–42.

Kingsolver, Barbara. 1989. *Holding the Line: Women in the Great Arizona Mining Strike of 1983.* Ithaca, N.Y.: ILR Press.

Lamphere, Louise. 1992. "Introduction: The Shaping of Diversity." In *Structuring Diversity: Ethnographic Perspectives on the New Immigration,* ed. Louise Lamphere, 1–34. Chicago and London: University of Chicago Press.

La Puente Planning Department. 1972. *The Comprehensive General Plan*. La Puente, Calif.
La Puente Valley Historical Society. 1976. *La Puente Kaleidoscope Part 1*. Whittier, Calif.: Gateway Printers.
———. N.d. "Walnut Industry in La Puente Valley." La Puente, Calif.
Lieberson, Stanley. 1980. *A Piece of the Pie*. Berkeley: University of California Press.
Lindholm, Kathryn. 1995. "Theoretical Assumptions and Empirical Evidence for Academic Achievement in Two Languages." In *Hispanic Psychology*, ed. Amado Padilla, 273–287. Thousand Oaks, Calif.: Sage.
Lofland, John, and Lyn H. Lofland. 1984. *Analyzing Social Settings: A Guide to Qualitative Observation and Analysis*. Belmont, Calif.: Wadsworth.
Lopez, David. 1996. "Language: Diversity and Assimilation." In *Ethnic Los Angeles*, ed. Roger Waldinger and Mehdi Bozorgmehr, 139–163. New York: Russell Sage Foundation.
Lopez, David, and Yen Espiritu. 1990. "Panethnicity in the United States: A Theoretical Framework." *Ethnic and Racial Studies* 13 (2): 198–224.
Lopez, David, and Ricardo D. Stanton-Salazar. 2001. "Mexican Americans: A Second Generation at Risk." In *Ethnicities: Children of Immigrants in America*, ed. Rubén G. Rumbaut and Alejandro Portes, 57–90. Berkeley: University of California Press.
Los Angeles County. 1994. Records. Voter Registrar-Recorder, County Clerk. Norwalk, Calif.
———. 1996. Records. Voter Registrar-Recorder, County Clerk. Norwalk, Calif.
Lucas, Douglas P. N.d. "A Complete History of Hudson and Central Elementary Schools: Puente, California From 1887 to 1936." Manuscript. Hacienda–La Puente United School District. City of Industry, Calif.
Madrid, Arturo. 1995. "Missing People and Others." In *Race, Class, and Gender*, ed. Margaret L. Anderson and Patricia Hill Collins, 10–15. Belmont, Calif.: Wadsworth.
Madsen, William. 1964. *Mexican-Americans of South Texas*. New York: Holt, Rinehart and Winston.
Maldonado, Lionel. 1991. "Latino Ethnicity: Increasing Diversity." *Latino Studies Journal* 2 (3): 49–57.
Martínez, Elizabeth. 1995. "Beyond Black/White: The Racisms of Our Time." In *Sources: Notable Selections in Race and Ethnicity*, ed. Adalberto Aguirre Jr. and David V. Baker, 79–88. Guilford, Conn.: Dushkin Publishing Group.
———. 1998. *De Colores Means All of Us: Latina Views for a Multi-Colored Century*. Cambridge, Mass.: South End Press.
Martínez, Elizabeth Sugar. 2000. "Ideological Baggage in the Classroom: Resistance and Resilience among Latino Bilingual Students and Teachers." In *Immigrant Voices: In Search of Educational Equity*, ed. Enrique T. Trueba and Lilia I. Bartolomé, 93–106. Lanham, Md.: Rowman and Littlefield.
Martínez, Rubén. 1998. "The Shock of the New." In *The Latino Studies Reader: Culture, Economy and Society*, ed. Antonia Darder and Rodolfo D. Torres, 170–179. Malden Mass.: Black.
Massey, Douglas S., Rafael Alarcón, Jorge Durand, and Humberto González. 1987. *Return to Aztlán: The Social Process of International Migration from Western Mexico*. Berkeley: University of California Press.

McIntosh, Chester S. 1960. "McIntosh Reviews Early Days." Reprints from the 50th Anniversary Edition 1910–1960, *La Puente Valley (Calif.) Journal* and supplementary articles, Oct. 6, 1–2.

McIntosh, Peggy. 1995. "White Privilege and Male Privilege." In *Race, Class, and Gender,* ed. Margaret L. Anderson and Patricia Hill Collins, 94–105. Belmont, Calif.: Wadsworth.

McLemore, Dale, and Ricardo Romo. 1985. "The Origins and Development of the Mexican American People." In *The Mexican American Experience: An Interdisciplinary Anthology,* ed. Rodolfo de la Garza, Frank D. Bean, Charles M. Bonjean, Ricardo Romo, and Rodolfo Alvarez, 3–32. Austin: University of Texas Press.

McWilliams, Carey. 1990. *North from Mexico.* New York: Praeger.

Melville, Margarita B. 1978. "Mexican Women Adapt to Migration." *International Migration Review* 12: 225–235.

Menchaca, Martha. 1989. "Chicano-Mexican Cultural Assimilation and Anglo-Saxon Cultural Dominance." *Hispanic Journal of Behavioral Sciences* 11 (3): 203–231.

———. 1995. *The Mexican Outsiders: A Community History of Marginalization and Discrimination in California.* Austin: University of Texas Press.

Méndez-Negrete, Josephine. 1999. "Awareness, Consciousness, and Resistance: Raced, Classed, and Gendered Leadership Implications in Milagro County, California." *Frontiers: A Journal of Women Studies* 20 (1): 25–44.

Mendoza-Denton, Norma. 1999. "Fighting Words: Latina Girls, Gangs, and Language Attitudes." In *Speaking Chicana: Voice, Power, and Identity,* ed. D. Letticia Galindo and María Dolores Gonzales, 39–56. Tucson: University of Arizona Press.

Menjívar, Cecilia. 2000. *Fragmented Ties: Salvadoran Immigrant Networks in America.* Berkeley: University of California Press.

Miller, Lawrence W., Jerry L. Polinard, and Robert D. Wrinkle. 1984. "Attitudes toward Undocumented Workers: The Mexican American Perspective." *Social Science Quarterly* 65: 482–494.

Mills, C. Wright. 1959. *The Sociological Imagination.* New York: Oxford University Press.

Mindiola, Tatcho Jr., and Max Martinez. 1986. "Introduction to Chicano-Mexicano Relations." In *Chicano-Mexicano Relations,* Mexican American Studies Monograph No. 4, Mexican American Studies Program, ed. Tatcho Mindiola Jr. and Max Martinez. Houston: University of Houston, University Park.

Mirandé, Alfredo. 1985. *The Chicano Experience: An Alternative Perspective.* Notre Dame, Ind.: University of Notre Dame Press.

Monto, Alexander. 1994. *The Roots of Mexican Immigration.* Westport, Conn.: Praeger.

Moore, Joan, and Diego Vigil. 1993. "Barrios in Transition." In *In the Barrios: Latinos and the Underclass Debate,* ed. Joan Moore and Raquel Pinderhughes, 27–49. New York: Russel Sage Foundation.

Mora, Pat. 1984. "Legal Alien." In *Chants.* Houston: Arte Público Press.

Morris, Aldon D. 1984. *The Origins of the Civil Rights Movement: Black Communities Organizing for Change.* New York: Free Press.

———. 1992. "Political Consciousness and Collective Action." In *Frontiers in Social Movement Theory,* ed. Aldon D. Morris and Carol McClurg Mueller, 351–373. New Haven, Conn., and London: Yale University Press.

Muñoz, Carlos Jr. 1989. *Youth, Identity, Power: The Chicano Movement*. New York: Verso.

National Council of La Raza. 1997. "Out of the Picture: Hispanics in the Media." In *Latin Looks: Images of Latinas and Latinos in the U.S. Media*, ed. Clara E. Rodríguez, 21–35. Boulder, Colo.: Westview Press.

Naples, Nancy A. 1998. *Grassroots Warriors: Activist Mothering, Community Work, and the War on Poverty*. New York: Routledge.

Nelson, Candace, and Marta Tienda. 1997. "The Structuring of Hispanic Ethnicity." In *Challenging Fronteras*, ed. Mary Romero, Pierrette Hondagneu-Sotelo, and Vilma Ortiz, 7–29. New York: Routledge.

Niemann, Yolanda Flores, Andrea J. Romero, Jorge Arredondo, and Victor Rodriquez. 1999. "What Does it Mean to Be 'Mexican'? Social Construction of an Ethnic Identity." *Hispanic Journal of Behavioral Sciences* 21 (1): 47–60.

Nyden, Philip, Anne Figert, Mark Shibley, and Darrly Burrows, eds. 1999. *Building Community: Social Science in Action*. Thousand Oaks, Calif.: Pine Forge Press.

Oakes, Jeannie. 1985. *Keeping Track: How Schools Structure Inequality*. New Haven, Conn., and London: Yale University Press.

Oboler, Suzanne. 1995. *Ethnic Labels, Latino Lives: Politics of (Re)Presentation in the United States*. Minneapolis: Minnesota Press.

Ochoa, Gilda Laura. 1999. "Everyday Ways of Resistance and Cooperation: Mexican American Women Building Puentes with Immigrants." *Frontiers: A Journal of Women Studies* 20: 1–20.

Ochoa, Gilda Laura, and Enrique C. Ochoa. Forthcoming. "Education for Social Transformation: The Intersections of Chicana/o and Latin American Studies and Community Struggles." *Latin American Perspectives*.

Oliver, Melvin L., James H. Johnson Jr., and Walter C. Farrell Jr. 1993. "Anatomy of a Rebellion: A Political-Economic Analysis." In *Reading Rodney King, Reading Urban Uprising*, ed. Robert Gooding-Williams, 117–141. New York: Routledge.

Omi, Michael, and Howard Winant. 1994. 2d ed. *Racial Formation in the United States*. New York: Routledge.

O'Neil, Stephanie. 1994. "Casa, Sweet Casa." *Los Angeles Times*, Dec. 4.

Orellana, Marjorie Faulstich, Lucila Ek, and Arcelia Hernández. 2000. "Bilingual Education in an Immigrant Community: Proposition 227 in California." In *Immigrant Voices: In Search of Educational Equity*, ed. Enrique (Henry) T. Trueba and Lilia I. Bartolomé, 75–92. Lanham, Md.: Rowman and Littlefield.

Orfield, Gary. 1996. "The Growth of Segregation." In *Dismantling Desegregation: The Quiet Reversal of Brown v. Board of Education*, ed. Gary Orfield, Susan E. Easton, and The Harvard Project on School Desegregation, 53–71. New York: New Press.

Orfield, Gary, and John T. Yun. 1999. *Resegregation in American Schools*. Boston: Civil Rights Project, Harvard University.

Orozco, Cynthia E. 1992. "The Origins of the League of United Latin American Citizens (LULAC) and the Mexican American Civil Rights Movement in Texas with an Analysis of Women's Political Participation in a Gendered Context, 1910–1929." Ph.D. diss., University of California, Los Angeles.

Ortiz, Vilma. 1996. "The Mexican-Origin Population: Permanent Working Class or Emerging Middle Class?" In *Ethnic Los Angeles*, ed. Roger Waldinger and Mehdi Bozorgmehr, 247–277. New York: Russell Sage Foundation.

Padilla, Felix M. 1985. *Latino Ethnic Consciousness: The Case of Mexican Americans and Puerto Ricans in Chicago*. Notre Dame, Ind.: University of Notre Dame Press.

Pardo, Mary. 1991. "Creating Community: Mexican American Women in Eastside Los Angeles." *Aztlán* 20 (1–2): 39–71.

———. 1998. *Mexican American Women Activists: Identity and Resistance in Two Los Angeles Communities*. Philadelphia: Temple University Press.

Park, Robert. 1950. *Race and Culture*. Glencoe, Ill.: Free Press.

Parsons, Talcott. 1951. *The Social System*. Glencoe, Ill.: Free Press.

Piatt, Bill. 1990. *Only English? Law and Language Policy in the United States*. Albuquerque: University of New Mexico Press.

Pinheiro, Eugene Arthur. 1960. "A Historical Study of the City of La Puente." Master's thesis, Whittier College, California.

Pitt, Leonard. 1966. *The Decline of the Californios: A Social History of the Spanish-Speaking Californians, 1846–1890*. Berkeley: University of California Press.

Polinard, Jerry L., Robert D. Wrinkle, and Rodolfo de la Garza. 1984. "Attitudes of Mexican Americans Toward Irregular Mexican Immigration." *International Migration Review* 18: 782–799.

Portes, Alejandro, and Robert L. Bach. 1985. *Latin Journey: Cuban and Mexican Immigrants in the United States*. Berkeley: University of California Press.

Portes, Alejandro, and Rubén Rumbaut. 1990. *Immigrant America*. Berkeley: University of California Press.

———. 2001. *Legacies: The Story of the Immigrant Second Generation*. Berkeley: University of California Press.

Poston, Dudley L., Richard G. Rogers, and Ruth M. Cullen. 1986. "Income and Occupational Attainment Patterns of Mexican Immigrants and Nonimmigrants." In *Mexican Immigrants and Mexican Americans: An Evolving Relation*, ed. Harley L. Browning and Rodolfo O. de la Garza, 72–84. Austin: University of Texas Press.

Puente Parents. 1996. "Mission Statement." July 22. Photocopy. La Puente, Calif.

Radford, Claire. 1984. *Footsteps to the Past: True Tales of the San Gabriel Valley*. La Puente, Calif.: La Puente Valley Historical Society.

Ramirez, Deborah A. 1996. "Multiracial Identity in a Color-Conscious World." In *The Multiracial Experience*, ed. Maria P. Root, 49–62. Thousand Oaks, Calif.: Sage.

Ramírez Berg, Charles. 1997. "Stereotyping in Films in General and of the Hispanic in Particular." In *Latin Looks: Images of Latinas and Latinos in the U.S. Media*, ed. Clara E. Rodríquez, 104–120. Boulder, Colo.: Westview Press.

Riley, Edward Franklin. 1962. "A History of the Organization and Administration of the Elementary Schools in the La Puente High School District." Master's thesis, Claremont Graduate School, Calif.

Robnett, Belinda. 1997. *How Long? How Long? African-American Women in the Struggle for Civil Rights*. New York: Oxford University Press.

Rocco, Raymond. 1997. "Citizenship, Culture, and Community: Restructuring in Southeast Los Angeles." In *Latino Cultural Citizenship: Claiming Identity, Space, and Rights*, ed. William V. Flores and Rina Benmayor, 97–123. Boston: Beacon Press.

Rodríguez, Clara E. 1997. "Latinos on Television and in the News: Absent or Misrepresented." In *Latin Looks: Images of Latinas and Latinos in the U.S. Media*, ed. Clara E. Rodríguez, ed. 13–20. Boulder, Colo.: Westview Press.

Rodriguez, Jaclyn, and Patricia Gurin. 1990. "The Relationships of Intergroup Contact to Social Identity and Political Consciousness." *Hispanic Journal of Behavioral Sciences* 12 (3): 235–255.

Rodriguez, Nestor. 1986. "Chicano-Indocumentado Work Relations: Findings of The Texas Indocumentado Study." In *Chicano-Mexicano Relations*, Mexican American Studies Monograph No. 4, Mexican American Studies Program, ed. Tatcho Mindiola Jr. and Max Martinez, 72–84. Houston: University of Houston, University Park.

Rodriguez, Nestor, and Rogelio Nuñez. 1986. "An Exploration of Factors that Contribute to Differentiation Between Chicanos and Indocumentados. In *Mexican Immigrants and Mexican Americans: An Evolving Relation*, ed. Harley L. Browning and Rodolfo O. de la Garza, 138–156. Austin: University of Texas Press.

Rojas, Patrisia Macías and Rebecca Gordon. 1999. "Just Facts: Racial Resegregation and Inequality in the Public Schools." *Color Lines* (spring): 10.

Rollins, Judith. 1985. *Between Women: Domestics and Their Employers.* Philadelphia: Temple University Press.

Romo, Harriett D., and Toni Falbo. 1996. *Latino High School Graduation: Defying the Odds.* Austin: University of Texas Press.

Rosaldo, Renato, and William V. Flores. 1997. "Identity, Conflict, and Evolving Latino Communities: Cultural Citizenship in San Jose, California." In *Latino Cultural Citizenship: Claiming Identity, Space, and Rights*, ed. William V. Flores and Rina Benmayor, 57–96. Boston: Beacon Press.

Rowland, Leonore. 1958. *The Romance of La Puente Rancho.* Covina, Calif.: Nielson Press.

Rubin, Karen. 2001. "La Puente to Publish Bilingual Newsletter." *San Gabriel Valley* (Calif.) *Tribune*, July 26.

Ruiz, Vicki L. 1987. *Cannery Women, Cannery Lives: Mexican Women, Unionization, and the California Food Processing Industry, 1930–1950.* Albuquerque: University of New Mexico Press.

———. 1998. *From out of the Shadows: Mexican Women in Twentieth-Century America.* New York: Oxford University Press.

Sabagh, Georges, and Mehdi Bozorgmehr. 1996. "Population Change: Immigration and Ethnic Transformation." In *Ethnic Los Angeles*, ed. Roger Waldinger and Mehdi Bozorgmehr, 79–107. New York: Russell Sage Foundation.

Saito, Leland T. 1998. *Race and Politics: Asian Americans, Latinos, and Whites in a Los Angeles Suburb.* Urbana: University of Illinois Press.

Saito, Leland T., and John Horton. 1994. "The New Chinese Immigration and the Rise of Asian American Politics in Monterey Park, California." In *The New Asian Immigration in Los Angeles and Global Restructuring*, ed. Paul Ong, Edna Bonacich, and Lucie Cheng, 223–263. Philadelphia: Temple University Press.

Sánchez, George J. 1993. *Becoming Mexican American: Ethnicity, Culture and Identity in Chicano Los Angeles, 1900–1945.* New York: Oxford University Press.

Sandoval, Thomas Frank Jr. 1994. "The Multiethnic Struggle for Community in the La Puente Valley." Senior history thesis, Claremont McKenna College, Calif.

Santos, Gonzalo. 1997. "Somos RUNAFRIBES? The Future of Latino Ethnicity in the Americas." In *Latinos and Education: A Critical Reader*, ed. Antonia Darder, Rodolfo D. Torres, and Henry Gutiérrez, 203–224. New York: Routledge.

Sassen, Saskia. 1998. *The Mobility of Labor and Capital*. Cambridge: Cambridge University Press.

Schlesinger, Arthur. 1991. *The Disuniting of America: Reflections on a Multicultural Society*. New York: Norton.

Schmid, Carol. 1992. "The English Only Movement: Social Bases of Support and Opposition among Anglos and Latinos." In *Language Loyalties: A Source Book on the Official English Controversy*, ed. James Crawford, 202–209. Chicago: University of Chicago Press.

Seidman, I. E. 1991. *Interviewing as Qualitative Research: A Guide for Researchers in Education and the Social Sciences*. New York: Teachers College Press.

Sethi, Rita Chaudhry. 1995. "Smells Like Racism." In *Race, Class, and Gender in the United States*, ed. Paula Rothenberg, 89–99. New York: St. Martin's Press.

Shah, Sonia. 1994. "Presenting the Blue Goddess: Toward a National Pan-Asian Feminist Agenda." In *The State of Asian American Activism and Resistance in the 1990's*, ed. Karen Aguilar-San Juan, 147–159. Boston: South End Press.

Shannon, Sheila M. 1986. "Minority Parental Involvement: A Mexican Mother's Experience and a Teacher's Interpretation." *Education and Urban Society* 29 (1): 71–84.

Shannon, Sheila M. and Silvia Lojero Latimer. 1996. "Latino Parent Involvement in Schools: A Story of Struggle and Resistance." *Journal of Educational Issues of Language Minority Students* 16: 301–319.

Shor, Ira. 1992. *Empowering Education: Critical Teaching for Social Change*. Chicago: University of Chicago Press.

———. 1996. *When Students Have Power: Negotiating Authority in a Critical Pedagogy*. Chicago: University of Chicago Press.

Simón, Laura Angelica. 1996. *Fear and Learning at Hoover Elementary*. Video. Distributed by Transit Media/Fear and Learning Library.

Skerry, Peter. 1993. *Mexican Americans: The Ambivalent Minority*. New York: Free Press.

Sleeter, Christine E. 1993. "How White Teachers Construct Race." In *Race Identity and Representation in Education*, ed. Cameron McCarthy and Warren Crichlow, 157–171. New York: Routledge.

Solorzano, Daniel G. 1995. "The Chicano Educational Experience: Empirical and Theoretical Perspectives." In *Class, Culture, and Race in American Schools: A Handbook*, ed. Stanley William Rothstein, 35–54. Westport, Conn.: Greenwood Press.

———. 1997. "Teaching and Social Change: Reflections on a Freirean Approach in a College Classroom." In *Latinos and Education: A Critical Reader*, ed. Antonia Darder, Rodolfo D. Torres, and Henry Gutiérrez, 351–361. New York: Routledge.

Soto, Lourdes Diaz. 1997. *Language, Culture, and Power: Bilingual Families and the Struggle for Quality Education*. Albany: State University of New York Press.

Sowell, Thomas. 1981. *Ethnic America*. New York: Basic Books.

Steinberg, Stephen. 1989. *The Ethnic Myth*. Boston: Beacon Press.

Stephan, Cookie White, and Walter G. Stephan. 1989. "After Intermarriage: Ethnic Identity among Mixed-Heritage Japanese-Americans and Hispanics." *Journal of Marriage and the Family* 41 (2): 507–519.

Sullivan, Teresa A. 1986. "Stratification of the Chicano Labor Market Under Conditions of Continuing Mexican Immigration." In *Mexican Immigrants and Mexican Ameri-*

cans: An Evolving Relation, ed. Harry L. Browning and Rodolfo O. de la Garza, 55–73. Austin: University of Texas Press.

Takaki, Ronald. 1989. *Strangers from a Different Shore: A History of Asian Americans.* Boston: Little, Brown.

———. 1993. *A Different Mirror: A History of Multicultural America.* Boston: Back Bay Books, Little, Brown.

Tienda, Martha, and Vilma Ortiz, 1986. "Hispanicity and the 1980 Census." *Social Science Quarterly* 67: 3–20.

Tse, Lucy. 2001. *"Why Don't They Learn English?": Separating Fact from Fallacy in the U.S. Language Debate.* New York: Teachers College.

U.S. Bureau of the Census. 1971. *Census of Population, 1970.* Washington, D.C.: U.S. Government Printing Office.

———. 1981. *Census of Population, 1980.* Washington, D.C.: U.S. Government Printing Office.

———. 1991. *Census of Population, 1990.* Washington, D.C.: U.S. Government Printing Office.

———. 2001. U.S. Census American Fact Finder. Online at http://factfinder.census.gov/servlet.

U.S. Department of Education. 1993. Office of Civil Rights. Investigative Report, July 12.

Unz, Ron. 1997. "English for the Children: A Project of One Nation/One California." Flyer. Palo Alto, Calif.

Valencia, Richard R. 1991. "The Plight of Chicano Students: An Overview of Schooling Conditions and Outcomes." In *Chicano School Failure and Success: Research and Policy Agendas for the 1990s,* ed. Richard R. Valencia, 3–26. London: Falmer Press.

Valenzuela, Angela. 1999. *Subtractive Schooling: U.S.-Mexican Youth and the Politics of Caring.* Albany: State University of New York Press.

Valle, Victor M., and Rodolfo D. Torres. 2000. *Latino Metropolis.* Minneapolis: University of Minnesota Press.

Vasquez, Melba J. T. 1997. "Confronting Barriers to the Participation of Mexican American Women in High Education." In *Latinos and Education: A Critical Reader,* ed. Antonia Darder, Rodolfo D. Torres, and Henry Gutiérrez, 454–467. New York: Routledge.

Vigil, James Diego. 1980. *From Indians to Chicanos: The Dynamics of Mexican American Culture.* Prospect Heights, Ill.: Waveland Press.

———. 1997. *Personas Mexicanas: Chicano High Schoolers in a Changing Los Angeles.* Fort Worth, Tex.: Harcourt Brace College Publishers.

Vila, Pablo. 1998. Review of *At the Crossroads: Mexico and U.S. Immigration Policy,* ed. Frank D. Bean, Rodolfo O. de la Garza, Bryan R. Roberts, and Sidney Weintraub. *Contemporary Sociology* 27 (2): 177–178.

Waters, Mary. 1990. *Ethnic Options: Choosing Identities in America.* Berkeley and Los Angeles: University of California Press.

———. 1999. *Black Identities: West Indian Immigrant Dreams and American Realities.* New York and Cambridge, Mass.: Russell Sage Foundation and Harvard University Press.

Weber, David J. 1982. *The Mexican Frontier, 1821–1846: The American Southwest Under Mexico*. Albuquerque: University of New Mexico Press.

———, ed. 1973. *Foreigners in Their Native Land: Historical Roots of the Mexican Americans*. Albuquerque: University of New Mexico Press.

Weber, Devra. 1994. *Dark Sweat, White Gold: California Farm Workers, Cotton, and the New Deal*. Berkeley: University of California Press.

Wildman, Stephanie M., with Adrienne D. Davis. 1997. "Making Systems of Privilege Visible." In *Critical White Studies*, ed. Richard Delgado and Jean Stefancic, 314–319. Philadelphia: Temple University Press.

Wilson, Glen A., High School. 2001. "Glen A. Wilson High School Course Catalog 2001–2002." Hacienda Heights, Calif.

Wilson, Williams J. 1978. *The Declining Significance of Race*. Chicago: University of Chicago Press.

Wollenberg, Charles. 1976. *All Deliberate Speed: Segregation and Exclusion in California Schools, 1855–1975*. Berkeley: University of California Press.

Yamato, Gloria. 1990. "Something about the Subject Makes It Hard to Name." In *Making Face, Making Soul/Haciendo Caras: Creative and Critical Perspectives by Feminists of Color*, ed. Gloria Anzaldúa, 20–24. San Francisco: Aunt Lute Books.

Yetman, Norman R. 1991. *Majority and Minority: The Dynamics of Race and Ethnicity in American Life*. 5th ed. Boston: Allyn and Bacon.

Zavella, Patricia. 1987. *Women's Work and Chicano Families: Cannery Workers of the Santa Clara Valley*. Ithaca, N.Y.: Cornell University Press.

———. 1993. "Feminist Insider Dilemmas: Constructing Ethnic Identity with Chicana Informants." *Frontiers*, 13 (3): 53–76.

———. 1994. "Reflections of Diversity Among Chicanas." In *Race*, ed. Steven Gregory and Roger Sanjek, 199–212. New Brunswick, N.J.: Rutgers University Press.

Index

affirmative action, 3, 23, 45, 221. *See also* California propositions: Proposition 209

African American(s), 23, 25, 34, 43, 60, 79; churches, 198–199; civil rights movement, 35; defined, 237n. 4; women, 124

Americanization, 14, 34, 52, 100; as experienced by Mexican American generation, 116–117. *See also* Central Avenue Americanization School

Americanness, 71, 100, 114, 220, 223

Anglo conformity, 34, 113, 245n. 8

Anglo superiority ideology, 15, 18–19, 24, 34, 112–113

Anglos. *See* Whites

anti-immigrant sentiment, 2–3, 7, 28, 32, 41, 45, 46, 65, 142; in the media, 76. *See also* California propositions: Proposition 187; Immigration Reform and Control Act; Operation Wetback; repatriations and deportations of the 1930s

Asian Americans, 60, 64, 73, 137, 143; Asian immigrants, 25; Chinese miners, 26; defined, 237n. 4; Filipinos, 34; Japanese Americans, 29, 51, 242n. 9

Assimilation in American Life, 245n. 8

assimilationist perspective, 18–24, 34, 36–41, 70, 85, 91, 110–112

banking method of education, 146

Beverly Hills, 78

bilingual education, 3, 37, 39, 46, 110–111, 246–247nn. 5, 6, 7; and race/ethnic relations, 172; respondents' attitudes toward, 105, 118, 140, 171, 176, 181, 198–202, 204–205, 207–208, 212–213. *See also* California propositions: Proposition 227; dual language immersion

biological deficiency perspective, 70, 85, 128

Blacks. *See* African American(s)

Black-White paradigm of race relations, 4, 73

both-and conceptual framework, 124

Bracero Program (1942–1964), 29–30, 41

Brown v. Board of Education, 53

California Civil Rights Initiative (CCRI). *See* California Propositions: Proposition 209

California gold rush, 26

California propositions: 1986 proposition declaring English the official language, 39, 113; Proposition 187, 3, 7, 32, 45, 126, 140–143, 190, 225, 241n. 1; Proposition 209, 3, 45; Proposition 227, 3, 39, 46, 171, 244–255n. 5; Racial Privacy initiative, 23, 221

Californios, 25–27, 48, 242n. 1

Catholic churches, 55-56, 98-99, 160-161; parent organizing in, 212; and priests, 59, 120; and Spanish masses, 99, 119, 161-163

Central Americans, 42, 43, 60

Central Avenue Americanization School, 50-55, 58-59

Chávez, César, 37-38

Chicana/o identity, 16, 35-36, 82, 84-86, 93-97, 131, 147, 243n. 5. *See also* Mexican Americans

Chicana/o movement, 35-38, 42, 95-96, 131, 183, 244n. 8

Chicano Spanish, 153. *See also* code-switching

Chicano studies, 37, 93, 131, 146, 147-148, 229

City of Industry, 6, 58, 62-63, 175, 242n. 15

code-switching, 153-154. *See also* Chicano Spanish

color-blind. *See* power evasive

Community Service Organization (CSO), 41-42

Connerly, Ward, 23

contact hypothesis of race/ethnic relations, 127

context of reception, 32-33

cultural deficiency perspective. *See* assimilationist perspective; cultural deprivation model

cultural deprivation model, 117. *See also* assimilationist perspective

cultural factors in race/ethnic relations, 15, 19-22, 38-39; defined, 239n. 15

cultural reinvigoration, 157-158

dominant ideologies: defined, 15, 34-35, 39, 42. *See also* Anglo superiority ideology; assimilationist perspective; Manifest Destiny; power evasive

dual language immersion, 171-172, 246-247nn. 6, 7

East Los Angeles, 43, 58, 78-79, 88, 90, 93

economic restructuring, 2, 6-7, 31, 32, 102. *See also* North American Free Trade Agreement (NAFTA)

El Monte, 116, 198

El Plan de Santa Bárbara, 146

empowering education, 146, 172

Encarnación Martínez, María de la, 48

English for the Children. *See* California Propositions: Proposition 227

English-only movement, 3, 34, 39, 46, 110-112, 200. *See also* California propositions: Proposition 227

Ethnic Myth, 23

European Americans. *See* Whites

European immigrants, as distinguished from Mexican immigrants, 18, 19, 22, 23-24, 134-135

free trade zones, 32. *See also* North American Free Trade Agreement (NAFTA)

Foreign Miners Tax (1850), 26

gender and political activism, 209-210, 216. *See also* good mothering; reproductive labor

GI Bill, 58

GI Forum, 36-37, 41-42

good mothering, 213

Great Depression, 28, 40, 45

Guadalupe Chapel, 55-56

Hacienda Heights, 6, 62, 144-145, 175, 178-181, 219

Hacienda-La Puente Unified School District (HLPUSD), 8, 68, 92, 131-132, 204-206, 248n. 14; bilingual education in, 176, 181, 208; demographics of, 103, 178, 244n. 3; inequality within, 144-145, 179-181, 183-188, 200, 214, 247-245nn. 4,8; recommendations for, 227-230; and school consolidation, 180-181, 192-193; structure of, 178-180, 247n. 7

Hayakawa, S. I., 110

Hispanic generation, 42

Hispanic label, 75

History of La Puente Valley California,
55–56
Hudson School, 50–53, 55

ideological processes, defined, 239nn.
15–17. *See also* assimilationist perspective; dominant ideologies
Immigration Act (1917), 28
Immigration Reform and Control Act
(IRCA) (1986), 31–32, 188
integrated power conflict perspective, 19,
20, 24. *See also* theoretical framework of study
internal colonialism, 24
intra-ethnic relations, defined, 238n. 7

King, Martin Luther, Jr., 45
King, Rodney, 43, 198
Koreatown, 43

La Opinión, 157
La Puente: anti-immigrant sentiment in,
64; Catholic churches in, 55–56, 59,
98–99, 119–120, 160–165, 245n. 10
(*see also* Guadalupe Chapel); City
Council of, 65–66, 219–221, 242n.
22; debates in, over Spanish language,
65–68; demographics of, 6–7, 59–
62, 180; history of, 7, 16, 46–63;
outsiders' perceptions of, 143–144;
schools in, 7, 8, 13, 50–55, 59, 66–
67, 92, 98–99, 103–109, 131–132,
140, 144–148, 165–173, 242n. 10
(*see also* Central Avenue American
School; Hacienda–La Puente Unified
School District; Hudson School);
segregation in, 9, 50, 56–58, 61, 101–
102, 242n. 14; Spanish-speakers in,
155–156; unequal resources in, 144–
146; voting record of, 46, 241n. 1;
walnut-packing plant in, 242n. 7
Latinas/os: attitudes of, toward Spanish
language, 246n. 14; and Catholicism,
160–165; defined, 237n. 2; demographics of, 3, 6–7, 60; educational

attainment of, 239n. 14; families of, 3,
30; and home ownership, 61; media
images of, 75–76; perceptions of,
regarding Mexican Americans, 81–85;
political consciousness of, 38–39; and
racial/ethnic identification, 73, 146; as
teachers, 172–173, 229; voting record
of, 45–46, 171; and women, 3, 30.
See also Central Americans; Mexican
Americans; Mexican immigrants
League of Latin American Citizens
(LULAC), 35–37, 41–42, 241n. 10
"Legal Alien," 71
Los Angeles, 6–7, 29, 30, 31, 57, 141–142;
archdiocese of, 161; demographics of,
114; founding of (1781), 113; Spanish-
speakers in, 155–156. *See also* East
Los Angeles; Koreatown; Pico-Union;
South Central Los Angeles
Los Angeles Uprisings (1992), 43
Lucas, Douglas P., 52

Manifest Destiny, 24–25
McCarran-Walter Act (1952), 30, 42
media images of Latinas/os, 75–76, 81–82
Mendez v. Westminster, 53
methodology of study, 7–12, 234–236,
238n. 10, 239n. 12; researcher's position, 233–236, 239n. 12. *See also*
qualitative research
Mexican American generation, 115–121
Mexican American–Mexican immigrant
relations: by age, 127–128 (*see also*
Mexican American generation); assimilationist perspective, role of in,
18–19, 40–41, 110–121, 124; challenging anti-Mexican sentiment,
158, 169–170; in churches, 4, 5, 99,
119–121, 160–165; by class position,
1–2, 26–27, 40–41, 48, 88, 136; and
conflict-solidarity continuum, 15,
100, 176, 224–225; examples of cooperation and solidarity in, 2, 37,
42, 43, 132–218, 221; and cultural
commonalities, 15, 39–40, 134; by

gender, 4, 17, 128–129, 226; historical patterns in, 39–43; and intergenerational relationships, 221–222; in the labor market, 4, 5, 128–129; around language, 1, 19, 39, 99–101, 104–107, 111, 112, 122–123, 161–163; limited scholarship on, 3–5; long-term immigrants, role of in, 183–187, 189–190, 204–205, 216, 226 (see also Parents for Quality Education; Puente Parents); mobilization of, 42, 142, 176–218; in neighborhoods, 4, 27, 150–160; power conflict perspective, role of in, 19, 36, 38, 133, 170, 182–218, 225; in schools, 4, 10, 12–16, 103–109, 165–173 (see also Parents for Quality Education; Puente Parents); structural factors and dominant ideologies, influence of on, 15, 19–20, 23–24, 27, 28–29, 40, 43, 100–130 (see also assimilationist perspective); tensions in, 1, 16, 99–130; women, role of in, 226 (see also Parents for Quality Education)

Mexican Americans: and Catholic churches, 55–56, 59, 98–99; as cultural brokers/buffers, 150; defined, 9, 237n. 2; distinguishing/distancing of, from Mexican immigrants, 88–89, 106–107, 114–115, 121–122; dominant stereotypes of, 75–76; educational experiences of, 13, 33, 36, 49–55, 92–96, 98, 107, 116, 131–132, 144–148, 165–173; internalized racism among, 140–141; Latinas'/os' conceptualizations of, 81–85; making connections with Mexican immigrants, 134–137, 148–149; in the middle class, 241n. 9; as outsiders within society, 124; prejudice and discrimination, impact of on, 137–140; racial/ethnic identities of, 71–97, 223, 244n. 7; and respondents' attitudes toward immigration, 111–113, 123–127, 135–136; respondents described, 9–12; and seg-

regated communities, 36, 50, 56–58; and the Spanish language, 10, 13, 23, 59, 82, 98, 150–156, 165–168 (see also Chicano Spanish; code-switching); Whites' conceptions of, 77–81, 137–140; work experiences of, 36, 48–50, 52, 56, 102–106. See also Chicana/o identity; Mexican American–Mexican immigrant relations

Mexican American War. See War of the North American Invasion

Mexican food, 64, 94

Mexican immigrants: class position of, 1, 3; defined, 9, 237n. 2; and demographics in La Puente, 60; as described by respondents, 10, 13; educational experiences of, 185–187, 199; English-language skills of, 1, 3; long-term, 177, 189–190, 203–205, 249n. 18; occupations of, in Los Angeles, 102; perceptions of Mexican Americans among, 81–85, 122–123; political activism among, 183–187, 189–190, 204–205, 216, 226 (see also Puente Parents; Parents for Quality Education); settlement of, 1–2, 149–150. See also Mexican American–Mexican immigrant relationships

Mexican music. See Spanish-language music

Mexicanness, 16, 71, 77, 80, 82–86, 114, 223, 243n. 2

Mexican-origin: and anti-Mexican sentiment, 26, 28–31, 34; defined, 237n. 2; families, 21–22; others' perceptions of, 13, 27–29, 138–140; parents, 13. See also Mexican Americans; Mexican immigrants

Mexican Revolution (1910–1920), 28

Mills, C. Wright, 225

Monterey Park, 136–137

Mothers of East Los Angeles, 160

Movimiento Estudiantil Chicano de Aztlán (MEChA), 36, 96, 202, 219–221

NAFTA. *See* North American Free Trade
  Agreement (NAFTA)
National Chicano Moratorium (August 29,
  1970), 36
Native Americans, 25, 47–48, 73
nativism. *See* anti-immigrant sentiment;
  California propositions: Proposition
  187
newcomer programs. *See* Americanization
North American Free Trade Agreement
  (NAFTA), 2, 32

occupied Mexico, 15, 18–19
"one-drop rule." *See* rule of hypodescent
Operation Wetback, 30, 42
oppositional consciousness, 96. *See also*
  Chicana/o identity

panethnicity, 38, 143, 160
Parents for Quality Education, 176, 203–
  218
Pedagogy of the Oppressed, 147
Pico-Union, 43
pocho, 82
power conflict perspective, 16, 18–20,
  23–25, 72, 87, 96; of respondents,
  133–134, 147–149, 187, 225–226
power evasive, 22–23, 34–35, 228, 240nn.
  1, 5
power sharing, 17
practical and policy recommendations of
  study, 17, 174, 227–230
Proposition 187. *See* California propositions: Proposition 187
Proposition 209. *See* California propositions: Proposition 209
Proposition 227. *See* California propositions: Proposition 227
Puente Parents, 176, 182–203, 214–218,
  248n. 10, 12

qualitative research, 238n. 9, 239n. 11. *See
  also* methodology of study

race/ethnicity, defined, 237n. 3
racial/ethnic hierarchy, 16, 20, 24, 25–

26, 33, 57, 71, 244n. 1; as linked to
  language, 112–113, 123–124, 165; in
  relations between Mexican immigrants and Whites, in which Mexican
  Americans serve as mediators/buffers,
  101, 103, 121; within schools, 107–
  108, 165
racial/ethnic identity in Mexican-origin
  population, 16, 26–27, 35–36, 39,
  40–41, 57, 71–97; and intra-ethnic
  relations, 72, 87, 97; institutionalized
  constructions of, 73–76; as linked to
  ancestry, 87–89; as linked to culture,
  89–91; as linked to experiences of
  racism and power conflict perspective, 91–97; among multiracial/ethnic
  respondents, 90
racial/ethnic lumping, 121–122, 140–143,
  245n. 12
Racial Privacy initiative. *See* California
  propositions
repatriations and deportations of the 1930s,
  29, 40, 134
reproductive labor, 203, 210, 226, 248n. 13
revolving door strategy of migration, 28,
  32
Rowland, John, 47–48, 241n. 4, 5
rule of hypodescent, 73

San Gabriel Mission, 47
Santa Paula, 42–43
Schleder, Anthony J., 53
school(s): advanced placement courses in,
  179–180, 247n. 3; Americanization
  programs in, 14, 52, 116–117, 165;
  assimilating pressures in, 94–95, 165–
  166; bilingual education in, 3, 13, 105,
  246–247nn. 5, 6, 7; challenging, 132,
  148, 166–173; curriculum tracking
  in, 14, 33, 106–107, 165; English-
  only policies in, 17; Eurocentric
  course curriculum in, 13, 36, 81–82,
  94; officials, and racial/ethnic gap
  with students, 103; segregated classrooms in, 33, 50–55, 240n. 6; Spanish
  language repression in, 13, 66–67,

116–117, 165, 199; standardized tests in, 104, 107, 230; teachers' stereotyped attitudes and actions in, 13, 55, 59, 92, 95, 106–108, 138, 145–148. *See also* banking method of education

Secularization Proclamation (1834), 47

Servicemen's Rampage (1943), 34

South Central Los Angeles, 43

Spanish language: attitudes of Latinos toward, 246n. 14; attitudes of respondents of Mexican American generation toward, 118–119; in Catholic churches, 161–162; debates over, 16, 110–114; in homes and neighborhoods, 150–156; maintaining and reclaiming, 16, 38, 41, 67–68, 93, 131, 150–156; protection of in Southwest by Treaty of Guadalupe Hidalgo, 113; ridicule of, 1, 3, 13, 82–83, 85, 122–123; in schools, 165–168; skills of respondents, 10, 98; speakers of, in the United States and Los Angeles, 155–156; subordination of, 13, 19, 22–23, 39, 46, 59, 64–68, 116–117. *See also* bilingual education; Chicano Spanish; code-switching; English-only movement

Spanish-language music, 89–90, 94, 121, 131, 154, 156–158, 224

Stafford, Jim, 242n. 15

straight-line theory of assimilation, 24

structural factors: defined, 15, 19–20, 38–39, 44, 239n. 15; and racial/ethnic identity, 85

theoretical framework of study, 15–16, 19, 24–39

Torres, Esteban, 66

Treaty of Guadalupe Hidalgo (1848), 25, 113, 243n. 1

UCLA (University of California, Los Angeles), 95–96, 148, 244n. 9

United Farm Workers (UFW), 35–38. *See also* Chávez, César

Unz, Ron, 110–112, 244–255n. 5

Urioste, Nicolasa, 48

USA PATRIOT Act (Uniting and Strengthening America by Providing Appropriate Tools Required to Intercept and Obstruct Terrorism), 220

Valinda, 178, 238n. 8, 247n. 1

War of the North American Invasion, 25

West Covina, 6, 62–63, 147

Whites, 24, 25–27, 43, 45, 46, 51, 54, 58, 60, 73; Americanization, views of, 116–117; Americans, seen as, 34, 91; in the Catholic Church, 164; defined, 237–238n. 4; occupations of, 102–103; perceptions of Mexicans among, 71, 75–81, 93, 121–122, 137–140; racial/ethnic identity of, 72, 74, 91; speaking Spanish, 155; as teachers, 228; supremacy of, *see* Anglo superiority ideology

Wilson, Pete, 142

windows into exotica, 79

Workman, William, 47–48, 241nn. 4, 5

World War I, 28, 49

World War II, 9, 21, 29, 56, 58, 116, 242n. 12

Zoot Suit Riots (1943). *See* Servicemen's Rampage

CPSIA information can be obtained at www.ICGtesting.com
Printed in the USA
BVOW022357070313

315004BV00001B/31/P